ST MARTIN'S
TRUE CRIME
CLASSICS

D0465336

PRAISE FOR GARY C. KING

BLOOD LUST

"Writer Gary King knows the dark side of the Northwest as well as anybody . . . an unflinching account of one of the most vicious reigns of terror by one of the sickest psychopaths in the annals of crime." —*Official Detective*

"Effective account of the worst serial killer in Oregon's history."   —*Publishers Weekly*

BLIND RAGE

"Gut-wrenching and gripping. . . . Solid, absorbing true crime."   —Clark Howard, author of LOVE'S BLOOD

DRIVEN TO KILL

"The first complete book about Westley Dodd's short but destructive career . . . a thorough, thoughtful, and unforgettable account of a profoundly disturbing case of pedophilia and murder."   —*Inside Detective* magazine

"Horrific . . . this story will leave you gasping."
—Jack Olsen, bestselling author of SALT OF THE
EARTH and HASTENED TO THE GRAVE

St. Martin's Paperbacks
True Crime Library Titles
by Gary C. King

The Texas 7
An Early Grave
Murder in Hollywood

AN EARLY GRAVE

GARY C. KING

St. Martin's Paperbacks

AN EARLY GRAVE

ISBN: 0-312-97926-6
EAN: 80312-97926-3

Printed in the United States of America

St. Martin's Paperbacks edition / May 2001

10 9 8 7 6 5 4 3 2

For Kirsten and Sarah

ACKNOWLEDGMENTS

I would like to gratefully acknowledge the following people for their support and assistance during the writing of this book:

First and foremost, a very special thanks to my agent, Peter Miller, of PMA Literary and Film Management in New York, truly a true crime writer's best friend in the business, especially at a time when the genre has become so competitive and overcrowded. "You the man, Peter!" Thanks also to Delin Cormeny, vice president and literary manager at PMA who helped button down the deal; and to Kate Garrick and Elaine Gartner, development associates at PMA, who continually hold my hand along the way and put up with all of my annoying phone calls.

Thanks also to the Las Vegas Metropolitan Police Department for their cooperation during the writing of this book, especially to homicide Detective James Buczek and Lieutenant Wayne Petersen.

I am also deeply indebted to my editor, Charlie Spicer, for inducting me into the St. Martin's Press True Crime Library, and to his assistant, Joe Cleemann, for all of his hard work on a truly masterful job of fine-tuning the manuscript.

I am also grateful for the efforts of producer/screenwriter Frank Abatemarco for his support and faith in this project and I am happy in knowing that I've made a good friend through our endeavors.

I am also indebted to my wonderful parents, Curtis and Eunice King of Pahrump, Nevada, who assisted me in my efforts for that leg of the story.

I would also like to thank Virgil and Dixie King for their love, moral support, and encouragement along the way

And to my terrific wife, Teresita, I thank her from the

bottom of my heart for her continued support, encouragement, and, most of all, her love, without which projects such as this would be impossible for me to accomplish.

I am also grateful to my friends at *Gothic Landscape, Incorporated*, especially Brian Meehan, Chris Chapman, Mike Georgio, Ron Georgio, and Jon Georgio, and many others too numerous to mention here (you know who you are!), for all of their kindness and support which helped make this book possible.

Also, special thanks to David Lohr for helping me get the word out about my books.

Last, but not least, I am grateful to my brother, Don Moody, whose occasional prodding, suggestions, support, and faith in me helped push me into tackling this difficult project, as well as those that came before it, and helped me come to realize over the years that success should only be measured by one's love of what one does and one's ability to do it.

Why, man, he doth bestride the narrow world
Like a Colossus; and we petty men
Walk under his huge legs, and peep about
To find ourselves dishonourable graves.
Men at some time are masters of their fates:
The fault, dear Brutus, is not in our stars,
But in ourselves, that we are underlings.

—William Shakespeare
Julius Caesar

AUTHOR'S NOTE

This is a complex story of suspicious death that unfolded over nearly a two-year period. It is based on hundreds of hours of research of public documents, trial accounts, interviews, and news sources. The dialogue included herein came from a variety of sources, including interviews, trial proceedings, police affidavits, court documents, and news sources. I would be remiss as an author if I did not provide attribution to the news sources where some of the dialogue and quoted material first appeared: *Las Vegas Review-Journal*; Las Vegas *Sun*; KLAS-TV; KVBC-TV; and Court TV, all of which did an outstanding job in their reporting of this very unusual case. Every attempt has been made to present the story in the order that it was believed to have unfolded, except for a few events presented out of chronological sequence for easier reading and understanding of the facts of this complicated case. None of the names have been changed.

There were many people involved in this investigation, and I have included as many of them as possible. However, for clarity of reading, I have made Detective James Buczek, the lead investigator, a composite character of sorts in an effort to smooth out the narrative so that readers would not have to keep a checklist at hand to refer to who did what. To include everything that everyone did, and identify each individual as such would have required a juggling act on my part and that of the reader and would have greatly diminished the dramatic aspects of this case. Utilizing Detective Buczek as the lead central investigative character should not be construed that he did *all* of the work, and it was not my intention to diminish in any way the fine work of all the other people who helped bring this case to a successful conclusion. Rather, I made Detective Buczek a composite character to more readily enable the reader to visualize the case from the investigators' perspective. Make no mistake, however. Detective Buczek did much of the work and was involved in the case from start to finish, and it should be recognized that this was *his* case.

—G.C.K.
September 2000

INTRODUCTION

*"You know my motto. Outlive every sonofabitch. And
I've outlived a lot of them."*

—Lester "Benny" Binion,
shortly before his death in 1989

I was just a couple of months shy of 17 when I first set
foot in Binion's Horseshoe Hotel and Casino in November
1970, during a time when certain factions of the New York
and Chicago crime families still ran most of the city. I had
driven nearly a thousand miles to Las Vegas from the Pacific Northwest with a friend in his 1959 light blue Dodge
pickup truck, carrying a bottle of King George IV scotch
whiskey behind the seat. Our motivation for the trip was to
see Dean Martin at the Riviera Hotel and Casino, to party
heartily and, hopefully, to get laid. At Dean Martin's dinner
show, we did meet a couple of good-looking divorcees
from New Hampshire, who accompanied us later that evening to the Landmark Hotel for a midnight show that head-
lined singer Trini Lopez and comedian John Byner, but
alas, despite the fact that every opportunity had been afforded us, we did not get laid, due to our naivete and sexual
inexperience. We did make it downtown to Second Avenue
and Fremont Street where the Horseshoe was located. After
about an hour of slot play we were politely ejected, not
because we were underage but because we were not observing "gambler's courtesy" by playing a follow-up coin
after a win to turn off the winner's light atop the machine
so that the next player would not know that the machine
had just paid off. As we left, dejected and disappointed, I
never in my wildest dreams ever imagined that I would
write a book some thirty years later detailing the suspicious
death of one of the heirs of the Binion gambling "money

machine." Perhaps it was fate that played a hand in that eventuality, just as it would play a hand in Lonnie "Ted" Binion's ultimate demise.

That teenage trip in November 1970 began my life-long love affair with the neon oasis in the middle of the Mojave Desert known as Las Vegas. I found that I could not resist its allure not because of the gambling—I am not a gambler—but because of the excitement that this city generates, the pleasant year-round weather, the entertainment, the food, the astounding growth and healthy economy it has enjoyed and, of course, its compelling history. Whenever possible I found myself visiting the gambling mecca twice a year, sometimes for two days, other times for two weeks, until, some twenty-five years later, and barely three years before Ted Binion's untimely death, I finally moved my wife and family to "Sin City."

You know what they say. You can't fight fate.

Although she no longer works there, my wife obtained employment at the Horseshoe as a claims specialist for several months for their in-house employee health insurance program. Though she didn't know it at the time, she was meeting many of the people who made the Binion "money machine" turn on a daily basis, a few of whom would play an integral part in the yet-to-be trial of the century. Her high standards and ethics, however, precluded her from being a valuable source for my project. Along similar lines I soon found myself reading about slain mobster Herbert "Fat Herbie" Blitzstein, a one-time lieutenant of Chicago mobster Anthony "The Ant" Spilotro, a character immortalized by actor Joe Pesci in the Martin Scorsese film *Casino*, and I began learning about Blitzstein's associations with Ted Binion. As it turned out, through my own inquisitiveness I was slowly being drawn into a case that hadn't even occurred yet, a case that no one saw coming. At the time I was on a self-imposed hiatus from true crime, burned out from years of writing five to six stories a month for the U.S. version of the now defunct *True Detective* magazine, and had no idea that this story was coming down the pike. When it finally came zooming toward me in September 1998 I knew, without question, that I would dive headfirst right into the passenger seat. As I began my research of this fascinating tale, I realized that my hiatus was over. It was time to go back to work.

However, before we get started and delve into the "meat" of this fascinating and sensational story, a brief history of the Binion family and the evolution of the Horseshoe seems appropriate to help set the stage.

The Horseshoe, I soon learned, wasn't always so named. Its meager beginnings can be traced back to 1930, when the Apache Hotel opened on Second Avenue and Fremont Street, some sixty-five years before Fremont Street was ambitiously converted into a covered gambling mall of sorts at a cost of some $60 million. The Apache Hotel was a sleepy little club nestled among a few cafes and slot joints at a time when Las Vegas was little more than a gasoline stop for tourists on their way to Los Angeles. Although the Apache would undergo several changes in the years that followed, including a name change to the El Dorado Casino, it would remain virtually unknown to the world until Lester "Benny" Binion, a tough cowboy gambler, bootlegger, and racketeer, born on November 20, 1904, in Pilot Grove, Texas, came to Las Vegas in October 1946.

According to the old-timers, Benny arrived in Las Vegas with a suitcase that contained more than $100,000. Some estimates run as high as $2 million. No one really knows for sure how much money he brought with him to Las Vegas, and that is a secret that Benny took with him to the grave.

It was no secret, however, that during the Depression, Binion earned his money from bootlegging and illegal gambling. As a boy, Benny was no stranger to gambling. He would accompany his father on horse-trading trips at age nine, and would watch with fascination as his father and other cowboys sat around the campfire at night and played cards. He soon found that he had become hooked, even before reaching adulthood.

According to the FBI, he had become a "big-time gambler, ruthless racketeer and hoodlum in the Fort Worth and Dallas, Texas, areas" by the time he was a young adult. Although his known criminal activities began with bootlegging, he eventually graduated into organized gambling. He used specially constructed craps tables made out of crates that were labeled as if they contained hotel beds, which enabled his operation to clear out if given notice of an impending raid. The FBI characterized Binion as the "type of person who wanted to kill all opposition," and who formed a group that became known as the "Southland Syndicate," which had "complete control" of all the rackets in the Dallas area during the war years. His operations caught not only the eyes of the feds, but of a number of rivals as well.

Throughout much of his life, Binion was known to carry three pistols, two .45 automatics and a .38 revolver. In 1931, long before he was to leave for Las Vegas, Binion had begun to suspect that Frank Bolding, a black bootlegger, was stealing liquor from him. Binion himself, at that time, was known to rob fellow bootleggers of their liquor, and then demand a ransom for the stolen goods. When Binion confronted Bolding about stealing from him, Bolding came toward him and Binion's perception was that Bolding was going to stab him with a knife. Binion, fearing for his life, pulled one of his guns, shot Bolding through the neck, and killed him. It turned out that Bolding was indeed carrying a knife, but investigators determined that he hadn't pulled it on Binion. Although Binion was convicted of the slaying, he only received a two-year suspended sentence due to Bolding's unsavory reputation. Five years later, in 1936, Binion killed another man, Ben Frieden, a competitor of Binion's gambling operations. But because Binion was also wounded in the gunfire the case was considered self-defense and Binion wasn't charged.

Some say Binion was on the run from the Texas mob, a faction of a larger organized crime syndicate that was attempting to strong-arm a piece of his Texas gambling operation, which he and his "Southland Syndicate" had been resisting. Others say that he took his share of the Texas gambling operation stake and moved to Las Vegas on the advice of mobster Meyer Lansky before things became too "hot" for him in Texas. Binion himself said in later years that it was the increased heat from Dallas law enforcement and the feds that precipitated his relocation to Las Vegas, leaving his wife and children behind temporarily.

"The politics [of Dallas] changed a bit, but not in my favor," Binion once said. "So I left. . . . When I realized how good it could be up here, I said, 'Let 'em have Texas.' "

Shortly after he arrived in Las Vegas in his powder blue Cadillac, Binion purchased a six-acre ranch on Bonanza Road for $68,000, a huge price to pay for land in that area in 1946. The split log and stone home had been built in 1938 and, until Binion purchased it, was rented to out-of-state people who wanted to obtain a "quickie" Nevada divorce but first needed to establish their Nevada residency, which took six weeks. Prior to purchasing the home, Binion made certain that there were no out-of-sight corridors on the ranch and that he had a clear view of the approaches to the house from nearly every window. Because of the past that he was trying to leave behind, Binion held deep-seated fears that his children might be kidnapped and he wanted them safe and secure when they arrived. The following year, 1947, Binion brought his vigorous wife, Teddy Jane, and their five children, Jack, Ted, Barbara, Brenda and Becky, to Las Vegas.

The Binion presence would soon change not only the face of downtown Las Vegas, but the way in which Las Vegas gambled.

When Benny Binion finally purchased the El Dorado

Casino on August 15, 1951, he promptly renamed it the Horseshoe Club. At a time when the population of Las Vegas was barely 18,000 and downtown's "Glitter Gulch" didn't have much glitter, the Horseshoe Club became the first real gambling hall and saloon in town. Among the first casinos to have carpet installed on its floors and foot rails added to its bars, the Horseshoe Club began to take on an identity all its own. Binion's simple philosophy of "good food, good whiskey, and good no-limit gambling" made the Horseshoe famous almost overnight, and the fact that it was the first casino-hotel to pick up visitors at the airport in limousines and to provide free drinks to slot machine players helped its success story. For a long time the Horseshoe would be considered the most successful gambling hall in Las Vegas.

Despite the obvious success of his new casino, Binion's past continued to catch up with him. In 1951, a former gambling rival of Binion's, Herbert "The Cat" Noble, so named because of his uncanny ability to escape death, was arrested at the airport in Tucson, Arizona, piloting a plane en route to Las Vegas. According to the FBI, Noble believed Binion was out to get him. Because of a gang war that had developed when Binion was still in Texas, he and Noble feuded, sometimes violently. An FBI memo indicated that individuals from both Binion's "Southland Syndicate" and Noble's gang were murdered or disappeared without a trace. Noble survived having been shot in the back; escaped without a scratch from another incident in which his car was riddled with a spray of machine gun fire; discovered dynamite wired to his car's starter; and survived being shot during a high-speed car chase. In yet another attempt on Noble's life, someone blew up his car. Trouble was it was Noble's wife who got into the car, not Noble. She was killed, and Noble blamed Binion for her death. In his mind at least, there was a score to even.

When Noble was apprehended in Tucson, according to the FBI, he was in the process of equipping his plane with two bombs weighing at least five hundred pounds each, one of which was a high explosive and the other an incendiary device. He also had a map in his possession that detailed Benny Binion's home on Bonanza Road. There was no doubt that Noble was out to get Binion. His plans cut short, he would not be afforded another chance to rub out his rival. Although Noble escaped or survived seven attempts at assassination, he would not escape the eighth. He was finally killed in 1951 from a bomb that was detonated in front of his mailbox. Even though the FBI suspected Binion of at least some of the attempts on Noble's life, Binion swore on his children's lives that he never tried to kill Noble, and the feds were never able to bring a case against him for violence.

The fact of the matter was that the feds didn't have anything *solid* on Binion, at least not yet. They had connected him by association to Jack Dragna, head of the California branch of La Cosa Nostra and the man who got the Mafia involved in the entertainment industry, and to Mickey Cohen, a Hollywood shakedown criminal who used sexual blackmail tactics on 1930s-era movie stars that earned his group the moniker of the "Mickey Mouse Mafia." Although so-called "associations" with the Los Angeles mafia would continue to haunt the Binion family for years to come and would carry over to affect Benny's youngest son, Ted, as will be shown, the feds were never able to garner enough evidence to put Binion away for his purported ties with mob elements.

It wasn't until 1952 that they had the goods on him, but the evidence they had gathered was for tax evasion. Not exactly what they wanted, but they had enough to make the charges stick. Binion was indicted for not paying $14,000 in federal income tax on money he made from his various ventures in Texas, and was convicted and sentenced to Leavenworth prison for four years. While Benny was away in prison, family friend Harry Claiborne, who would later become a federal judge and be driven from the bench by scandal, acted as a surrogate father to Benny's children. After getting out of prison, Benny had to sell his majority interest in the casino in order to pay his legal bills, and not until 1964 would the Binion family regain controlling interest. At that point Jack Binion was appointed president; young Ted Binion, who had spent much of his childhood following his father around the casino dressed in cowboy clothes like his dad, was made manager, and Teddy Jane Binion controlled the casino cage. It was clear that Benny did not want his daughters involved in the casino business; not until after Benny's death would his daughter, Becky, play any kind of a major role in the casino's operations. Because of his conviction and prison sentence, Benny Binion could not hold a gaming license, though it was obvious that he still ran things as the casino's "consultant."

"I went to the penitentiary for income tax," Binion once said. "But there's not a scratch against me since I've been here [in Las Vegas]. It's all on the up and up."

J. Edgar Hoover did not believe him. He ordered that Binion and his family be placed under surveillance, and informants wearing wires were hired to try to obtain information that connected Binion and his gambling operation to mobsters. They even watched Binion's children as they trained horses on the Bonanza Road ranch. Binion was quick to catch on to the surveillance, and at first was concerned that he was being followed by an enemy from earlier days. He soon realized that those tailing him were not old rivals, but the feds. He began to taunt them by outrunning them, trying to stop them to ask questions, and on one occasion he asked the FBI if they were in fact following him. He said he wanted to know because if it was the feds, he could breathe easier.

According to historian Allan May, mobster Louis Strauss, also known as "Russian Louie," attempted to blackmail Binion during the early years but did not know of Binion's alleged association with Jack Dragna. According to May's account in Crime Magazine online (see *www.crimemagazine.com*), Binion purportedly assured Dragna a 25 percent interest in a future casino if Dragna would take care of the problem. In April 1953, eighteen months later, Jimmy "The Weasel" Fratianno lured "Russian Louie" into a house in California where Joe Dippolito grabbed Strauss around the waist in a bear hug that allowed Frank Bompensiero and Jimmy "The Weasel" to perform the Italian rope trick—each holding one end, they looped a rope around Strauss's neck and tightened it from both sides—strangling him to death.

Years later, after the purported casino deal failed to come to fruition, Jimmy "The Weasel" allegedly reminded Binion of the deal even though Dragna was by then deceased. According to May's account, Binion agreed to pay Fratianno $60,000 for Strauss's murder. Fratianno supposedly split the money between himself, Bompensiero, Dippolito, and "Milwaukee Phil" Alderisio, the gangster who had driven Strauss to the house where he was murdered. No criminal allegations or charges were ever brought against Binion for Strauss's death and nothing other than historical accounts of gangland activities ever connected him to these crimes.

"They checked me and checked me," said Binion, "and I said, 'You'll never get me again.'" And they didn't, despite years of nearly continuous surveillance.

In fact, Binion gained the respect of local city and state politicians, and he and the entire Binion family were soon being characterized as "very loyal Americans." Binion also became involved in the community, donating heavily to the Catholic Church after reportedly finding religion while in prison. He also made substantial donations to a local Jewish hospital, and supported the March of Dimes and other charitable organizations. On one occasion he purchased a bus for a Little League team, furnished them with a driver, and paid virtually all of their expenses. Binion was indeed doing well, and by this time in his life he had purchased a 400,000-acre ranch in the Missouri Breaks region of

Montana where young Ted spent most of his summers riding horses with his dad.

As the Horseshoe continued to prosper, it gained worldwide attention with its annual "World Series of Poker" event, started by Benny, and attracted high-stakes gamblers from all over. And as Binion's gambling success grew so did the size of the Horseshoe. The original Horseshoe was only seventy-five feet wide. However, its size changed rapidly. In 1960 the casino expanded by another fifty feet when Binion acquired the adjacent Boulder Club. The Horseshoe was once more remodeled in 1969, and in 1982 it grew again when it added the ever-popular coffee shop restaurant downstairs. In 1988, a year before Benny Binion's death, Binion's Horseshoe, still operating under Jack Binion's presidency, purchased the financially troubled Mint Hotel next door. The interior walls that separated the two establishments were torn down, and the Horseshoe's size was doubled. It now covered the entire block, and the acquisition of the Mint provided it with a 24-story, 296-room hotel tower.

As has been seen and as will continue to be seen in the pages that follow, the phenomenal success story of the Horseshoe and the Binion family was not always a happy one. It was often marred with a dark side of legal complications, family squabbling, and personal tragedy.

Barbara, the youngest daughter, failed at an attempt at suicide: she shot herself and was left with a badly disfigured face. She would die later of a drug overdose. A dramatic kidnapping attempt against young Ted Binion would be thwarted, leaving in its wake bodies lying in the desert. Ted would begin to run afoul of the law as early as 1986 over his own drug problems and be arrested for heroin trafficking, and his known associations with underworld mobsters would ultimately cost him his gaming license and force him to sell his share of the Horseshoe to his sister, Becky. Jack, too, would sell to Becky after a prolonged series of disagreements involving her accusations that he and Ted were mismanaging Horseshoe capital, Jack allegedly diverting money to finance Louisiana and Mississippi gambling operations not directly affiliated with the Horseshoe. In a lawsuit filed against her brothers, Becky also alleged that Jack had been luring players away from the Horseshoe so that he could fill the tables at his other franchises. Ted, in the meantime, would meet a bleached-blonde dancer at a cheesy topless nightclub and would move her into his home after his wife moved out. Distrustful of his sister and fearful that he might lose the millions in silver that he had stored in the Horseshoe's vault, Ted would befriend a young man he met at a urinal in the men's room at Piero's Restaurant, and would hire him to remove the silver from the Horseshoe's vault and to build him a new vault near his ranch in Pahrump, Nevada. And to top it all off, Ted would die mysteriously in the process.

So there you have it, dear readers, an ever-so-brief overview of the Binion family and an introductory *mise en scene* of sorts to the story that follows. Now we're ready to delve into the "meat" of this most fascinating and eye-opening examination of a real-life soap opera that will likely be playing out in the courts for years to come.

PROLOGUE

Sandra Renee Murphy blew into town from California with several of her girlfriends on Friday, February 24, 1995, just four days after her twenty-third birthday. Originally from the Southern California town of Bellflower, Sandy, as she preferred to be called, was a pretty bleached blonde who came to Las Vegas looking for a change of scene and hoping to win big. Upon their arrival Sandy and her friends gazed in wonder at all the lights, the fake Egyptian pyramid and the brightly lit Disneyland-like castle. The imitation New York skyline hadn't been built yet, nor had the two-thirds scale mock-up of the Eiffel Tower. But Sandy and her friends didn't need those phony Wall Street–financed creations to have a good time. There was plenty to do in the "Entertainment Capital of the World" without them. Eager to begin parting with their hard-earned cash, Sandy and her friends checked into their hotel rooms at Caesars Palace and headed directly for the casino.

Those who knew her generally regarded Sandy Murphy as a nice girl who stayed out of trouble and would come to the aid of a friend on a moment's notice. Many people also recalled her as a pageant princess. She had won as a runner-up in the Miss Bellflower beauty pageant in 1989 at the age of 17, and was proud to represent the working-class city as one of its own. She cherished her Miss Bellflower princess sash, and showed it to nearly everyone. But Sandy Murphy wanted more out of life—much more—and she was determined that she was going to get what she wanted.

Sandy came from a family of two brothers and one sister. Her father repossessed cars for a living—a repo man—and her stepmother was a homemaker. Little was known about her biological mother, and Sandy preferred not to talk about her. Instead she referred to her stepmother as her mother. Together her father and stepmother raised their children as best they could in Bellflower, an older, industrial suburb of south central Los Angeles whose neighborhoods consisted primarily of a proliferation of warehouses and auto repair shops. It wasn't the greatest environment for a child to grow up in, but it wasn't the worst, either.

While attending middle school, Sandy worked as a student clerk in her school's attendance office. Officials at the middle school recalled her as being pleasant, smart, and responsible. By the time she was fourteen her family had moved to nearby Downey. At Downey High School she was recalled as a beautiful and popular girl, a looker who caught the boys' eyes. Sandy began hanging out with the athletes and was soon dating the school's star running back. Together with her boyfriend and their friends, Sandy did all the typical things a California teenage girl might do— surf, swim, drive around, "park" with the boys, and go to the movies. Although she wasn't considered a "bad girl" in high school, Sandy was no stranger to the principal's office. Called in for usually minor disciplinary problems, Sandy had the gift of gab, an ability to talk herself into and out of just about any situation, and her trips to the principal's office were usually brief and the subsequent punishment negligible. .

But in her senior year, something happened to Sandy. Her grades fell drastically, and she began running in more mature circles than were appropriate for her age. She began dating a wealthy man named Richard, a family friend who was ten years older than her, and it wasn't long before she left home and moved in with him. Both of them possessed an entrepreneurial spirit, and they opened a business together called Alltech Mobile Security. Richard worked in the office, and Sandy went out and sold automobile security systems to local car dealerships. In between work hours Sandy attempted to go to school, but the job required too much of her time and she failed to complete two courses of the high school's required curriculum. As a result she did not graduate.

Their business prospered and they made enough money to afford to live in a posh home in Huntington Beach. Their typical workday began at 7 a.m. and lasted sometimes until 10 p.m. The long hours soon took their toll on Sandy, however, and despite the lavish lifestyle she was living she soon began wanting financial independence from Richard. As a result she found a job working as a finance manager for a Newport Beach auto dealership that specialized in imports, and before long she was driving around town in a brand new Corvette. She began "clubbing" regularly, broke off her relationship with Richard and moved into an upscale condominium.

By all appearances Sandy was successful despite her failure to graduate from high school. Most who knew her thought she had it made. At least that's how it seemed on the surface. Although she didn't know it yet, her newfound lifestyle and the financial independence that she had sought were taking her on a downward spiral. There seemed to be no stopping her, however.

Sandy basically had a clean record with law enforcement, with the exception of a growing number of traffic violations that she continued to ignore and which eventually resulted in her driver's license being suspended. Then, on February 11, 1994, she was arrested in Costa Mesa for driving on the suspended license. When she was pulled over she initially told the police officer that her name was Tiffany Luna, but he soon learned her real name. The policeman found in her possession a $1.3 million check that had been signed by a Huntington Beach department store security officer. The officer called the security guard and asked if he knew a woman who went by the names of Tiffany Luna or Sandra Murphy. The guard said that he did not recognize either name, and initially denied even writing the check. However, on follow-up the investigation revealed that the security guard did in fact write the seven-figure check, which, he added, he did not have the funds to cover. But he didn't write it to Sandra Murphy or Tiffany Luna. He wrote it to a Newport Beach business partner who, it turned out, also happened to be the owner of the Porsche Sandra was driving. The incident, particularly the part where she provided false information to the policeman was enough for the officer to charge her for suspicion of fraud. Her stepmother bailed her out of jail by putting up a $10,000 bond. A month later, apparently because of Sandy's increasingly irresponsible lifestyle and the fear that she would not show up at her scheduled court appearances, her stepmother withdrew the bond and asked that Sandy be placed back into the custody of the court system.

People began to wonder how Sandy could maintain such a lavish lifestyle on her salary as a finance manager. No one knew for sure what she did apart from her job to keep her life in the fast lane. She would become known later, however, for associating with exotic dancers. Although there was speculation that she danced in the evening for additional income, Sandy vehemently denied that she ever danced for money and said that she had never been employed by a topless club.

Sandy's skirmishes with the law didn't end, however, with her suspended license. She was arrested a year later, in February 1995, only a couple of weeks before her trip to Las Vegas, for driving a 1992 Lexus while under the influence of alcohol. Because of her prior charges she was sentenced to forty-five days in jail and was required to install an interlock ignition device on her Lexus that would prevent her from starting it prior to taking and passing a breath test. Sandy, however, did not report to jail. She went to Las Vegas instead, reasoning that things would be different there. She had no idea just how drastically her life would change following that fateful trip.

Accompanying her to Las Vegas was her life savings of $13,000, an unlucky number if ever there was one.

Enjoying the complimentary drinks that were brought to

them as long as they sat in front of a slot machine or joined in on the table games, Sandy and her friends played on into the night and early morning hours. Sandy preferred the table games, blackjack in particular.

At first Sandy's bets were minor and her losses negligible. But as the weekend wore on she moved progressively to the higher stakes tables and began placing maximum wagers, which she continued to lose. Determined to regain her losses, Sandy continued to play, which, just about any gambler will concede, is not a smart move. Before the weekend was over her determination to win could have been compared to that of Chevy Chase trying to beat dealer Wallace Shawn in the movie *Vegas Vacation*. But this was no movie, and it most certainly was not funny. Before the weekend came to a close she had double-downed one too many times and had lost everything. Her friends packed up and headed back to Los Angeles, but Sandy decided to stay in Las Vegas. She had to get her money back somehow.

Broke and about as depressed as a human being could become, Sandy recalled a contact she knew at Cheetah's, a topless bar located on Western Avenue just off The Strip. Though it is situated among a number of other topless clubs and all-nude establishments that dot Western Avenue and Industrial Road every few blocks, Cheetah's is considered one of Vegas's classier topless joints by tourists and locals alike. A short time later Sandy found herself working at Cheetah's dressed as a Dallas Cowboys cheerleader. By Sandy's initial accounts of her new employment she was only selling costumes to the customers, who would buy the $200 outfits for the dancers that they liked, and was modeling lingerie that was designed by a friend. She contended that she was not dancing topless or performing lap dances nor did the establishment officially employ her. However, it would later be revealed that she was in fact dancing topless, in addition to her other endeavors, in her attempt to earn back all the money that she had lost.

A few nights after Sandy started working at Cheetah's,

53-year-old moon-faced Ted Binion walked into the club with a friend, mobster Herbert "Fat Herbie" Blitzstein, and a fellow gaming executive. On this particular evening, Ted was at a low point in his life, more than half-drunk and depressed about marital problems and ongoing troubles with the state Gaming Control Commission over his gaming license. Because of his drug and alcohol problems and known associations with Herbie Blitzstein, Binion had so many stipulations attached to his license that he feared that his lucrative career in the casino business was nearly over. Ted's favorite haunts were "titty joints," as he often referred to them, and he frequently conducted business at such establishments as Cheetah's, Club Paradise, and the Olympic Garden. He particularly enjoyed Cheetah's because he'd had prior success there picking up female dancers who sometimes went home with him, and he figured that spending the evening there might cheer him up. The girls who worked there loved Ted Binion. Known for his generosity, it wasn't unusual for him to tip the girls $500 or more on any given evening. It was no wonder that some of them would spend the night with him.

Sandy Murphy sat at the table next to Binion's that evening, and was telling all of her troubles to "Nick the Kick," one of Cheetah's bouncers. Ted overheard part of her conversation—about how her boyfriend had recently dumped her for an aerobics trainer—and he quickly became interested in her: it appeared that they shared something in common.

Sandy was introduced to the customers that evening as "The Irish Venus." Ted was immediately taken by her good looks, and it wasn't long before Sandy was sharing a booth with him at his invitation. Ted was a steadfast party animal who seemed to live for the Las Vegas nightlife, and he often wouldn't go home until he'd spent the pocketful of cash that he always carried with him. This particular night would be no different for the millionaire playboy in the twenty-four-hour city that he loved.

Sandy Murphy had no idea who Ted Binion was. She was not particularly impressed by him, but she might have been had she known that he was the son of audacious casino legend Benny Binion. Nonetheless he was friendly, and a paying customer, so she remained with him and humored him as he drank Absolut vodka on into the night. Obviously attracted to "The Irish Venus," Binion tried his best to impress Sandy. At one point he attempted to push a wad of cash that amounted to about $1,700 into her hand, but ended up insulting her instead. Furious, even though she desperately needed the money, she threw it back into his face. Ted stuffed the money back into his pocket and left. He commented later to friends and family members that he had been impressed by this woman's actions because, he thought, he had found someone who was not interested in him only for his money. Most women would have taken the cash, he said, but not Sandy.

It wasn't long before Sandy found out who Ted Binion was. She soon learned that Binion was worth an estimated $50 million. When Ted showed up at Cheetah's again a couple nights later he specifically requested her company. Sandy quickly made up for the impudence she had shown him on their first meeting and happily accepted a date with him for a night on the town.

On another evening she attended a dinner party at Ted's house. He had invited Sandy and one of her friends, having brought another date for himself. Embarrassed, Sandy blew up and made a scene. She told Binion that she thought that she had been his date for the evening, and taunted him that it was going to be her or no one.

Ted and Sandy soon made up, and it wasn't long before the two were being seen together all over town. Even though Sandy by now realized that Ted was a wealthy man, she still had no idea what he did for a living and knew nothing of his background or his family.

On another of their earliest dates, Ted, tired of Sandy referring to him as "Bunion," took her downtown to the

Fremont Street Experience. They stopped in front of the Horseshoe.

"You always call me *Bunion*," Ted said as he pointed towards the club and the sign that read *Binion's Horseshoe*. "It's *Binion*, and I own that casino."

He walked Sandy over to the entrance to the Horseshoe and called a security guard to the door. He instructed the guard to tell her who he was and that he was one of the owners of the casino.

"Ted, you don't have to do that," Sandy insisted.

"I'm sorry, sir," replied the security guard. "But I've never seen you before." The guard was new, and was telling the truth. He hadn't seen Ted Binion before, and with Ted's problems with the gaming commission, which stipulated that he could not enter the casino or be active with the day-to-day management of the establishment, there was no way that the guard could have known him.

As Ted walked away from the Horseshoe with Sandy it was obvious that he was disappointed. He had failed, again, to impress the young woman to whom he had taken such a fancy.

A few days later Ted's wife, Doris, overheard her husband making a date with Sandy on the telephone. Following a heated argument, she promptly packed her bags and moved herself and their 15-year-old daughter, Bonnie, to Texas. She had already filed for a divorce over Ted's continuous use of heroin and his occasionally abusive ways, but this latest incident left no room for reconciliation. She had finally had enough. Ted, by now consuming nearly a full bottle of Southern Comfort or Absolut vodka each day—depending upon his mood—and being the up-and-down impulsive doper that he was, didn't seem particularly bothered by his wife's sudden departure. It was almost as if he had been expecting it.

One evening soon after, Ted went out looking for Sandy, but couldn't find her despite searching all night long. It turned out that she had decided to spend the evening with friends, but when Ted finally caught up with her he was clearly angry and agitated.

"I don't ever want to not know where you are," Binion purportedly told Sandy.

The next day, on March 7, 1995, almost immediately after Doris and Bonnie had moved out, Ted instructed two of his friends to pack up Sandy's scant belongings and move them, as well as Sandy, into his home at 2408 Palomino Lane. The move was easy. Sandy only had three outfits to her name, and few other personal belongings. In the nearly two weeks that she had worked at Cheetah's Sandy had made back all of the money she had lost playing blackjack at Caesars, and then some. No longer having a reason to continue working as "The Irish Venus," she quit her job at the strip club.

Within two weeks Sandy's life had undergone an unimaginable metamorphosis. She had recovered her money, met and moved in with a multi-millionaire, no longer had to work, began enjoying comps at a number of casinos, was allowed to use the Horseshoe limousines, and began racking up huge credit card bills on shopping sprees at Versace and Neiman Marcus. She also soon had a nose job and a breast augmentation at Binion's expense. There was no way that she would even consider returning to the life she left behind in California. Las Vegas had panned out for her after all.

Suddenly she had it all, and she wasn't about to let any of it go, under any circumstances. Sandy Murphy had finally gotten what she wanted out of life—and a whole lot more.

CHAPTER 1

Las Vegas, Nevada, has not always been comprised of gambling joints, glamour, and glitz. Its beginnings were, in fact, quite meager. With its boundaries situated on the eastern perimeter of the Mojave Desert, the southern edge of the Great Basin Desert, and the northern perimeter of the Sonoran Desert, Las Vegas is, without question, one of the hottest and driest cities in the United States. It was founded by Mexican explorers and traders in 1830 who were in search of a shortcut between Santa Fe and Los Angeles. Surrounded by miles of scorching sand and omnipresent arid heat, they had veered off the Old Spanish Trail and were many miles from the nearest watering hole when, in the middle of nowhere, they stumbled upon a series of artesian springs bubbling up out of the sand and caliche. As they pressed onward they soon discovered an oasis made up of cottonwood trees, mesquite trees, tall grass, and a number of small creeks that flowed outward from the springs. They aptly named this oasis *Las Vegas*, which means "The Meadows."

In 1843 explorer and cartographer John C. Fremont surveyed the area. His surveys, in part, kicked off the momentum that brought the railroads to town. By 1905, Las Vegas had become a true railroad town, a stop along the route from Salt Lake City to the West Coast.

In 1930, the U.S. government decided to dam up the Colorado River and create one of the largest man-made lakes in the world. Their project was Hoover Dam, and their creation became known as Lake Mead. While the rest of the country was mired in the Great Depression, Las Vegas, for the most part, prospered. And grew.

Although Glitter Gulch and The Strip had not yet materialized, politicians in Carson City, Nevada's capital, were working fervently to enact laws that would legalize gambling and make getting a divorce in the Silver State an easy, not to mention quick, matter. As a result of the new laws, casinos began to pop up in the downtown area and, by the 1940s, New York and Chicago crime families decided they wanted their share of the prosperity that Las Vegas was enjoying. Meyer Lansky soon sent Benjamin "Bugsy" Siegel to Las Vegas, where Siegel opened the Flamingo Hotel. The Strip, for all intents and purposes, was born. There are no signs on the highways leading into town proclaiming that Las Vegas was built by criminals, though truer words couldn't be written.

As the Flamingo prospered, several rival entrepreneurs, many of them underworld bosses, decided that they, too, wanted a piece of the action. Over a ten-year period the Tropicana, the Stardust, the Sands, the Riviera, the Desert Inn, and Caesars Palace all opened on The Strip. Las Vegas's sudden prosperity had a price, a negative element that would long be remembered. Most of the new ventures had been financed by mob money, which brought with it a somewhat violent era. Bugsy Siegel had by this time been rubbed out by the mob for skimming profits from the Flamingo and for sending his girlfriend, Virginia Hill, on shopping sprees to Europe where she deposited much of the money into Swiss bank accounts for him. Similarly, Gus Greenbaum displeased his bosses at the Riviera, and his body was found, along with his wife's, in their Las Vegas home, their throats cut. Frank "Lefty" Rosenthal, characterized by actor Robert De Niro in the movie *Casino*, ran things at the Stardust for a while with Anthony "The Ant" Spilotro and nearly lost his life to a car bomb outside a Tony Roma's restaurant on East Sahara. And more recently Herbert "Fat Herbie" Blitzstein, a one-time lieutenant of Spilotro's, was murdered in his townhouse when the Los Angeles mob decided it wanted to take over the loan sharking business and auto insurance scams that they believed he was running.

But Las Vegas is evolving. The mobster element is still there, to be sure, though markedly less visible than it was twenty years ago, and nowadays the politicians and the corporations have assumed a new posture for themselves and for Las Vegas. Las Vegas has become known, today, as a Disneyland for adults, although it has become more "family friendly," too. It has also become known as the setting for one of the most diabolical and intricately plotted murder schemes in the annals of this city's crime history, if the prosecutor's charges are correct.

On Thursday, September 17, 1998, a thick, grayish brown cloud of smog and dust ringed the far-reaching boundaries of Clark County, Nevada, and the Las Vegas Valley, just as it did on most days in recent history, and the temperature was still in the scorching low one-hundreds. Gone were the days of clear dark blue skies, now only faded memories for the few life-long native Las Vegans who remain here, but an accepted fact of life for the hundreds of thousands of new transplants who have settled here in their quest for a better life. Some call it progress. Those who know what it used to be like here call it a shame. Although he was not a native Las Vegan, Lonnie "Ted" Binion grew up here in the desert dust and was one of those who knew what Las Vegas used to be like.

Ted Binion, a slightly built man, lived in the fast lane, in many respects much like his infamous father, Lester "Benny" Binion, and possessed some of the same bravado. Binion was also a cowboy in many respects. He loved horses, and had been an accomplished horseman even before he turned ten years old. But unlike his father, who lived to the ripe old age of 85, Ted lacked much of Benny's insight and common sense and couldn't see trouble coming when it was only around the corner. He was smart, though, in other ways. He loved history, and was a whiz at math with an uncanny ability to analyze gambling odds and come up with the house take in seconds, all without the use of a calculator or even a pencil. He also loved to schmooze with the patrons at the Horseshoe, and could be seen on any given day sitting at the bar trying to put the make on women whose husbands were gambling away the family fortune. Ted had a knack for always being able to find trouble, and he took one of life's routes that led him down the highway to hell. Despite his tremendous wealth and a sense of fairness toward those he liked, despite his being known to help others who were less fortunate, Ted had difficulty in helping himself and eventually became his own worst enemy. Although he performed his job well, there were many occasions when he would be above the casino floor smoking pot, utilizing the "eye in the sky" to keep watch on the gaming action and the casino dealers. The dealers always knew when he was there because of the pungent, telltale odor of the marijuana smoke. But his lifestyle had a price. By the time of his untimely death, Ted looked older than his fifty-five years, and his teeth had become stained an ugly brown from the years of smoking tar heroin and marijuana. His lifestyle led to a number of decisions that would first cost him his status in the gaming community as a casino giant and then, ultimately, would cost him his life.

When Ted Binion's longtime gardener, Tom Loveday, showed up on Thursday morning, September 17, he couldn't have known that something terrible was amiss behind the walls of Binion's 8,000-square-foot palatial home. Binion's expansive gated ranch-style home resides in an older, upscale Las Vegas neighborhood, centrally located near Rancho Drive and Charleston Boulevard, only minutes from downtown where the Horseshoe is located. Thursday was Loveday's regular day to mow the grass. It was about 9 a.m. when he arrived and at first it didn't seem any different from any of the other 500 or so times that he had taken care of Binion's grounds during the last fourteen years. It didn't take him long, however, to begin to sense that something wasn't quite right.

He knew that Sandy Murphy, Binion's live-in girlfriend for the past three and a half years, always parked her shiny black 1997 Mercedes in the garage. This particular morning, however, Loveday noticed and thought it peculiar that her car was parked in the side driveway. He noticed, too, that Binion's three dogs, Pig, Buddy, and Princess, were not themselves. Instead of following Loveday around the yard as they usually did, the dogs remained close to the back door, unable to gain access to the house through the doggie door that was now either locked or jammed shut from the inside. It appeared that they wanted to go inside, but no one would let them in.

Loveday walked around the perimeter of the house, a stroll that afforded him, at best, a cursory examination. He first noticed that the living room curtains were closed—he had never seen the curtains closed at any time on past workdays. As a result he could not see into the den where Binion spent most of his time when he was at home. He looked through the kitchen door near where the dogs were staying put, but he couldn't see anything there, either. The house was too dark. Similarly, he went to Binion's bedroom window and peered in through the opened drapes. Binion's bed was made and there were no articles of clothing on the floor. Knowing that Binion and Sandy Murphy had separate bedrooms, Loveday made his way around to Sandy's room. On Thursdays it wasn't unusual for Sandy to open her bedroom window and talk to Loveday. Her drapes were open, too, and, like Binion's, her bed was made. Where was everyone? he wondered. Where was the maid, Mary Montoya-Gascoigne? She had usually shown up for work by the time Loveday got there. Although concerned over his observations, Loveday decided that he had learned all that he could from his scrutiny of the premises and went about his business.

On occasion, since Sandy hung out with exotic dancers, Loveday would see large-busted girls who liked showing off what they had walking around the house, often wearing only T-shirts. The girls Sandy hung out with were a vain lot, and Loveday would sometimes see them with bandaged noses following plastic surgery. Sandy was certainly pretty enough with her voluptuous lips, dancer's legs, buff body, and those brown bedroom eyes. Ted Binion had particularly liked her ass, and was known to point out that she had a "nice ass" to his friends. The way that Sandy flaunted it she didn't need to be told. She knew it was a nice one. At five-feet eight-inches tall and weighing in at one-hundred eight pounds, Sandy, her hair no longer blonde but now a light brown, closer to her natural color, was certainly an inviting young woman. Sandy had even told him that Ted hadn't made love with her for a long time due to his drug use, and blatantly said to Loveday that she needed sex. She had even invited him in to smoke marijuana with her, but he had declined the offers. Sandy was Ted Binion's girl, and no one in his right mind dared to mess with Binion's girl. However, there was no Sandy and no flirting on this particular day. Nothing was going on at the Binion house that day that Loveday could see or hear, no scantily clad young women were running around the house and there were no apparent signs of other visitors. It was quiet—all too quiet for the Binion residence.

Loveday finished his work and left Ted Binion's home sometime between 1 and 1:30 p.m. He wouldn't know until later why he had sensed that something was wrong.

Sometime after Loveday left the grounds, Sandy Murphy emerged from the house with one of Binion's associates, Rick Tabish, and they drove to Horseshoe Gaming's administrative offices without an appointment. Sandy wanted to see Kathy Rose, Ted Binion's personal secretary. The receptionist told her that Rose was in a meeting, but Sandy asked her to interrupt the meeting so that she could give Rose a check that needed to be deposited into Ted's account.

Rose came out of the meeting and met Sandy in the

reception area. Sandy looked tired, almost haggard, like she
had been up all night. She certainly did not look the show-
girl type, as she normally appeared. After greeting her and
giving her a once-over, Rose thought it was odd that Sandy
would be bringing in a check for Ted. She had never done
that before. Sandy explained to Rose that Ted was sleeping.
Besides, she said, she left the house to go out and get something to eat which made it convenient for her to drop off
the check. Afterward, she said, she was going to go home
to check on Ted. Sandy told Rose that Ted had obtained a
prescription drug to assist him in getting off heroin once
again. After losing his gaming license for good because of
his associations with known mobsters and because of his
drug problems, Ted had become depressed and had started
smoking heroin again. Sandy explained that she had in fact
stayed up all night with him at his request.

A short time later Sandy called Kathy Rose again, and
asked her for the phone number of one of Binion's associates. She didn't say why she needed the number, but Rose
gave it to her anyway. Rose heard the sound of a male voice
in the background on Sandy's end, and did not press her
further about why she wanted the phone number. In retrospect, Sandy's contact with Rose that day had seemed out
of character, even strange, because she rarely had an occasion to speak to her, much less see her in person.

A short time later, at 3:55 p.m. the Las Vegas Metropolitan Police Department's emergency communications
department received a 911 call from a woman who was
obviously distraught and quite hysterical.

"My husband has stopped breathing," was all that she
had said, and then had abruptly hung up. Although the call
was immediately disconnected, the dispatcher was able to
trace it to 2408 Palomino Lane, Ted Binion's residence.

CHAPTER 2

Las Vegas Fire Department paramedic Kenneth Dickinson was the first to arrive at Palomino Lane. Two other emergency medical technicians accompanied him, and a second team of paramedics arrived moments later. They parked on the street in front of the expansive gated home, and walked up the driveway where a hysterical young woman came running toward them screaming nearly unintelligible words when she met them. Between her sobs and carrying on, they were able to discern part of what she was saying: "He's not breathing! He's not breathing!" One of the paramedics, Steven Reincke, remained outside for a few moments and tried to calm down the hysterical woman while Dickinson and the other technicians entered the house. In the process Reincke learned that her name was Sandy Murphy.

"What is your relationship to the patient?" Reincke asked.

"I'm his wife," Sandy responded.

"When was the last time you saw your husband?" Reincke wanted to establish a timeframe for his report.

"It was this morning," Sandy sobbed.

Reincke left Sandy with another technician and entered the home.

Inside, Dickinson and Reincke found a man lying on his back in the den in the southeast quadrant of the house. It was Ted Binion, all right. There was no mistake about that. Ted's remarkable moon-shaped face was known all over town. He was lying on a small mattress atop a throw rug in front of the television. A comforter had been draped over his lower legs, and there was an empty medicine bottle labeled *Xanax* lying on the floor beside him. His skin appeared ashen and gray, and he wasn't moving. Their first thoughts were that he was dead. Reincke walked over to the body, reached down and felt for a pulse in one of Binion's carotid arteries. There was none. The body was cold to the touch and it was apparent that rigor mortis was present in the area of his jaw though strangely absent from the rest of his body.

In the next moment Sandy Murphy ran into the room, dropped to the floor, and attempted to embrace the body. It was all the paramedics could do to keep her off and away from the deceased, but they finally managed to escort her out of the room. One of the technicians remained with her in an attempt to console her as she continued rambling on hysterically.

Dickinson and Reincke promptly hooked up Binion's body to a monitor, but he was a flatliner. There was no need for a chest rub or other attempts at resuscitation. It was clear to them that Binion was dead, and had been for some time. Just how long was difficult to say, but they guessed that it had been several hours.

One of Binion's neighbors, Janice Tanno, saw the activity and wanted to know what was going on and if she could help out in any way. Shocked at the news of Binion's death, Tanno wanted to know how he had died. She was informed that at this point the cause of death had not been determined.

Sandra Murphy, meanwhile, was still hysterical. Amid all the crying and emotional outbursts, it was difficult to comprehend anything she was saying. At one point she composed herself enough to stop babbling and stated, "I don't want to hurt Teddy." Although little attention was given to the statement at that time, investigators would later wonder why she was speaking in the present tense. Why would she make such a statement? Had she merely repeated something she had said to someone earlier—perhaps during an attempt to refuse to do something that someone else wanted her to do—that had been indelibly embedded in her mind? It had seemed like a strange thing to say, but then, people often say unusual things and act strangely under these circumstances.

Because of her seemingly uncontrollable and unmanageable hysteria, having stated to one of the paramedics that she wanted to kill herself, and after she began to hyperventilate, it was decided that Sandy should be taken to the hospital. She was placed onto a gurney and transported by ambulance to Valley Hospital a few blocks away. Janice Tanno accompanied Sandy in an attempt to console her.

It was 5:29 p.m. when Sandy was seen in the emergency room by Dr. Brian Kominsky. Dr. Kominsky wrote in his chart notes that, aside from being hysterical, Sandy Murphy appeared healthy and otherwise normal. He recommended that crisis counselors should evaluate her. Another emergency room physician prescribed Valium to calm her down but, when nurse Larry Krev attempted to administer the medication, Sandy refused it and her hysteria continued.

"Boy, a little overdramatic, eh?" Krev said to a detective waiting outside Murphy's room. Krev would further characterize Sandy's behavior as "almost theatrical." Approximately twenty minutes later, Krev noted that Sandy had calmed down considerably without the Valium.

Minutes later a young man, 33-year-old Richard "Rick" Tabish, arrived at the hospital. Tabish, carrying a cellular telephone, explained that he was a friend of both Ted Binion's and Sandy Murphy's. He met Janice Tanno in the waiting area and explained to her that he had been on his way to the airport when he heard the news about Binion and wanted to see if there was anything he could do to help Sandy through her difficult time. However, Las Vegas Metropolitan Police Department (LVMPD) Detective Jim Mitchell of the general assignment detail, the detective who had been waiting outside her room, was interviewing Sandy. A few minutes later Tanno's son, Alex, came out and announced to those waiting to see Sandy that a police interview was being conducted. Tabish, upon hearing this information, said his goodbyes and promptly left the hospital.

During the interview with Detective Mitchell, Sandy explained that Binion had begun using drugs again shortly after his gaming license had been revoked, and claimed that he was suicidal. She said that she had seen him stick a gun inside his mouth when he was high on drugs. She explained that he had gone into her bedroom and awakened her in the middle of the night to tell her that he was going to try to go to sleep, but that he was fearful and wanted her to watch him.

"Sandy, can you tell me what happened this morning up until this afternoon, when you found Ted?" Mitchell asked.

"He said that he might be sick . . . more stuff so he could . . ." Sandy trailed off, breathing heavily.

"When you say 'more stuff,' what does he mean by 'more stuff'?" Mitchell asked.

"No. I don't wanna . . . I don't wanna, I don't wanna mention it," Sandy replied, crying.

"Sandy, Sandy, just calm down. Sandy, did you give him any heroin today?"

"No. I was looking for it for him and I couldn't find it. He couldn't find it," Sandy said, still crying.

"Sandy, there's a window that's open in your bathroom back in the bedroom where you were, in the northwest corner of the house. Can you tall me why that . . . bathroom window is open?" Mitchell asked.

"I locked myself out last night," Sandy replied between sobs. "I don't have my key . . . and he was asleep and he wouldn't answer the door."

"Okay. Can you tell me why there's a white chair underneath the . . . window?"

"Because I had to stand on the chair . . . because it [the door] was locked."

"Okay. I'm gonna ask you again, Sandy, did you give him any drugs today?"

"I don't . . . I gave him . . . He asked me, so I opened his [unintelligible] for him," she responded. Her crying made it difficult for Mitchell to understand everything that she was saying.

"What type of pills did you give him?" Mitchell asked.

"I didn't give 'em to him, I just brought 'em to him and . . ."

"What type of pills were they?"

"I don't know. He got 'em from my neighbor."

"Were they pills that he got from a doctor?"

"My nei . . . My neighbor's a doctor and my neighbor used to give him that shit before when we were [unintelligible] and I told him, 'If you ever give him that stuff again' . . . And he give him some more last night. I don't know . . . He gave him more."

"What's the doctor's name, Sandy?" Mitchell repeated the question twice because Sandy didn't answer at first, and only continued crying.

"Dr. Lacayo," she finally responded.

"He lives next door to you?"

"Yes."

"Which house does he live in? Does he live to the west of your house or to the east of your house?" Mitchell pressed.

"The east."

"Can you spell his last name for me?"

"L-A-C-A-Y-O. I don't know . . ."

"Do you know his first name?"

"Yeah. Enrique. . . . And he got some other pills from Dr. . . . a couple weeks ago when he tried to get straight. He told me that this is the last time and he wasn't gonna do it ever again . . ."

"When did Dr. Lacayo give him the pills?" Mitchell asked.

"Last night," Sandy said.

"Did Dr. Lacayo see him last night?"

"I—He had to get him the pill."

"Do you know what the pills are? Are the pills in his bedroom?"

"Some are. I think Xanax. But he got some other pills, I don't know what they're called, a couple weeks ago from another doctor."

"Were there any pills left over in the room that we found him in?"

"I don't know. I didn't look. I don't know . . ."

"Sandy, when was the last time you saw him alive?"

"When I left . . . morning . . . the last time I . . . I thought he was alive. He looked like he was sleeping. I thought he was sleeping and he wouldn't wake up, he wouldn't wake up, he wouldn't wake up . . . Oh God! Oh God! Oh God!" Sandy exclaimed, sobbing uncontrollably.

"Sandy, after you found him, Sandy . . ."

"Oh, God! I'm so sorry."

"Sandy, after you found him . . ." Mitchell tried again.

"I'm so sorry."

"Did you clean the room after you found him?" Mitchell asked.

Sandy didn't respond to the question, but continued crying.

"Did you pick anything up in the room?" Mitchell asked.

"I, I, I don't think so . . . Oh, I don't know. I don't think so. I don't know. I found him and he wouldn't wake up and I panicked and I was trying to make him breathe and he wouldn't breathe . . . Oh God! Oh God! Oh God!" Sandy sobbed.

"Sandy, do you remember what time you found him when you came back home?"

"I don't know what time it was," Sandy responded, now breathing heavily. "My watch stopped . . . I don't know what time it is . . . I don't know . . ."

"You said he asked you earlier to sit up with him that night. Do you remember what time that was?" Mitchell probed.

"I don't know . . . He woke me up in the middle of the

night . . . and wanted me to watch him sleep," Sandy explained, breathing heavily.

"Did you see him again after he woke you up in the middle of the night? What did he say to you after . . . he woke you up in the middle of the night?"

"He told me that he was gonna try to . . . that he might be sick and he wanted me to watch him sleep . . . He said he might have a seizure, and to please watch him. I should've never left. I should've never left. I'm so sorry. I'm so sorry. Oh God! Oh God!"

By this time Binion was lying on the mattress on the floor inside the den. It seemed a bit odd, even contradictory, to the detective that someone who was suicidal would be concerned enough about the possibility of having a seizure that he would want someone to remain with him.

"After he woke up, what did you do?"

"I went and laid with him."

"Did you fall back asleep?"

"Oh, for a little while."

"But then when you left the house, he was fine, right?"

"Yes. Well, he was just sleeping."

"How long were you gone from the house?"

"For a few hours. I don't know."

"You don't remember what time you left the house?"

"No."

"Was it in the morning?"

". . . the morning and then I came back and then he was sleeping and I just laid on the sofa and just watched him sleep for a little while and I was tired because he had kept me up all night and then I went and got dressed and then I went to Kathy's and then I went to . . . [unintelligible] and then I came home and I . . . and he was still sleeping and he wouldn't wake up." Sandy was rambling and crying at the same time. ". . . and he wouldn't wake up and I tried to make him breathe and he wouldn't breathe, he wouldn't breathe, he wouldn't breathe. He wouldn't breathe . . ."

* * *

While Detective Mitchell was interviewing Sandy at the hospital, Rick Tabish drove back to Ted Binion's residence accompanied by one of his associates, Michael Milot. Richard Wright, one of Binion's attorneys, was at the residence when Tabish and Milot pulled up in front in Tabish's black Mercedes.

"I'm just totally shocked," Wright said. "I saw him last night, and he was in fine spirits. We talked about the future and what he always talked about, looking for a new ranch." Binion, Wright said, was also looking forward to appealing the Nevada Gaming Commission's revocation of his gaming license. Binion, he said, had been a loyal friend for a long time.

"I was on the way to the airport to fly home to my family in Montana," Tabish said, "when I heard the news and headed over here . . . I know he was happy his sister took over the casino, and he hoped she would do a good job. He was trying to stay out of the limelight, do some more fishing and advance his relationship with his girlfriend . . . It's just such a tragedy . . . I never had any bad dealings with the man . . . What a tragedy. I know he was trying really hard to change his life."

After introducing Milot to Wright and explaining that Milot was an executive in Tabish's business, MRT Transportation of Nevada, a company that specialized in hauling sand, Tabish explained that the police were interrogating Sandy at the hospital. He asked Wright to accompany him back to the hospital to demand that the police interrogation be stopped. Wright agreed. However, by the time Tabish, Milot, and Wright reached the hospital, Detective Mitchell had concluded his interview with Sandy.

Meanwhile, at Binion's residence, after an already long day at work, LVMPD Detective Pat Franks had taken charge of the suspicious death scene. As part of his preliminary survey, Franks noted the names of the paramedics and fire department personnel and anyone else, including Sandy Murphy, who had entered the scene prior to his arrival. As he continued his observations, Franks noted that the living room drapes, which hung ceiling to floor, were drawn, causing the room to be quite dark. He then walked through the living room and passed by a grand piano as he made his way down a hallway that led to other rooms of the house. It was a cursory examination, but he wanted to get a feel for the layout of the house as he found his way back to the southeast den, located a few feet east of the front door. Lying on the floor were a pair of sunglasses and a set of keys, which he later determined belonged to Sandra Murphy. Franks observed Binion's body lying face-up on the mattress, his head resting on a white pillow.

Binion's arms were at his sides, and his legs were straight. His body was clad only in a pair of briefs and an unbuttoned long-sleeve shirt. Franks observed a pair of jeans and a pair of loafers to the left of Binion's knees, an empty pill bottle labeled *Xanax* to the right of Binion's head, an open package of Vantage cigarettes, two disposable cigarette lighters, and a remote control unit, all of which were next to Binion's body. Although Franks had observed a number of firearms in some of the other rooms of the house, there were no weapons present in the den.

Criminalists were ordered to the home and they arrived a short time later to begin processing it in the usual manner that is required when a death has occurred under suspicious circumstances. Crime scene analyst Mike Perkins examined the doors and windows and found all of them secured except for a window in one of the rear bathrooms. He observed the chair beneath the window on the outside of the home that, he presumed, someone had used to stand on to gain entry into the house through the bathroom window. He would later learn the details about the use of the chair that Detective Mitchell had obtained from Sandy Murphy during his interview with her at the hospital.

When Perkins entered the adjacent bathroom, he soon discovered what he suspected was narcotics paraphernalia. A large knife with brown residue on its blade lay on a small table. Next to the knife was what appeared to be a clean piece of aluminum foil, as well as an ashtray. Perkins found what looked like a small piece of a red rubber balloon on the floor next to the table. When he checked inside the trash can he found another piece of balloon, this one pink in color, as well as several pieces of crumpled aluminum foil. He suspected that the brown substance on the knife was heroin, and reasoned that the aluminum foil had likely been cupped and formed into a spoon-like shape in which to smoke the drug. He knew from his training and his experience with addicts that some users place the heroin onto the foil, heat it with a flame, and inhale the smoke that is produced. Addicts commonly referred to this procedure as *chasing the dragon.* Perkins and Franks bagged, marked, and impounded all of the items for additional analysis at the crime laboratory.

As the evening wore on and police investigators and crime scene analysts continued with their work, friends and associates of Ted Binion's showed up at his home to try to to find out what had happened. One of those who showed up was the famous defense attorney, and soon-to-be mayor of Las Vegas, Oscar Goodman, whose claim to fame was defending mobsters. "This is a sad, sad time," said Goodman of his friend's death. "He was one of the best guys I ever met."

Becky Binion-Behnen, Binion's sister, also showed up wanting to know what had happened to her brother. LVMPD Sergeant Jim Young told her that even though Binion's death was considered suspicious, they could not say whether foul play was involved or not.

"At first glance," said Young, "the scene indicated that this was not intentional. We're not one hundred percent certain that it was accidental or intentional, but there is no evidence to make us believe it was intentional." Young indicated that investigators had reason to believe that Binion had been taking prescription medication for possible stress-related problems, and cited the empty bottle of Xanax found next to Binion's body.

"That was not Ted," said Binion-Behnen, who told investigators that she had never known her brother to take prescription drugs. "Ted would be the first to tell you that his drug of choice was heroin."

The investigators recalled that it was his heroin and cocaine use that had caused Binion problems with the gaming commission a few years earlier, and that it was also brought up again more recently, in early 1998, when Binion's gaming license was revoked for good. But during his fight to retain his license, Binion had continuously insisted that he had remained drug-free and he had the results of more than 160 drug tests that backed him up, despite the fact that he had once shown up with his head and body completely shaved, which would make it impossible to remove hair samples to properly administer the test. The investigators reasoned that it was possible, however, that he had relapsed within the past few days.

When the condition of Binion's mental state and the possibility of suicide were brought up, Binion's sister was quick to discount it.

"I talked to him all week," said Binion-Behnen, "and he was not despondent. Ted would never take his own life." She said that although Binion had been fighting with Sandy Murphy all week, he indicated that he still aspired to regain his share of the Horseshoe and return to the business he loved. "Ted was one of the most knowledgeable people in the gaming industry," she said.

Ted Binion, according to those who knew him, was indeed a knowledgeable man whose interests went beyond gaming. He was known to intelligently discuss guns, biology, history, and various types of animals, particularly horses, with just about anyone, even strangers he would meet at the casino. Now he was dead, and by the end of day one of the investigation the police were leaning toward declaring accidental drug overdose as the cause of death.

Even though Binion's sister urged the police to treat her brother's death as a homicide there wasn't, at this point, enough evidence to support such an investigation. If there were answers that would lead them toward homicide, they would likely only materialize through an autopsy and associated toxicology tests. For now, Binion's death was listed as "undetermined," according to homicide Lieutenant Wayne Petersen.

CHAPTER 3

The investigators continued their work throughout the night of September 17 at Ted Binion's home. It was busy with detectives and crime scene technicians coming and going, and security was posted to keep out the merely curious. Outside, above the entrance to the house, they had earlier observed a Halloween decoration that read "R.I.P." Although crime scene analyst Michael Perkins had thought it was strange to have such a decoration posted outside a month and a half before Halloween, which he so noted in his report, no one had had time to pay it much thought because of all the other work they were doing. As he went room-to-room in his search for clues as to what had happened there, Perkins found another identical decoration inside the house. Had Binion been preparing for Halloween this early? he wondered. Or was this just a cruel joke perpetrated by someone with a morbid sense of humor? If so, who besides Sandy Murphy would have had access to the house to put up the displays?

At another point Perkins observed that someone had disabled Binion's burglar alarm by removing some of the wiring. He didn't know whether Binion had done it himself, or whether someone else had, for possibly sinister reasons.

As they analyzed the scene, it seemed to forty-two-year-old Detective James Buczek, an eleven-year veteran of the Las Vegas Metropolitan Police Department who had been assigned to homicide detail for the past two-and-a-half years, and who had also been brought into the Binion case as the lead investigator, that perhaps Binion's body had been cleaned, along with the crime scene, prior to his death being reported. The manner in which the body was found contrasted greatly to those in other deaths by drug overdose—both accidental and suicide-related—that they had investigated. Usually in such cases there are signs of heavy purging, or vomiting, from the victim. But in Binion's case there were only traces of such evidence in the immediate area of his body. They were also uncomfortable because of the way Binion's body was lying when they arrived. He was on his back, his head resting peacefully on a pillow, his arms straight at his sides. Strangely, it seemed like someone had deliberately placed his body in a mortuary-like position. Often when someone has succumbed to death by poisoning or drug overdose, the victim goes into convulsions prior to death. This didn't appear to be the case here, and they wondered why. To Franks and Buczek, the scene looked like it had been staged. Proving it, they knew, would be another matter. Even though there were many circumstances which indeed appeared suspicious, and Binion's sister, Becky, continued to urge them to treat his death as a homicide, Franks and Buczek knew that the facts of the case at this point could not support such an investigation.

At another point the detectives noticed that the audiocassette tapes had been removed from the telephone answering devices inside the house and were missing. Why, they wondered, would anyone remove the tapes from their answering machines when such devices can easily be turned off or disconnected?

After the criminalists and the detectives had concluded their work at Binion's home and Binion's body had been taken to the morgue, the residence was turned over to Public Administrator Jared Shafer. Shafer, accompanied by one of his investigators and attorney Richard Wright, inspected the interior of the home to determine if there were any valuables that needed securing. Binion was known to keep plenty of cash in the house, sometimes a million dollars at a time, and he had a very valuable coin collection of rare silver dollars that he kept in the den. He was also known to keep jewelry and several guns in the house. However, there were no valuables that they could find. It would be reported later that another collection of very rare silver dollars, minted in Carson City, Nevada, in the late 1800s, estimated to be worth between ten and fifteen million dollars, was also missing. They did find several of Binion's guns, but because of the suspicious nature of the missing valuables, Wright, on behalf of Binion's estate, hired a security company to post guards at the front and back of the residence until the situation could be resolved.

When Sandy Murphy was released from the hospital later that evening, Janice Tanno and attorney Richard Wright agreed to take responsibility for her for the night. At first Rick Tabish had planned to get her a room at the Desert Inn, but after discussing the situation, it was decided that Sandy would spend the night at Tanno's house. Tabish and Wright drove her there.

By this time Sandy had calmed down considerably, and she and Tanno talked for a while before retiring for the evening. Sandy told her that she'd had lunch with Rick Tabish and her lawyer, William Knudson, at Z'Tejas Grill on Paradise Road, near the convention center, earlier that day before coming home and finding Binion's body. Sandy said that she had left the restaurant at 3:45 p.m., when Tabish had driven her home, and that after being dropped off, she remembered that she had left her purse in Tabish's car. Although Tanno didn't realize it at the time, there was something wrong with the timeframe that Sandy had just described. Z'Tejas Grill was more than halfway to the airport from Ted Binion's home, toward the southeast part of the city from Binion's centrally located home, and it would have been difficult, if not impossible, for her to have left the restaurant at 3:45 p.m. and arrive home in time to notify the police of Binion's death at 3:55 p.m., particularly with the usual heavy afternoon traffic.

An hour or so after Sandy had gone to bed, Linda Carroll, 41, her friend in California who had accompanied her to Las Vegas in February 1995 and a former Cheetah's employee herself, showed up at Tanno's home asking to see Sandy. Carroll told Tanno that she had heard about Binion's death on the news and had driven from California to see her friend. Although Sandy had begun crying again, the two women talked for about half an hour. Afterward Carroll left to find a hotel room and Sandy went back to bed. Although they would meet and talk again, that evening was the only time that Carroll would recall observing Sandy display any emotion over Ted Binion's death.

The next morning, Friday, September 18, Tanno left Murphy sleeping at her home while she went to Mass at a nearby Catholic church. When she returned home at 8:25 a.m., Rick Tabish was there talking to Sandy in the cabana. They told Tanno they were going for a ride where they could talk alone, and were gone for approximately fifteen minutes. Sandy appeared to be her old self again. After being totally out of control the night before, shaking, crying, and rambling hysterically, unable to even walk by herself, it seemed to Tanno that Sandy had made a remarkable recovery and had regained her composure.

Throughout the morning Sandy made several telephone calls from Tanno's home. During one of those calls Tanno overheard Sandy talking to James J. Brown, an attorney and a longtime personal friend of Ted Binion's. During the conversation Sandy expressed concern that she was not going to get the Palomino Lane house. When she finished her call with Brown, she called attorney Richard Wright, and explained to him that she was the beneficiary of a one-million-dollar insurance policy on Ted's life. She asked Wright for advice on how she could file a claim, but Wright told her that he was not aware of the policy to which she referred.

Later that same afternoon, Ted Binion's 18-year-old daughter, Bonnie, who had been attending an exclusive boarding school in Connecticut, asked for and received permission from the authorities to enter her father's house to remove some of her personal belongings as well as photos that the family wanted to display at Ted's funeral. Attorney Jim Brown accompanied her. She also removed several of her father's watches and his wallet, which, oddly, contained no cash. While Bonnie was gathering her father's personal items, Sandy Murphy showed up and demanded access to the house to obtain her personal belongings. Attorney Bill Knudson, her friend Linda Carroll, and Tanya Cropp, 23, one of Binion's secretaries, sometime maid, and also Sandy's friend, accompanied her. Brown refused to grant Sandy and her companions access to the house, and an argument ensued.

Knudson called the police, and patrol officers from the downtown precinct responded a short time later. Sandy explained why she was at the residence, and provided the officers with identification, including a driver's license and vehicle registration, which showed 2408 Palomino Lane as her legal address. After verifying that the information Sandy provided was correct, the officers informed Brown that he would have to leave and provide Sandy access to the house unless Brown had a court order giving him possession of the property. Brown promptly left to try and obtain the order.

When Linda Carroll and Sandy Murphy went to the southeast den where Binion's body had been found, Carroll was suddenly overcome by an eerie feeling, likely an emotional reaction resulting from the fact that a man had died in that room. She noticed, however, that Sandy did not seem bothered by entering the den; she failed to show any observable reactions or emotions, appearing almost detached from what had happened there. Sandy's lack of emotion seemed strange, since this was a room where she had spent many an evening with the man she presumably loved for the past three years.

As they went through the house, Sandy complained to Carroll that twenty thousand dollars in cash was missing, as well as other valuables. When the missing answering machine tapes were mentioned, Sandy told Carroll that she had disposed of them but did not offer an explanation as to why.

While attorney James Brown was away attempting to get the court order, Rick Tabish arrived with a video camera and handed it to attorney Bill Knudson. He advised Knudson that a videotape of the interior of the house should be made to inventory everything. Tanya Cropp would later recall that "Tabish was pissed" about something, but she didn't know what. Tabish stayed for only a short time, and before he left he called Sandy aside.

"I'll talk to you later," Tabish was reported as having said. "I've got to go take something before Jim Brown gets his hands on that, too." He then left to go to the site of one of the companies that he did business with, the equipment yard of All Star Transit Mix, where Michael Milot was instructing employees to load an excavator onto a lowboy trailer so that they could transport it to Tabish's MRT equipment yard at 9555 South Las Vegas Boulevard.

Two hours later James Brown returned to Ted Binion's home with an order signed by Clark County District Court Judge Jack Lehman that appointed Brown as the administrator of Binion's estate. The order effectively gave Brown exclusive control of Binion's Palomino Lane home. He showed the order to Knudson, at which point Knudson proceeded with the videotaping of the interior and contents of the house. When told of the missing cash and other items, Brown and Bonnie Binion denied removing any of them. When Knudson finished with the videotaping he, Sandy, Linda, and Tanya left the residence.

Meanwhile, at 5 p.m., several truck drivers and other employees were waiting for their paychecks to arrive at Tabish's MRT equipment yard. MRT employee Willie Alder normally delivered the checks to the yard. As the afternoon wore on, the employees became disgruntled when Alder failed to show up. They were finally told that the checks would be very late because Alder was busy working on a project for Rick Tabish. The employees were not told what Alder was doing, but the truth of the matter was he was experiencing difficulty loading the excavator onto the trailer.

As the employees continued to wait, they observed Rick Tabish, Michael Milot, and Steve Wadkins huddling around a belly dump truck. They were speaking in hushed voices so that they couldn't be heard by anyone except themselves as they examined the size of the large vehicle. One person also later reported seeing several plastic cases, the type that are used to store coin collections, in the back of a truck near where Tabish and the others were huddled together. A short time later Milot instructed Alder to drive the excavator to the Union 76 truck stop just off Interstate 15 and Highway 160, also known as Blue Diamond Road, the direct route from Las Vegas across the Spring Mountains to the desert town of Pahrump.

CHAPTER 4

On a chilly morning in February 1998, Ted Binion stood in an alley behind the Horseshoe Hotel and Casino with a sawed-off shotgun in his hand and his faithful dog, Princess, by his side. Dressed as usual in a casual shirt, jeans, and cowboy boots, Binion warmed himself by a fire he had started in a large barrel just outside the casino. Because of all of the problems he was having with the state Gaming Control Board, he wasn't allowed inside the Horseshoe under any circumstances. So he stood by his pickup truck, a white Ford, and watched as armed guards loaded sacks of silver and heavy silver bars, some seven million dollars' worth, onto the trailer that was hooked to the back of a rental truck that was parked behind his own pickup. When the guards had finished loading all of Ted's silver onto the trailer, they hauled it under Ted's supervision, with Ted riding shotgun, so to speak, and unloaded it in the garage of his Palomino Lane home where it remained until the following June.

While some would consider it extremely risky, keeping seven million dollars in silver stored inside his garage was not uncharacteristic of Ted Binion's style. Most people would consider such a move risky, even foolish, and some would say that Ted was downright crazy to do such a thing. But that was Ted Binion's way. He had plenty of guns there with which to protect his precious silver, and he had dogs and a security system for those times when he wasn't at home. Ted was known to keep many valuables at his home, including an abundance of cash and his coin collections. He had been known to keep a million dollars on hand at times, and according to his daughter, Bonnie, he had at least a hundred thousand dollars in the house at any given time. He was also fond of burying things in his back yard. It wasn't unusual for his gardener to discover bags of marijuana that Binion had buried in the rose beds, and sometimes he would do the same thing with bags of cash. It would later be said that such eccentricities had caused him to believe that he was invincible, untouchable, and that it was precisely that type of thinking that got him into trouble with the law and the Gaming Control Board and, ultimately, cost him his life.

One of the primary reasons that Ted had removed his silver from the Horseshoe was that he knew he would likely lose his gaming license at a hearing that had been scheduled for the following month. He was being investigated for his close ties to known mobster Herbert "Fat Herbie" Blitzstein, who was found murdered in his Las Vegas townhouse on January 6, 1997, slumped over in a chair with three bullets in his head. The gaming regulators were also investigating a questionable one-hundred-thousand-dollar loan that Binion had made to Peter "P. J." Ribaste, a convicted felon alleged to have ties to the Kansas City, Missouri, arm of La Cosa Nostra. The loan was for a part ownership of a used car lot on Decatur Boulevard in Las Vegas, and it was made with a handshake. No signatures, no paperwork. The deal had been done Ted Binion–style all the way.

Six months after Blitzstein's slaying there was talk that Ted had offered to pay a man named Alfred Mauriello fifty thousand dollars to have his sister, Becky, killed. According to the FBI, he was unhappy about her attempts to take over the Horseshoe from him and his brother, Jack, and sought to put an end to the family squabbling over the casino by hiring Mauriello. Mauriello was the reputed mobster who was eventually charged with hiring two men to kill Blitzstein as part of a scheme engineered by the Los Angeles Mafia so that they could take over the street rackets they believed Blitzstein was running. But Ted reportedly had changed his mind about having his sister killed and had backed out of the deal. Word on the street was that his decision had angered the mob and that a hit on Teddy Binion had been ordered. Others were saying that his sister, Becky, had ordered the hit. The truth of the matter was that no one really knew for sure who had ordered the purported hit or, for that matter, if one had actually been ordered.

A week later, however, on Wednesday, June 4, 1997, the front of Binion's house was sprayed with machine gun fire. The house was damaged, as was a Ford Explorer that was parked in the driveway. Ted was out gambling at the time, but Las Vegas police had previously made him aware of the proposed hit. He wasn't aware that talk on the street indicated that the mob wanted to kill him so that they could steal millions of dollars that they believed he had stashed in his house some seven months *before* he moved his silver out of the Horseshoe. It would seem that if the mob had wanted Ted dead, whether because someone had actually ordered a hit or because of someone's own interests in wanting a piece of Ted's fortune, they would have taken a more direct, decisive approach to killing him rather than merely spraying the front of his home with bullets. It seemed more likely that someone was just trying to scare him, for reasons known only to the perpetrators.

Ted would later tell people that he thought that it had been his young nephew, Benny, Becky's son, who had fired the shots at his home while out screwing around with his friends. Benny denied it, and suggested that Ted may have done it himself. There was no evidence to suggest that Benny had fired the shots, but it was known that Ted frequently played with his guns when he'd been drinking. It was left as a mystery that probably would never be solved.

Ted, more because of the purported mob hit than the gunshots fired at his house, was now much more fearful for his life, and some said that he had become a bit paranoid. In addition to keeping more than ten rifles, pistols and shotguns inside his house, as well as keeping near constant watch with his state-of-the-art security and video monitoring system, Ted installed rear-view automobile mirrors on each of his bedposts. His friends didn't know if his drug use had made him this paranoid or if he had just lost his mind. Whatever it was, Ted suddenly seemed to be taking fewer chances with his life and belongings.

The Gaming Control Board had tried to work with Ted Binion despite his problems through the years. In 1986, Binion was busted for possession of narcotics outside of a Las Vegas drug house, and quickly became the focus of a police narcotics investigation into heroin trafficking. Because they were unable to build a strong enough case against him, Binion was able to plead guilty to a lesser charge, a misdemeanor, and the Gaming Control Board saw fit to only suspend his gaming license until 1993.

In 1990, however, Ted was brought up on a federal indictment, along with seven other people, some of whom were employees of the Horseshoe. The indictment alleged that Binion and Horseshoe employees robbed, kidnapped, and beat a number of Horseshoe customers, several of whom were black, that they had deemed "undesirable" to the Horseshoe's normal standards. These would include drunk and disorderly customers, gamblers who tried to welsh on bets and gambling debts, and those who became threatening to the dealers when they lost their money at the tables. Binion and some of his security guards were accused of taking the customers to a back room of the Horseshoe and roughing them up. Binion found that luck was with him again when the federal case fell apart and the indictment against him and the others was thrown out. Nonetheless, the Horseshoe ended up settling with the victims by paying $675,000 in a civil lawsuit.

Ted's gaming license was reinstated in 1993 after he reached an agreement to undergo random drug testing. Things went well for him until 1997. He regularly tested negative and seemed to be clean of drugs, and he performed community service at a rehabilitation center for drug addicts that even involved bathing some of the patients. He reportedly enjoyed the experience and commented to others that he found it rewarding. Following some of the drug rehabilitation meetings, Binion would often take a group of his fellow patients out for a night on the town in the Horseshoe's limousines. He also returned to nearly non-stop drinking.

When he showed up out of the blue for a drug test with his entire body shaved so that the lab personnel could not obtain the needed hair samples to conduct the test, he helped seal his own fate with the Gaming Control Board. He soon found himself being investigated for possession of cocaine and marijuana, and in May 1997 he admitted to using those drugs again. It was also determined that he was allowing Sandy Murphy to smoke marijuana inside his home whenever she wanted. As a result his gaming license was suspended again, thus marking the beginning of the end to Ted Binion's gaming career.

If he didn't have enough problems already, Ted Binion's tribulations escalated on Sunday, August 10, 1997. According to police reports, a man got into an argument with a 20-year-old male gas station attendant, Thomas Lee Woodward, over pumping gas at a Texaco station on Charleston Boulevard, just off Interstate 15 and only minutes from Binion's home. The argument intensified to scuffling between the two men inside the station, and soon escalated to pushing and shoving, accompanied by a foul-mouthed shouting match. According to the reports, the attendant, feeling threatened, squirted pepper spray into the man's face, after which the man left. The man returned about an hour later, with a shotgun. He purportedly pointed the shotgun at the attendant and identified himself as Ted Binion.

The two men scuffled again and, according to police reports based on the attendant's statements, Woodward was able to grab the shotgun and take it away from Binion. Woodward pepper-sprayed Binion again and Binion fled in what was reported as a sport utility vehicle. This time the attendant and another witness obtained the Nevada license plate number, 839-HKJ, and called the police. The police quickly determined that the vehicle was registered to Ted Binion.

When officers showed up at Binion's home at 7:15 p.m., Binion told them that he had indeed been to the gas station in question, but insisted that he had not pointed the shotgun at anyone. Instead, he told the officers, the gas station attendant had gone out to his vehicle and removed the shotgun, bringing it with him into the station at which time Binion tried to take it away from him. The officer observed pepper spray residue on Binion's face, and called paramedics to the scene to remove the chemical. Another officer, in the meantime, brought Woodward to Binion's home where he identified Binion as the person who had pointed the shotgun at him. The other witness told one of the officers that he had also observed a handgun tucked into Binion's waistband during the brawl. Binion was read his Miranda rights and booked into the Clark County Detention Center on charges of burglary and assault with a deadly weapon. He was released a short time later after posting bail of five thousand dollars on the burglary charge and three thousand dollars on the assault charge.

Although police didn't know it at the time, Woodward had given them a false name when he filed the complaint against Binion. When they became aware that his real name was Woodward, investigators learned that he had an outstanding arrest warrant from North Las Vegas police stemming from an incident that dated back to November 26, 1996, in which he had allegedly pointed a gun at another man and told him that he was a police officer. Woodward had also allegedly handcuffed the man against his will.

According to authorities, Woodward pleaded guilty to two misdemeanors in a plea bargain arrangement that netted him probation instead of jail time. However, a few weeks later, Woodward was arrested again. This time he was charged with murder in connection with the beating death of a homeless Hispanic man the previous March, whom police still have not identified to this day. Woodward did not become a suspect in that case until a witness came forward and told police that he had watched Woodward beat the homeless man to death with a portion of a log as the man begged for his life behind a bank building near Cheyenne Avenue and Las Vegas Boulevard North. As it turned out, the witness who reported the beating death of the homeless man was the same witness who had corroborated Woodward's account of the incident involving Ted Binion at the Texaco station. The witness was also a close friend of Woodward's. Woodward subsequently pleaded guilty to a reduced count of voluntary manslaughter and was sentenced to a minimum of eight years, and a maximum of twenty years in prison.

To Binion's benefit, police had found another witness to the Texaco gas station incident who had been in the station at the time. The new witness told the investigators that the altercation hadn't occurred the way that Woodward had reported it. In fact, Woodward had asked his friend to lie for him against Binion. The new witness told police that Woodward was the one who had taken the shotgun from inside Binion's vehicle, just as Binion had said, and then had sprayed Binion with pepper spray *after* Binion tried to take the weapon away from Woodward. As a result, the charges against Binion were dropped. However, his woes with the Gaming Control Board were not over.

On Monday, March 24, 1998, the Gaming Control Board determined that Ted Binion had violated state gaming regulations by associating, both socially and in business, with Herbie Blitzstein. They found that Binion had rekindled his relationship with Blitzstein as early as 1994 and had maintained it through November 1996 with the knowledge that Blitzstein had ties to the Chicago mob and had served time for credit card fraud. Binion told the board that they had met in front of Binion's house in 1994 after having not seen each other for some time. Blitzstein had been driving a Rolls Royce that was similar to one that Binion owned, which was in need of repair, and Binion had stopped him when he saw him drive by and invited him in for a drink. As they renewed their friendship, Blitzstein made arrangements to have Binion's car fixed at his auto repair shop, Any Auto Repair, and would later service other vehicles for Binion. Binion also admitted that it was Blitzstein who had introduced him to a contractor who remodeled Binion's home, who turned out to be a longtime mob figure who later became an FBI informant and fingered one of Blitzstein's killers.

The board also determined that Binion and Blitzstein went to dinner together on at least four occasions, and at other times met at two Las Vegas topless clubs, Club Paradise and Cheetah's. On two such occasions Blitzstein gave Binion a ride home afterward. The gaming regulators also determined that Binion assisted Blitzstein in cashing two auto insurance claims checks at the Horseshoe on New Year's Day 1995, one for five hundred dollars and another for eleven thousand dollars, despite the fact that Binion was prohibited from having any involvement with the Horseshoe. Binion denied any wrongdoing in any of the instances of association with Blitzstein, and characterized Blitzstein as an old man who was trying to straighten out his life. Binion compared Blitzstein to his father, Benny, an ex-felon who by most accounts had been rehabilitated.

The board also determined that Binion had engaged in business dealings with Joe DeLuca, who co-owned Any Auto Repair shop with Herbie Blitzstein. DeLuca was another mob associate who had pleaded guilty to racketeering charges and also became a government informant. In the arrangement he had with DeLuca, Binion's personal vehicles were serviced and repaired at the shop as were several limousines owned by the Horseshoe. It was unfortunate for Binion that all of this had come about at a time when a national commission had been formed to study gambling, and Nevada was being scrutinized to see how well it regulated its mainstay industry. Any other time, the Gaming Control Board might only have chosen to slap his hands, issue a fine, give him another suspension, or even look the other way. This time, because all eyes were on Nevada, they had to take decisive action.

On Monday, March 23, 1998, citing a state regulation—one that had never been applied before—that prohibits licensees from associating with people of "notorious or unsavory reputations or who have extensive police records," the Gaming Control Board voted 4–0 to permanently revoke Ted Binion's gaming license.

"It's not the end of the world," Binion said as he left the meeting with his lawyers. But it was clear that he was devastated by the board's decision, and friends would say that he never got over it.

But Ted Binion couldn't seem to stop associating with ex-felons. A few months before he lost his license he had met Rick Tabish at a urinal in the men's room of Piero's Italian restaurant, an upscale eatery located on Convention Center Drive just off The Strip that attracts many of the local business people as well as wannabe dealmakers in their quest for money. Binion was there having lunch with Sandy Murphy, and he had invited Tabish, an ex-felon, to join them. Of course there wasn't any way for Binion to have known that Tabish was an ex-felon, but even if he had known, given his past practices, Binion probably would have asked Tabish to join him anyway.

Tabish, a burly-looking, smooth talker from Montana, had been actively looking for investors for his business projects and he had begun frequenting Piero's in the hope of meeting and becoming acquainted with someone with a lot of extra cash to throw around. Ted Binion had certainly fit the bill, and it wasn't long before the two men had become friends, and for a time their friendship seemed to flourish.

Thirty-three-year-old Richard "Rick" Tabish was born March 15, 1965, in Missoula, Montana, to Frank and Lani Tabish, the second of three boys. His father owned and operated a petroleum distribution company and was one of the wealthiest men in Missoula. As a result, his sons never had to want for anything and were afforded a childhood of comfort and opulence. After graduating from Big Sky High School in 1983, Tabish entered the University of Montana in Missoula but dropped out after only two quarters of attendance. Afterward, he became a familiar face at the Missoula County Jail. Most of his early offenses were for drinking, driving, and fighting, prompting the cops to characterize him as a wild kid with more money than brains, and a Missoula bartender to portray him as one of the "three baddest motherfuckers in the city." His favorite pastimes soon included chasing women, working out, and being unemployed, and he seemed to relish the "don't-fuck-with-me" persona that he had developed for himself.

By the time he was twenty, Tabish had stolen a seventeenth-century painting valued at more than $600,000 from the home of a prominent Missoula attorney who also happened to be a family friend. After being caught for the crime, Tabish confessed and returned the painting. As part of the plea-bargain arrangement, he received a three-year suspended sentence and did not serve any jail time.

Two years later, in November 1987, Tabish was involved in a motor vehicle altercation that began when another driver had purportedly given him "the finger" as he passed him. Tabish caught up with the other driver, pulled him over to the side of the road, and physically assaulted him as the prevailing party during a fistfight. Tabish was subsequently charged with aggravated assault for the attack, was convicted and sentenced to six months in jail, and ordered to pay eight hundred dollars in restitution. Except for forty-one days that he had to serve in jail, the rest of the sentence was suspended.

On another occasion, also in the 1980s, Tabish allegedly stole $2,500 from a restaurant owned by one of his friends. The case was handled out of court, the restaurant's owner was repaid, and Tabish was not charged with the theft.

In 1988 Tabish moved to Arizona for a short time.

Along with two other men, he was suspected of operating a drug ring in Montana. Following surveillance and an investigation, Tabish and his cohorts were arrested for shipping a quarter-pound of cocaine from Arizona to Montana in a Federal Express package. In 1988 Tabish pleaded guilty to the charges and was sentenced to ten years in prison, with seven years suspended. He served nine months, then was paroled and placed on probation for the remainder of his sentence, which formally ended in 1997.

While on parole and probation, Tabish obtained a job for a rock-crushing business. He met the owner's daughter, Mary Jo Rehbein, married her in 1991, and fathered two children with her. During the 1990s Tabish started a number of small businesses, including Telepro, a telecommunications company; Wash Works, Incorporated, a truck-washing business; and finally a truck-hauling company that he called MRT Transport, which provided trucks and equipment for use on construction jobsites in Montana, Nevada, and Oregon. Although characterized as a hard worker, Tabish encountered cash-flow problems with each of his ventures.

After his probation was up, he decided to head for Las Vegas to make a new start, hoping to break his string of bad luck. He left Mary Jo and the kids in Montana, planning to send for them after becoming established in Nevada. Things did not work out the way that he had planned, however, and Mary Jo and the kids remained in Montana. Rick only saw his family when he'd come home on an occasional weekend.

After arriving in Las Vegas, he quickly set up and started MRT Transportation, a subsidiary of his Montana trucking operation, as well as MRT Contracting and MRT Leasing. Always carrying a cellular telephone, Tabish quickly made a name for himself within the business community of Sin City. In his feverish drive to succeed, he quickly made contacts and soon found that he was meeting even more people through those initial contacts in his

search for an investor with money to spend. He had heard
about Ted Binion, and when he met him in the men's room
at Piero's it was as if fate had dealt him a winning hand.
Little did he know that meeting Binion would ultimately
bring about his undoing. Given the characteristics of his
personality, however, even if he had known, he likely
would have forged ahead to cement his relationship with
the gambling icon.

As time went on, Tabish and Binion became closer. Tabish was known to visit Binion and Sandy Murphy at their
home, and they would socialize together publicly. Sometimes Ted would even ask Rick to tag along with Sandy
when she went shopping, to keep an eye on her. Rick Tabish's name came up during conversations that Binion held
with an acquaintance, a part-time building contractor, who
told him that Tabish had a reputation as a contractor. As
he continued to build Binion's trust, it wasn't long before
the subject of Binion's silver arose, and Binion began talking of wanting to move it out of his garage to a location
near his ranch in Pahrump, a small desert town about sixty
miles southwest of Las Vegas.

That property consisted of several acres right in the center of town about a mile from his ranch, where Highway
160 intersects with Highway 372, the road to Death Valley.
On one side was a Terrible Herbst casino known as "Terrible's Town," owned by the Herbst family, and on the
other a Burger King and a Smith's Food King supermarket.
A McDonald's restaurant was located across the highway,
as was a gas station and convenience store. It was the bus-
iest intersection in Pahrump, where people came and went
day and night. In keeping with his penchant for burying
things, Binion wanted to build an underground cement vault
on the site's northwest corner where he could store his
seven million dollars in silver. Binion eventually asked Tabish to build the vault for him and, after surveying the area
with Binion, Tabish agreed. When construction of the concrete vault was completed, Tabish, Binion, and a group of

men who worked for Tabish transported Binion's silver to Pahrump on July 4, 1998, and sealed it ten feet underground. Afterward, Tabish asked Binion if he wanted to change the combination to the vault's lock so that only Binion would know it. Binion had declined, and said that he trusted Tabish.

However, after the transfer of the silver had been completed, Binion called Sergeant Steve Huggins of the Nye County Sheriff's Department, and expressed concern that the people who knew of the vault's location, including Rick Tabish and his employees, might attempt to steal it. He asked Huggins to patrol the area for him, and Huggins assured him that he would.

Binion also asked his ranch manager, David Mattsen, to keep an eye on the vault. Mattsen, who had been hired by Binion in September 1994 for one thousand dollars a month, lived, room and board free, on Binion's Pahrump ranch with his wife. Even though Mattsen, 52, who rarely had more than two dollars in his pocket at any given time and had a reputation for always borrowing money from his friends, had frequently complained about being underpaid, Binion considered him trustworthy.

Ted Binion knew a great deal about many things, including history, math, making money, having a good time, and living the high life. However, as has been shown, he didn't seem to know much about how to wisely choose his friends or whom to trust.

CHAPTER 5

Pahrump has been said to mean "one hundred dollars per rump" by some of the locals, who try to find levity in the fact that a number of legalized whorehouses, including the Chicken Ranch and Madame Butterfly's, are located nearby. In reality, Pahrump is a Paiute Indian word and has been loosely translated to mean "water rock" or "place where big waters flow," and is a somewhat strange name, not so much because of the way it is pronounced, but because of the town's location in the Mojave Desert. However, there appears to be some accuracy to the name, as studies have shown that Pahrump sits atop a huge aquifer of approximately twenty-two million acre-feet of water.

Despite the fact that thirty-five thousand people now live in the ever-growing community, it is still by and large a Western-style town. The Pahrump Valley, surrounded by Mt. Charleston and the Spring Mountains to the east and the Nopah Vista Mountains to the west, still boasts a rural, country-like atmosphere with clean fresh air, very little crime, and breathtaking sunsets, and is home to the Pahrump Valley Vineyards, Nevada's only winery and producer of award-winning wines. Although modernized in many ways with conveniences of shopping and fast food, cable television and the Internet, its citizens still have a deep love of the Old West, and instead of romanticizing about cowboys, roping cattle, riding horses, and galloping off into the sunset, many of Pahrump's denizens actively "live it" and actually enjoy a plate of beans and biscuits or a deep-pit barbecue for dinner. It is in that spirit that the annual Harvest Festival is held. On Friday evening, September 18, 1998, two and a half months after Ted Binion had built his concrete vault in the center of town, Pahrump kicked off the celebration with the annual Harvest Festival parade, rodeo, and fair at the fairgrounds on the north end of town.

While Ted Binion's body lay in a refrigerator unit in the Clark County Morgue sixty miles away in Las Vegas less than two days after his death, his ranch manager, David Mattsen, and his wife, Thressa, attended the Harvest Festival rodeo. After the rodeo, Mattsen ran into Sheriff Wade Lieske, an eighteen-year veteran of the Nye County Sheriff's Department, who had twice been elected sheriff and was purportedly a good friend of Ted Binion's. They spoke alone for about five minutes, out of earshot of Mattsen's wife. Afterward, Mattsen and Thressa returned to the Binion ranch on Wilson Road.

Later that evening the telephone rang. Thressa Mattsen answered it and recognized the voice of Rick Tabish, calling to speak to her husband. After Mattsen and Tabish spoke for a few minutes, Mattsen left the ranch. A security guard who had been posted at the front gate by Binion's estate after Binion's death noted that it was 10:00 p.m. when Mattsen drove away. Upon his return the guard noted that the time was 10:30 p.m.

Two hours later, by then Saturday morning, September 19, 1998, Mattsen left the ranch again, this time driving a tow truck. Mattsen told the security guard that he had received a telephone call from a friend who needed help towing his car. The security guard noted that the time was 12:25 a.m. Mattsen never returned to the ranch that morning.

At 2:10 a.m. Nye County Sheriff's Department Sergeant Ed Howard was out on routine patrol when he received a call from Detective Sergeant Steve Huggins who instructed Howard to drive by and check on Ted Binion's vault. There had been reports of a disturbance at the site. When Howard arrived a short time later, followed in another patrol car by Deputy Dean Pennock, he observed two pickup trucks, an excavator, lots of dust, and three men, one of whom was operating heavy machinery. He also observed a tractor with a trailer for hauling heavy equipment, and a belly dump truck. As he turned off Highway 160 and into the area of the vault, he observed that a man operating the excavator was attempting to smooth out the dirt that had been disturbed near the road. Howard observed two men he would later identify as Rick Tabish and David Mattsen standing by, as the other man, Michael Milot, operated the excavator. Wondering what these men could possibly be doing at this hour of the morning, Howard parked his patrol car. Before he could get out, Mattsen approached the vehicle.

"We'll be done here in a few minutes," Mattsen told Howard as he leaned into the patrol car. "We're just moving some stuff." Mattsen explained that they were cleaning up some "ordnance" that had been stored on the property. "Where's Wade?" Mattsen asked, referring to Sheriff Wade Lieske. He explained to Howard that he had spoken to Lieske earlier and that Lieske was aware of what they were doing on the property.

Tabish then walked up to Howard's car and reiterated that they would be finished with their work shortly. He explained that they were removing concrete from the site because the property was being sold to the Herbst family. Tabish also explained to Howard that he had spoken to Sheriff Lieske and that "everything is okay . . . the sheriff knows we're doing this." Howard, recalling how Ted Binion had told Sergeant Huggins to keep an eye on the vault for him, and wondering why Mattsen had told him that they were removing "ordnance" and Tabish had told him that they were removing concrete, decided that he'd better have a look for himself. He got out of his patrol car and walked toward the tractor-trailer and the belly dump.

"What's inside the big truck?" he asked.

"Nothing," Tabish responded.

Howard didn't believe him. One look at the truck and he could see that it was nearly buckling under the weight of its load. He and Deputy Pennock climbed up and pulled back the tarp that covered it. Inside, they saw a huge stash of silver in bars and coins. One look was all that it took for him to know that it was Ted Binion's buried fortune.

"There's a shitload of silver in there!" Pennock declared.

Howard looked toward Tabish for an explanation.

"Okay, I lied," Tabish said to Howard.

Tabish then told Howard that he was Ted Binion's good friend and had built the vault for him. He claimed that Binion told him that if anything happened to him, Tabish should retrieve the silver, move it to the ranch or take it to Los Angeles, liquidate it, and deposit the money he got for it in a trust account for Binion's daughter, Bonnie. Tabish reiterated that he had previously spoken to Sheriff Lieske about what he was doing and insisted that everything was okay. He said that he had tried calling the ranch to let security know that they were bringing over the silver, but insisted that he could not get through. He presumed that the phones had been cut off by Binion's estate. Howard wondered why he just didn't drive over there and ask the security guard to let him in. After all, he reasoned, if this was all on the up-and-up, security would have been notified in advance.

Sergeant Steve Huggins arrived at the scene a short time later, and it was decided between Huggins and Howard that Sheriff Lieske should be called and asked to come out. Maybe, they thought, he could help clear things up. While waiting for Lieske to arrive, Tabish continued to talk to the two lawmen and revealed that he had been at Ted Binion's home on the day he died. He talked briefly about Binion's addiction to heroin, and the plans Binion had made to kick his habit.

"Ted Binion told me that he was going to take a whole bottle of Xanax tablets and lay down to go to sleep," Tabish said, "and when he woke up his body would be cleansed of all the drugs."

According to the police, Tabish also stated that Binion had authorized a payment of up to one hundred thousand dollars to Sheriff Lieske for allowing him to excavate the vault and retrieve the silver. When Lieske arrived he was briefed by the two sergeants about what had occurred and the statements Tabish had made. He approached Rick Tabish.

"You told me that you were a business partner of Ted's, and that you were coming out here to pick up *your* property," Lieske said.

Tabish quickly denied saying that he was Binion's business partner, and instead insisted that he had told Lieske that he had business dealings with Binion. Tabish further denied that he had said that the property belonged to him, and said that Lieske had told him that he could come out and "take the stuff."

"I never said that," Lieske replied.

"Wade, I told you that we were gonna take care of you as soon as we were done with this," Tabish responded. Following that statement Tabish, Mattsen, and Milot were promptly arrested and booked on burglary, grand larceny, attempted grand larceny, suspicion of theft, attempted embezzlement, and conspiracy to commit grand larceny. The three men were each held on one hundred thousand dollars bond.

After the trio was taken to jail, Lieske called Detective Christine Redmond to inventory the silver, and hired a private security company to retrieve the silver and haul it away for safekeeping in an armored vehicle.

"There's a lot of people who would kill you, who would even kill a police officer, for that kind of money," Lieske remarked.

Later that morning, attorneys Richard Wright and Jim Brown drove to Pahrump and met with Sheriff Lieske who asked Wright if Ted Binion had included Lieske in his last will and testament. "Ted said that he would take care of me," the sheriff claimed.

After Wright told Lieske that Binion had not bequeathed anything in his estate to him, they spoke about the suspected silver heist and the charges against Tabish, Mattsen, and Milot. Lieske related to Wright and Brown what Tabish had told him regarding Binion's purported instructions about retrieving the silver and moving it to the ranch to liquidate it for Bonnie. Lieske said that he had received a phone call from Tabish, whom he'd never met, and had been surprised by the call.

"Tabish said he had instructions from Ted that if anything ever happened to him, that Tabish was to collect the assets that were his and Ted's," Lieske said. Lieske said that he had no authority over the silver in the vault. "I never told Tabish that he can remove it or, no, that he can't. . . . They were within minutes of getting away with it" when Sergeant Howard pulled up. The vault had been emptied completely, except for a single silver dollar that had been left behind.

"Tabish and Ted would have informed me of such instructions," Richard Wright added. "There was no written documentation. Ted was convinced the silver was perfectly secure where it was. That's why he put it on the main street and told the sheriff's office about what was buried there. If there was any excavation, the cops would know what was being dug up."

At 11:22 a.m., Rick Tabish was brought into an interrogation room with Sheriff Lieske, Sergeant Huggins, and Undersheriff Bill Weldon, for a taped interview. Tabish stated his name for the record, and Huggins read him his Miranda rights.

"I want you to give me your version of what occurred out here," stated Huggins.

"Should I have an attorney?" Tabish asked.

"That's your choice," Huggins responded.

"Is Rick Wright coming out?" Tabish asked. "Is he here yet?"

"Yes," Huggins replied.

"What you are saying is you want an attorney present before you give a statement. Is that what you're saying?" Weldon asked.

"Well, I've given a statement but . . . I think I should be

protected somehow. I haven't had a chance to call my attorney or anything."

"Do you know Ted's attorney?" Lieske asked.

"Rick [Wright]? Yeah."

"Does he know about any of this?" Lieske asked.

"Well, yeah, I mean I was supposed to get a hold of him or Jack [Binion] after I got everything to the ranch but Rick [Wright] had the ranch blocked off out there [with security]. So, I couldn't get to the ranch out there."

"Okay, well, if you want an attorney then we're going to quit the interview?" Huggins asked.

"I really don't have much to hide here," Tabish responded. "I'm being charged with grand larceny . . . I should think about what I'm doing here for a minute."

"Not a problem, if you want an attorney we'll get you your attorney, not a problem," said Weldon.

"I haven't been able to call one," said Tabish. "Have I been charged yet or what?"

"Yes," said Huggins. "Well, you've been arrested."

The interview lasted approximately twenty-eight minutes, and consisted mostly of Tabish reiterating his supposed instructions from Binion to dig up and liquidate the silver for his daughter, Bonnie, if anything happened to him. Tabish stated that his financial interest in the affair amounted to one hundred thousand dollars, but that in order for him to obtain it he had to involve one of Binion's attorneys. He also revealed that Binion had given him and David Mattsen the combination to the safe inside Binion's home.

Subsequent follow-up investigation revealed that David Mattsen was also known as David Eugene Gaeth. National Crime Information Center records showed that he had been convicted of armed robbery and sexual intercourse with a minor girl in 1972 in Milwaukee, Wisconsin. His record had been clean since, up until the present alleged crimes in Pahrump.

Following proper police procedure, Sergeant Steve Huggins performed an inventory of the contents of each of the vehicles left at the scene of Ted Binion's vault. One of the vehicles, a 1995 silver-and-teal Chevrolet with Montana license plates, was registered to Richard Tabish and MRT Transport, Inc. He would later determine that David Mattsen had been seen driving the truck a few weeks prior to Ted Binion's death, which would establish a link between Mattsen and Tabish that dated back farther in time than the investigators had originally believed. Because of Ted Binion's death, the alleged silver theft, and Mattsen's criminal record, it would be a point that would require further investigation.

Huggins discovered a briefcase in one of the other vehicles, inside of which was a newsletter for coin collectors and a combination for a safe, presumably Binion's. He also found a handwritten note to Tabish that was signed, "Love you! Sandy. P.S. I love my Lover."

At about the same time that Pahrump was having its Harvest Festival, Montana's Original Testicle Festival was occurring more than a thousand miles to the north on the grounds of the Rock Creek Lodge, just outside the town of Clinton, a small picturesque community located just southeast of Missoula near the Marshall Mountain ski area. The Testicle Festival, an annual gathering of people who love to eat deep-fried beer-battered bull testicles, drink beer, and frolic naked outdoors in the "big sky country's" pre-autumn air, has grown from more than three hundred attendees in 1990 to more than eight thousand nearly a decade later. Thirty-five-year-old Kurt Gratzer was one of those attendees in 1998.

Gratzer, a friend of Rick Tabish's since childhood, traveled to the Testicle Festival on September 18, 1998, along with his friend Terry Sweeney. Even though he didn't know Sweeney very well, Gratzer confided to him during the trip that Tabish had solicited him several weeks earlier with a "special mission" to kill a wealthy former casino owner in

Las Vegas. Tabish purportedly had told Gratzer that a man named "Ted" owed him thirteen thousand dollars for transporting silver to a vault in the desert. According to Gratzer's account, he and Tabish had discussed several ways in which to kill "Ted." One plan called for jumping out of a helicopter onto "Ted's" property and shooting him. Another called for shooting him with one of his own guns, of which there were many. Yet another plan called for forcing drugs down his throat to overdose him. Gratzer indicated that Tabish promised him an amount of money that ranged from one hundred thousand dollars up to three million dollars, as well as providing him with a new sports car.

While socializing at the festival, Gratzer spoke to yet another friend about Tabish's alleged solicitation to murder a man in Las Vegas. Although having gone so far as to call a pharmacist to make inquiries about lethal doses of specific types of drugs, Gratzer indicated that he had ultimately turned Tabish down on the offer. A short time later the second friend related to Gratzer how he had just heard that a casino owner was found dead in Las Vegas. Afterward, Sweeney turned to Gratzer and said: "Didn't you just say something about that to me?"

Two days later, at about 1:00 a.m. on Sunday, September 20, 1998, while still at the festival, the second friend told Gratzer that he had heard that Rick Tabish had been arrested for allegedly attempting to steal another man's silver in Nevada. Although the credibility of Gratzer's statements had now been greatly strengthened, his friends, fearing Tabish and his connections, decided for the time being not to report to the police what Gratzer had told them.

Following the Testicle Festival, according to police, Gratzer returned to Missoula where he spoke with one of Tabish's relatives. The relative asked Gratzer if the rumors involving Tabish were true and, without revealing specific details, Gratzer confirmed that they were. Later, Gratzer purportedly was told by the relative to keep his mouth shut. For the moment, Gratzer complied.

On Monday, September 21, a woman who identified herself as Sandra Murphy Binion showed up at the offices of A-Best Bail Bonds in Las Vegas. She indicated that she wanted to post bail of one hundred thousand dollars each for Richard Tabish and Michael Milot, who were in jail in Pahrump. For collateral Sandy pledged her 1997 Mercedes Benz 500SL convertible, a white metal ring with a large pear-shaped stone, two white metal earrings with forty-four diamonds in each, a yellow metal chain containing forty-eight diamonds, and a white-and-yellow gold watch. Following his release from jail, Rick Tabish posted bail for David Mattsen.

Tabish promptly hired well-known Las Vegas attorney Louis Palazzo to represent him on the charges that he tried to steal Ted Binion's silver. Palazzo was quick to characterize his client as innocent of the charges facing him, and told the media that Tabish was merely carrying out Ted Binion's instructions.

"Rick Tabish was told in very express terms by Ted, if anything happened to him, he needed to remove the silver," Palazzo told reporters for the Las Vegas *Sun* and the *Las Vegas Review-Journal*. When asked about a possible romantic relationship between Tabish and Sandra Murphy, Palazzo indicated that he knew of no such relationship and stressed that his client is a married man.

Nye County Sheriff Wade Lieske, on the other hand, told reporters that "we interrupted a burglary," and that his case against Tabish, Mattsen, and Milot looked like "an open-and-shut case."

Binion's attorney, Richard Wright, agreed with the sheriff, and said that he had told Nye County deputies right after Binion's death to keep an eye out for fortune seekers. "I told them to be on the lookout for any vultures looking for an opportune nest," Wright said.

Palazzo reasoned that if Tabish had really been trying to steal Binion's silver, why would they have used heavy equipment and made so much noise to draw attention to themselves? And why would Tabish have called Sheriff Lieske to inform him of what he was doing?

"They've got machinery the size of homes, they work for hours and hours and they're out there between a Burger King and a casino, with all kinds of onlookers all over the place," Palazzo reasoned. If Tabish had really wanted to steal some of the silver, why not just sneak in and quietly take some of it instead of taking all of it?

In retrospect, it was Lieske's opinion that Tabish made the calls to him ahead of time in order to "lend legitimacy" to their actions of digging up Binion's silver. By making the phone calls, Tabish and the others would also likely feel more comfortable with their actions, and would take their time so that they could remove all of the silver rather than just part of it.

"Why would Ted Binion trust anyone outside his family?" Lieske asked. "It defies reason."

But then, in fairness, much of what Ted Binion did throughout his life defied reason.

CHAPTER 6

Dr. Lary Simms, chief medical examiner for Clark County, viewed Ted Binion's unclothed body as it lay on the cold, stainless steel table inside the morgue at 1704 Pinto Lane, only a few blocks from Ted Binion's home. It was his job to perform the autopsy, as well as collect blood and other bodily fluid samples that might be used as evidence in the event that this "suspicious death" became a criminal case.

During the external portion of the postmortem, Simms noted the presence of beard stubble on Binion's face, and guessed that he hadn't shaved for a day or more prior to his death. Binion, he noted, had a condition known as *pectus excavatum*, in which the chest looks like a small bowl. The condition causes the sternum to depress and the ribs to grow inward toward the spine, giving the appearance that the ribs and surrounding tissue had caved in and never returned to their normal position. He also noted the presence of substantial lividity, the gravitational settling of blood after death, on the right side of Binion's body, including Binion's right arm and the right side of his face. This observation led Simms to believe that Binion had been lying on his right side for a minimum of four hours prior to the discovery of his body. His belief was based on prior experience and medical literature. Because Simms also observed fully developed lividity on Binion's back, he concluded that Binion had likely been lying face-up for an additional two to three hours before discovery of the body was reported. This raised the question of whether Binion's body had been moved by someone after his death but significantly before the paramedics had arrived.

As he continued with the external examination, Simms noted a small circular "erosion" in the center of Binion's chest, a faint discoloration nearly a half-inch in diameter—

about the size of a shirt button. Two fresh bruises on the right side of Binion's body and on the back area indicated recent blunt force trauma. Simms also noted postmortem discoloration and skin sloughing in the area of Binion's mouth, and reasoned that the cause could have been a result of chemicals or regurgitation of bodily fluids, but otherwise considered it unremarkable. Simms also observed a small patterned abrasion on the posterior side of Binion's right wrist that consisted of superficial lines and measured nearly one half-inch in length. There were also several single superficial scratches up to three-and-one-third inches in length pressed together in the proximity of the patterned abrasion.

After Simms opened Binion's body with the usual y-shaped incision, he observed a one-inch hemorrhage in the left chest. The tongue, epiglottis, and larynx showed no evidence of before-death injury. The hyoid bone was intact. In cases of strangulation, the hyoid bone is usually broken, and there is normally bruising if the victim was manually strangled and ligature marks if some kind of device, such as a cord, rope, or belt was used. Because the hyoid bone was intact, and because there were no bruises or ligature marks present in the neck area, Simms could safely rule out strangulation as a cause of death.

Similarly, when Simms examined Binion's esophagus he found nothing unusual. However, his stomach continued forty milliliters of a gray-brown fluid, but no digested food or food particles. Simms collected the gray-brown fluid and took samples of the peripheral blood, heart blood, vitreous humor, and liver tissue. Because Ted Binion was known to smoke tar heroin, he also collected samples of lung tissue for further testing.

When the collected samples were sent to an outside pathology lab for testing, it was determined that there was no trace of heroin in the lung tissue. The finding did not mean that Ted Binion had not smoked heroin sometime in the past, but it was an indication that he had not smoked it recently, at least not in the hours or perhaps even days before his death. The results of toxicology tests on the gastric fluids from Binion's stomach did, however, reveal a concentration of morphine of 1755 milligrams per milliliter of blood; 13,317 milligrams per milliliter of blood of 6-monogacetylmorphine, a metabolite of heroin; 81 milligrams per milliliter of blood of codeine; and 872 milligrams per milliliter of blood of alprazolam, also known as Xanax. As a result of the toxicology tests revealing high concentrations of heroin and Xanax, it was clear that Binion either ate the heroin and Xanax or nasally ingested it. It was Dr. Simms's opinion that Ted Binion died within one to two hours after ingesting the drugs, regardless of how he ingested them. Medical literature regarding oral heroin overdose has shown that death has occurred from significantly smaller amounts being ingested than the amounts found inside Binion's stomach.

It is significant to note that throughout all of Ted Binion's years of drug abuse, he was never known to snort heroin or to eat it. His preferred method of taking the drug was to smoke it. The fact that such a large quantity of heroin was found inside his stomach served to lend credence to his death being investigated as "suspicious." Although Dr. Simms was not able to determine a precise time of death, it was his opinion, based on the postmortem lividity to the right side of Binion's body, that he died sometime between 5:30 a.m. and noon on Thursday, September 17, 1998. He narrowed the time gap by stating that he believed that Binion *probably* died between 5:30 a.m. and 10:00 a.m., and his official conclusion was that Binion died because of a lethal dose of heroin and Xanax.

Dr. Ellen Clark, a deputy medical examiner with the Washoe County Coroner's Office in Reno, was subsequently asked to review all of the autopsy records regarding Ted Binion. Afterward, she related that it was her opinion that Binion's body was moved and cleaned by someone after he died. She cited that the abrasions on Binion's face near his mouth were "consistent with the face having been vigorously rubbed or cleaned . . . ," which differed from Dr. Simms's opinion that there was nothing remarkable regarding the "sloughing" by Binion's mouth. She also stated that the absence of purge, or vomit, on Binion's body suggested to her that it had been cleaned up after death. It was possible, Dr. Clark said, that changes in the postmortem lividity and pressure patterns on Binion's face could have been the result of "substantial blunt trauma in the form of sustained pressure" subjected to Binion's face, perhaps during cleaning. According to Dr. Clark, the injuries to Ted Binion's body, specifically the injuries to his face, wrist, and chest, were ". . . features of postmortem trauma, and therefore also suggest movement of the body after death but before the arrival of death investigation personnel." She believed that Binion's body was moved after death from a face-down position to a face-up position.

As part of his inquiry into Ted Binion's death, Dr. Simms paid a visit to Binion's 8,000-square-foot home. As he moved through the house he observed, from the dining room, which is adjacent to the main living area, that French doors opened onto a veranda that led to the large back yard and pool area. The French doors were where gardener Tom Loveday first observed Binion's dogs on the day of his death, the same doors that the disturbed dogs couldn't gain entry through and wouldn't leave alone. When he entered the den from the marble-floored dining room, Simms noted, from the point where the marble floor ended and turned to carpeting, several dried droplets on the carpeting that he recognized as a "gastric contents–like fluid" that ran in a linear manner and didn't stop until they reached the area where Binion's body was found, yet another suggestion that Binion's body had been moved to the location where it was "discovered."

Although Dr. Simms had earlier observed some discoloration inside Binion's lower eyelids during the autopsy, it was his opinion that these did not consist of petechial hemorrhaging, the telltale dots of blood that would indicate suffocation. He also noted that he did not find any fibers or anything else that would indicate that the drugs had been force-fed to Binion, nor did he find any other evidence that Binion had been suffocated. Even though he considered Binion's death suspicious, lacking any substantial evidence at the scene that would indicate foul play, Dr. Simms's official opinion as to cause of death was that Ted Binion had died as a result of drug intoxication due to an overdose of heroin and Xanax.

Ted Binion's family and his estate lawyers did not agree that Binion had died simply because of a drug overdose. The drugs certainly had played a part in killing him, but those who knew Ted also knew that he was experienced at using drugs, always smoked heroin and never injected it or ingested it by mouth, and would likely not overdose himself, either accidentally or intentionally. The primary reason that he smoked heroin was that he had known it was the safest way to take the drug, because a person would pass out before overdosing. Even though the police investigators believed that someone had positioned his body on its back on the den floor after he had died and had likely cleaned up the crime scene, the lack of additional evidence precluded them from calling his death a homicide.

Becky Binion-Behnen, however, made it known that she felt otherwise. "I just feel it should be treated as a homicide until proven otherwise," Becky said to a reporter for the Las Vegas *Sun*. Even though her brother was a heroin user, she said, he would never have mistakenly overdosed and would not have committed suicide. "He explained to me that the way he used heroin," Becky said, "was by smelling it or ingesting it through smoke." She said that he had told her that taking heroin in that manner would prevent him from overdosing. "I know Ted was very concerned that you could not use Xanax with heroin, and he even spoke to the drug dealer about it."

Becky said that when she had heard about the Xanax and the bedroll on the floor, it had alerted her to look at

her brother's death as a homicide. She said that it was uncharacteristic of Ted to sleep on the floor, and she wanted
to know if the crime scene had been staged.

After conferring with Ted Binion's estate lawyers, it was
decided that a private investigator should be hired to probe
deeper. As a result, private detective Tom Dillard, of Tom
Dillard's Professional Investigators, Inc., was hired, not by
Becky as has been commonly misperceived by the reading
public, but by brother Jack Binion and Ted's estate. Dillard,
a retired twenty-year veteran of the Las Vegas Metropolitan
Police Department, agreed to take the case with the condition that he be able to turn over anything he uncovered
to the authorities. Because he was a private investigator, he
could act without many of the legal restrictions that would
be imposed on a regular law enforcement officer. Dillard,
as a general rule, would not necessarily have to obtain a
search warrant or other court orders for him to carry on
with his work.

"The Binion family felt strongly that there was foul play
from the beginning," Dillard said. "They did not for a second believe that Ted Binion overdosed on drugs. He was a
very sophisticated and careful drug user."

Although it wasn't public knowledge yet, Dillard actually became involved in the case from a different perspective the day before Binion died. Late on the morning of
Wednesday, September 16, 1998, Ted Binion had placed a
telephone call to private investigator Don Dibble, a col-
league of Dillard's. During that phone call Binion indicated
that he suspected Sandy Murphy of cheating on him with
another man, and asked Dibble to conduct surveillance on
her. He said he would provide more details later, and left
a phone message for Dibble in the afternoon indicating that
he would call again the following day. In the meantime
Dibble's instructions were to begin the surveillance, and
Dibble asked Dillard to assist him. Binion never called
back, however. He was dead by the following day.

CHAPTER 7

Within days of Ted Binion's death, Las Vegas Metropolitan Police Detective James Buczek and his partner, Detective Tom Thowsen, contacted Binion's ex-wife, Doris, to obtain additional background information about Binion. Doris told the detectives that she had met Ted in 1965, when she was a teenager, and they began living together a year later. They didn't marry, however, until August 9, 1980. A year later they had a child, Bonnie, whom Ted adored.

Doris told Buczek that she was very familiar with Ted's drug usage. When she first met him he was smoking marijuana "every day," and although he experimented with opium and LSD, marijuana was his preference at that time. In 1980 he began experimenting with heroin, and it wasn't long before he became addicted to it. She said that he always inhaled the smoke of the heroin, and never ate it or injected it. "Ted hated needles," she said.

To her knowledge, Ted was always very careful when taking heroin and never mixed it with other drugs. Later on, however, when he attempted to kick his habit, he would take the prescription drug, Xanax, to help alleviate the discomfort associated with heroin withdrawal. During periods when he was not using heroin, in particular during the times when he had to submit to random drug testing to satisfy stipulations attached to his gaming license, Ted would drink alcohol. For a while beer seemed to satisfy him, but he soon began drinking hard liquor. Inevitably, he would return to the heroin. During the course of their marriage, she said, Ted had spent nearly $1 million on the drug.

According to Doris, Ted Binion was a creature of habit. She confirmed that he always kept a large amount of cash inside the house, anywhere from $50,000 to $1 million at a time. He also kept an extensive collection of gold coins there, as well as various denominations of Civil War currency and other antique coins, including a very valuable collection of silver dollars minted at Carson City. He was also known to bury some of his valuables in the back yard at the Palomino Lane residence as well as at the ranch in Pahrump, and even kept $250,000 inside the motor housing of his boat.

Doris related that Ted always kept a number of guns inside the house, including two shotguns, "one for each of us," on either side of their bed. "He usually carried a gun on him at all times" as well, Doris said. "In the house, if he was sitting down, he might take it out and put it on the table next to him . . . He liked to target-practice . . . He'd always collected guns so he had all kinds of guns." However, contrary to what other people were saying, Ted wasn't paranoid, just protective.

When asked about the drapes in the den being closed on the day of Binion's death, she said that they were never closed at any time that she could recall prior to that day.

Doris characterized her ex-husband as someone who would sometimes become irrational and violent when abusing drugs or alcohol. On one occasion he woke her up in the middle of the night and said strange, even perverted things to her. On another, he accused her of having an affair with her personal trainer, which she said had never occurred. When he became suspicious of her, he beat her, she said, with the open side of his hand, and kicked her in the ribs while she was on the floor. In order to get him to stop beating and kicking her she lied to him and said that she was having the affair. She said that she had suffered what seemed like ceaseless intimidation, and he once threatened that he would "get her" if she ever told anyone about the beating that she had sustained.

Doris said that she had taken Bonnie and left Ted on several occasions because of his abusive ways and his love of heroin.

"He said he'd shoot himself if I didn't come home and

that he would do everything he could to quit [heroin] and that everything would be all right," Doris said. Everything would be fine for a while, then before long Ted would return to his drug use and abusive nature. "He was destroying his life and ours."

Doris explained to the detectives that in March 1995 she'd finally had enough when she overheard Ted on the phone with Sandy Murphy. She said that she had heard them making plans to have lunch and spend some time together at Binion's ranch in Pahrump. That telephone conversation culminated with Doris and Bonnie moving out of the house on Palomino Lane, after which Doris filed for divorce.

Detective James Buczek, 43, is a no-nonsense investigator who moved to Las Vegas more than a decade ago from back east. Although the brown-haired, blue-eyed, large-framed detective loves his job, he is also a devoted husband and father who does his best to find a happy middle ground between family and work. Fortunately, his wife is understanding of the demands of his job, such as getting called out at just about any hour of the day or night, and he has an understanding with his little girl that Daddy will bring home presents after an extended, duty-related absence. Most times just the sight of Daddy is sufficient. A non-smoker, Buczek is fond of Italian food and, unlike the Las Vegas cops of yesteryear, he does not wear a cowboy hat or a fedora but instead dresses casually while maintaining a professional appearance. An honest policeman, he is soft-spoken and appears easy-going, but his mild-mannered demeanor should not fool criminals. Buczek is the type of investigator who doggedly runs down leads and doesn't give up until he has apprehended the perpetrators in a tightly-woven case that can be compared to a pit bull's grip—once ensnared, it's not likely that the criminal will get loose easily.

As he probed deeper into Ted Binion's past in what was turning out to become the biggest investigation of his career, Buczek learned of a plot to kidnap, and likely murder, a young Ted Binion—well known to have been Benny Binion's favorite child—in December 1967. Marvin Shumate, a cab driver with a long police record of mostly minor offenses, and a friend of young Ted's, had apparently been in on the kidnapping-for-ransom scheme with another cab driver. The other driver, who was not named in the reports, allegedly backed out and made a deal with Ted's father, Benny, providing details of the plot before leaving town for good. The last time that anyone ever saw Shumate alive was at a bar near Paradise and Flamingo Roads, where he often went after getting off work. Shumate's body was soon found on the far east side of town at the base of Sunrise Mountain, with a shotgun blast to his chest and a .357 bullet in his head. Although the police at the time had interviewed dozens of people, they had been unable to solve the case.

The trail had eventually led to a man named Tom Hanley who, police believed, had played a part in Marvin Shumate's murder. Hanley and his son, Gramby, were known to have done a number of dirty jobs for the culinary union, such as firebombing restaurants that resisted unionization, at a time when the union was under the control of the mob. They were arrested a year after Shumate was killed for the slaying of culinary chief Al Bramlett in what police suspect was a Mafia-ordered hit. Both of the Hanleys pleaded guilty to Bramlett's slaying and were whisked off into the federal Witness Protection Program after they pledged to tell all that they knew about the Mafia and its connections to the culinary union. The police had been told by Hanley's bodyguard, Alphonse Bass, that Tom Hanley had played a part in Shumate's death. Not too surprisingly, Bass was also found murdered a short time later. Police suspect that Tom Hanley, who died in prison after flunking out of the Witness Protection Program, had ordered that Bass be killed to silence him. Hanley knew that Bass had been talking to the investigators who were looking into Shumate's murder, and Bass was only one of two people who could link Hanley to the slaying. The other witness against Hanley was also slain.

Although strong police suspicions exist to this day that point toward Benny Binion ordering the hit on Shumate, there was never sufficient evidence to positively link him to the crime and he was never charged. Similarly, Tom Hanley was never charged, and the murders of Marvin Shumate, Alphonse Bass, and another witness remain, at least officially, on the books of the Las Vegas Metropolitan Police Department as unsolved cases.

While gathering information on the case, Detective Buczek learned that a man named Peter Sheridan had supplied Ted Binion with heroin for the past eighteen years. When Buczek tracked him down, Sheridan, by that time addicted to methadone instead of heroin and receiving his "fixes" at a clinic, confirmed that he had been Binion's supplier. Sheridan told Buczek that he last saw Binion on the evening of September 16, 1998, when he delivered twelve balloons of tar heroin to him at home. Sheridan said that Binion normally only purchased three to five balloons of the drug, each of which consisted of about one quarter of a gram of heroin. On this particular evening, however, he had asked for twelve. Sheridan said that he had to borrow nearly $200 from his mother so that he could pay his heroin supplier.

When he delivered the heroin at about 9 p.m., he was greeted at the door and let in by Sandy Murphy. He said he had had few words with Sandy, and she had left him and Ted alone. Sandy never witnessed the drug and money exchange, nor had she talked to him about it. He said that Binion had appeared normal, except that he seemed like he was already "stoned" when Sheridan arrived. In response to Buczek's questioning, he said that Binion had not appeared despondent or suicidal. Binion paid him for the heroin from a large bundle of cash he had in his pocket, and he also gave Sheridan about thirty Xanax tablets as a tip. Sheridan said he cautioned Binion that he should not mix heroin with other drugs, and Binion acknowledged that he understood.

Buczek pondered the information that he had just been told regarding the twelve balloons of heroin. He recalled that when Binion's house had been processed by crime scene technicians, they had only found remnants of two balloons that they believed—and crime lab tests confirmed—contained heroin. He asked Sheridan if he was absolutely certain about the number of balloons he had delivered, and Sheridan acknowledged that he was.

So where was the rest of the heroin? Buczek wondered. If it had been used, as they now believed it had because of the contents of Binion's stomach, where were the balloon remnants?

Sheridan explained that Binion had been making plans to go to Pahrump for a while to ride some of his horses. It was possible, Buczek reasoned, that Binion had ordered additional heroin as a "stash" for the planned visit to his ranch. But if that were the case, why hadn't they found it at his house? And why did he have so much of it in his stomach? It just didn't add up.

As he responded to Buczek's questions, Sheridan said that Binion never purchased anything but tar heroin from him, and that he always smoked it. He *never* injected it or ate it. Sheridan explained that tar heroin has a very bitter taste and that he had never known anyone to eat it.

Although Peter Sheridan could have been charged with murder under Nevada law if it could be proven that he supplied the illegal drugs that killed Ted Binion, he was not charged or even arrested. In order to make any charges stick against him, the authorities felt that they would need corroborating evidence, which they did not have, to go along with his admissions.

As the investigation continued, Detective Buczek concentrated on reconstructing the last few hours of Binion's life.

He turned to Binion's gardener, Tom Loveday, for additional information.

Loveday said that when his suspicions prompted him to try and see inside the windows of Binion's home, everything appeared normal in the rooms that he could see into. He said that both Binion's and Murphy's bedrooms appeared immaculate. He explained that he could even see lines on the carpet in both rooms, as if they had been recently vacuumed, despite the fact that the maid, Mary Montoya-Gascoigne, had not reported to work that day. He said that he had checked the doors and windows and found them all to be locked except for the window to Murphy's bathroom. Buczek recalled that a white chair had been found outside, beneath that window, but when he asked about it, Loveday said that there was no chair there that morning. Had it been placed there later in the day, sometime after he left the property at 1 p.m.? Buczek wondered.

When Buczek contacted Mary Montoya-Gascoigne, he asked her to recount details of the last times that she had seen Ted Binion. Mary recalled that Binion had seemed happy in the days prior to his death, and that he was pleased that he was going to be visited by then-mayor Jan Jones. Jones had made an appointment to see Binion on September 16, 1998, to receive a $40,000 contribution, in cash, for her upcoming political campaign for governor.

On that particular day, Binion was in a good mood when Mary arrived for work. In his excitement over the impending visit, Binion had asked Mary to straighten up the house and make it presentable before the mayor arrived. She said that she had made Binion's bed, as well as Sandy Murphy's, in her customary manner. Mary said that Binion had shown her large amounts of cash and had even let her see part of the extensive coin collection he kept in his safe in the garage. She said that as far as she knew, only Ted Binion and Sandy Murphy had the combination to the safe.

Mary told Buczek that she had received a phone call from Sandy Murphy at 9 a.m. that morning, as she was preparing to leave for work. She said that Sandy had told her, "You don't need to come in today. Ted isn't feeling very well. Ted and I stayed up all night and we're going to stay in and sleep all day."

Mary said that she had thought that Sandy's instructions were somewhat unusual because she had worked inside the house on prior occasions when Binion was sick or not feeling well. Why not on this occasion? she had wondered.

Only days before Binion died, Mary said that she had seen Binion removing bullets and shells from the guns that he kept in the house. She said that he explained to her that he did not want Sandy to be able to use any of them when she became angry, and indicated that he was concerned that Sandy might grab one and shoot him. Ted explained that if she grabbed an unloaded gun, "I'll already be on top of it." Although she claimed never to have witnessed any acts of domestic abuse inside Binion's home, Mary did say that she had seen Ted and Sandy arguing at times, mostly over Ted's drug use. "They argued about it because she didn't want him to do it." Mary said that she knew of Binion's drug use, but had actually seen him using on only one occasion, when she watched him spread heroin onto aluminum foil, which he heated with a flame and subsequently inhaled the smoke. Mary also said that Binion hated taking pills, that he would rarely take aspirin even when he needed it.

She said that she also maintained a close relationship with Ted's family. She had even borrowed money from Ted's sister, Becky, shortly after Ted's death to make ends meet until she could find another job.

On the day before Binion's death, Mary said, Rick Tabish was at the residence meeting with Binion. She said that Binion had paid Tabish in cash that afternoon for a job that Tabish had done for him. She did not know what job Tabish had done, but Buczek reasoned that it could have been moving Binion's silver to Pahrump two months earlier. There had been some conflict or dispute over the amount of money that Tabish had charged Binion for that job, and it was possible that they had finally reached an agreement that afternoon and settled up. However, Buczek couldn't be certain at this point.

At about 2:30 p.m., as she was cleaning, Sandy had confronted her. She appeared upset and told Mary that she didn't trust her anymore, and ordered her to leave the residence at once. Mary said that she had complied with Sandy's order, and when she went to say goodbye to Ted, he offered to pay for her services. She politely declined his offer and told him, "I'll catch you tomorrow." Ted agreed, and when Mary left the residence the only persons present were Ted Binion, Sandy Murphy, and Rick Tabish.

In response to questioning, Mary described another confrontation with Sandy Murphy a few months earlier, in March 1998. She said that she had been in Binion's home during the evening with her husband while Binion and Sandy were away at the ranch in Pahrump. She was on the phone calling the ranch because she was worried that they hadn't returned yet, when Ted and Sandy walked in. Sandy was angry that Mary and her husband were there so late, and demanded her keys to the house. "She just took them off my key chain," Mary said.

On another occasion, Mary said that Sandy had shown her a pair of thumb cuffs. Murphy, she said, indicated that the cuffs were sometimes used to collect debts.

"I'm going to loan them to a friend," Mary quoted Sandy as having said. ". . . Sometimes you have to force people to pay you back."

Mary didn't know what she meant or even whether she had been referring to anything or anyone specific regarding the collection of debts, but indicated that she had seen the thumb cuffs around the house on different occasions while she was cleaning. Mary knew, however, that they were Binion's. Three days before his death, said Mary, Binion was looking for them. He liked to play around with them occasionally, and he sometimes kept them on a shelf in his den. Despite her efforts to locate the thumb cuffs for Binion, they were nowhere to be found.

One thing was certain, however. Although he had occasionally been known to get involved in roughing someone up, like the instances where he and others were investigated for beating patrons whom they felt didn't belong in the Horseshoe, it just wouldn't have been Ted Binion's style to use thumb cuffs on a person to collect a debt.

Mary said that Ted Binion was very good to her, and described her relationship with him as close and loyal, close enough that they often talked to each other. Right after he had lost his gaming license, she said, he had gone back to using heroin and she had expressed concerns to him.

"He was a really strong person, a strong man," Mary said. "He once told me, 'Don't worry, I'll never kill myself. I'm not that stupid.' . . . He promised to take care of me when I got old," she said.

When Buczek asked Mary if Binion had been depressed or appeared suicidal on the days prior to his death, she again indicated that he would never have taken his own life. She said that if he had been suicidal, he would have paid her before killing himself. It was his nature to take care of those with whom he was close.

"I miss him," Mary said. "Maybe if I had been there things would have been different."

When Buczek asked her if she had ever seen Binion use a mat to sleep on the floor, Mary said she had seen him use it only on one prior occasion. She said that Binion had told her that he used it to perform massages on Sandy.

Buczek asked Mary about the mayor's visit with Binion. According to Mary, while Ted was waiting for Mayor Jones to arrive, Tanya Cropp had shown up unexpectedly. Binion, having known Cropp for a considerable time, had hired her to take over some of Kathy Rose's personal secretarial duties because Rose was resigning and planned to leave the state. Binion had explained that he couldn't see her just yet because he was waiting for the mayor to arrive, and asked Cropp to return in about an hour. Mayor Jones arrived with her assistant just as Cropp was leaving.

Detective Buczek subsequently interviewed Mayor Jan Jones regarding the meeting. Jones explained that she had received a telephone call from Binion a few days earlier in which he had asked her to come to his house because he wanted to make a contribution to her campaign for governor. When she arrived at approximately 10 a.m., Binion greeted her. She said that he had been dressed in jeans and a plaid, button-down shirt. Jones said that she had observed that the living room drapes were open which allowed her to see all the way into the back yard.

Jones described Binion as happy and upbeat; he appeared to have enjoyed speaking with her. At one point he seemed to have gotten into a nostalgic mood and talked about his father, Benny, and Las Vegas history, and had shown her several old family photographs. "He was talking about how he was going to get straight and get his gaming license back," Jones said.

He had given her a tour of his house, Jones said, and had proudly shown her his coin collection. Jones told Buczek that at no time during her meeting with Binion had he seemed depressed or suicidal, and when she got ready to leave he gave her the $40,000 in cash.

"I know he didn't want me to leave," Jones later told a journalist. "But I was going to a speech. I felt bad about leaving."

Following his interview with Jones, Buczek spoke with Tanya Cropp. Cropp told him that she had returned to Binion's residence with her boyfriend following Binion's meeting with the mayor, and he seemed to have been in a very good mood and did not appear to be under the influence of any drugs. In addition to describing his meeting with the mayor, Binion talked about his future plans, as he had with Jones and others. They also talked about his addiction to heroin, and he had shown her a bottle of Xanax

that he had just had filled at Lam's Pharmacy from a prescription he had obtained from Dr. Enrique Lacayo, his next
door neighbor and friend. He had explained to her that they
were to help him get off heroin. She explained that Binion
was very careful in his use of Xanax and was aware of the
potential hazards of mixing it with heroin. Binion told
Cropp's boyfriend that he always waited for a safe period
of time after taking Xanax before he smoked heroin again.

"I got to be so careful," Binion had said to Cropp's
boyfriend. "I can't take one of those pills after I get high
because it would kill me."

At about noon that same day, Buczek subsequently
learned, Roy Price, one of Binion's ranch hands from Pahrump, had visited him. According to Price's account of his
meeting with Binion that afternoon, Binion had been in a
good mood. By this time Sandy Murphy and Rick Tabish
were already there, seated in the living room. Binion had
gestured to Price by pointing toward Murphy and Tabish
and had said, "They got me the best shit I have had in a
long time." Price said he inferred that Binion's statement
meant that Tabish and Murphy had supplied the drugs to
him. However, he said that Binion had not used any drugs
in his presence. He stated that Binion was very smart with
drugs and that he did not like Xanax.

If Tabish and Murphy had supplied Binion with heroin
that afternoon, why had Binion called Peter Sheridan later
that day to order twelve more balloons of it to be delivered
to him that evening? Had Tabish and Murphy brought Binion another kind of drug, perhaps marijuana, and that had
been what he was referring to when he had spoken to Price?
Buczek could only guess at this point as he continued listening to Price's account.

"She is closer to him than a cheap suit," Binion had told
Price as he gestured toward Tabish and Murphy. It was
obvious to Buczek that Binion's opinion of his live-in girlfriend had diminished considerably.

Price said that Sandy Murphy had made comments that

Binion was not providing for her sufficiently in his will, and that he was hiding assets from her. Price had observed Binion with a large wad of $100 bills, and Binion told him that he had $50,000 in cash with him.

While meeting with Binion, Price told him that he had seen a suspicious van parked near Binion's ranch two days earlier, on Monday, September 14, 1998. He told Binion that he had seen the van's occupants taking photographs of the area. When the van left, Price said he followed it to the location of Binion's vault on Highway 160. At one point while Price was relating to Binion what he had observed, Tabish interrupted and suggested that the silver should be moved to another location. Binion quickly dismissed the idea and ignored Tabish for the remainder of the meeting with Price.

When Price left, he said, the only people remaining were Binion, Tabish, Murphy, and Mary.

Since the mayor had already been there and had left with her $40,000 campaign contribution, Buczek wondered what had happened to the large amount of cash that Price had described. It certainly hadn't been found in the house when they searched it. With each person he interviewed, it seemed that he was only generating more questions instead of receiving answers to the growing mystery behind Ted Binion's sudden and unexpected demise.

CHAPTER 8

When Detective Buczek interviewed Enrique Lacayo, the doctor informed him that he had spoken with Binion on the morning of September 16, 1998. Binion had told him that he was feeling anxious, and said that he had been trying to stop drinking and taking heroin. He had asked for more Xanax, which the doctor had prescribed for him in the past. Dr. Lacayo gave him a prescription for 120 pills of a low dosage, to be taken four times a day. It was enough to last Binion for a month if taken as directed.

Although Binion had seemed excited about his impending visit with the mayor, Dr. Lacayo also said that he had seemed angry with himself, frustrated over his addiction, and indicated that he was going to kick his heroin habit on his own. Although the doctor had provided Binion with the prescription, he told him that he would have to come into the office later for an official visit and examination.

Buczek determined that among the last persons to see Binion alive was Dr. Lacayo's housekeeper, Eunice Altamirno. She said that she had seen a black car, presumably Sandy Murphy's Mercedes, pull into Binion's driveway at approximately 11 p.m. on September 16, and that it was still there when she saw Binion in front of his house at 5:30 the next morning. She said that she had greeted him good morning and handed him his newspaper, and he had seemed normal at that time.

"He was like a person who had just woke up," she said. "I didn't see anything wrong."

As he continued to trace Binion's movements during the early morning hours of September 17, Buczek learned that Binion had seen John Rieker, a friend for 25 years, who lived only a few blocks away. Binion was waiting at Rieker's place of employment when Rieker arrived for work at 4 a.m. Buczek determined that Rieker had told Binion approximately a week earlier that he had heard employees at a Smith's Food King supermarket, a few blocks from Binion's house, say that a relative of Sandy Murphy's had been seen in the store cashing in a number of coins. When he met Rieker early on the morning of September 17, Binion thanked him for passing along the information. He also related to Rieker that he knew that Sandy and others were stealing from him, and indicated that he believed Sandy Murphy was cheating on him. Binion purportedly told Rieker that he was going to "get rid of the broad and her family."

Buczek learned that, after speaking with Rieker, Binion had driven to a 7-Eleven convenience store near his home on Charleston Boulevard and Rancho Drive. According to Marvin Reed, the graveyard clerk, it had been about 5 a.m. when Binion entered the store. Reed said that Binion had appeared very agitated and didn't have much to say, except that he thought that his girlfriend was cheating on him. He asked Binion if he was okay.

"I'll be okay," Binion had responded. He then purchased two packs of cigarettes and left.

Reed said that Binion was a regular customer, and was always friendly with him.

"I've heard every story he ever told," Reed said. Reed said that Binion had not looked like he was high on drugs at the time.

Buczek learned that Binion was known to frequently purchase cigarettes and other items at that store, and in his generous nature it wasn't at all unusual for him to pay for his purchases with a $100 bill and tell the clerk to keep the change. He would sometimes return a short time later to grab a half-gallon of ice cream or some other item, and would tell the clerk to just take it out of the $100 bill he had just given him or her.

As Buczek continued to delve deeper into the case, he soon learned that Binion had been looking at some real

estate, specifically commercially zoned land, out on North
Rancho Drive, near the Fiesta and Texas Station hotel-
casinos. He had been talking with Las Vegas real estate
agent Barbara Brown, and the two of them had exchanged
at least ten telephone calls during the week prior to Binion's
death. When Buczek contacted Brown, a blonde, middle-
aged woman, he learned that she and Binion had spoken
by telephone during the evening of September 16 and were
planning a meeting for Friday, September 18. Binion had
seemed like he was in a good mood that evening, and had
been jovial to the point of telling her jokes.

Brown said that she had called Binion's home at 12:04
p.m. on Thursday, September 17, to confirm their meeting
for the next day and also because she wanted to talk to Ted
regarding one of her clients who was seeking advice about
the casino business. Sandy Murphy, sounding somewhat
hysterical, quickly answered the phone after it rang only
once. Barbara identified herself and asked to speak to Ted.

"Barbara, he's out of it, he can't talk right now," Brown
quoted Murphy as having said. It had sounded to Brown
like Sandy was upset and was crying.

"Are you okay?" Brown had asked.

"No," Sandy responded. "Nobody understands what it
has been like living with a drug addict." Buczek noted that
Sandy had referred to living with Ted Binion in the past
tense. According to Brown's account of the telephone call,
Sandy went on in a near-hysterical manner. "I have this
mess to clean up in this bathroom." She went on to say that
a doctor had given Ted "some pills" to take. Brown offered
to come over to help Sandy, but she declined.

"No," Brown quoted Sandy as saying. "He doesn't want
anybody to come over here, Barbara. He has lost so much
weight that he doesn't want anybody to see him. And if
you insist on coming over, don't bring anyone with you.
He'll be very upset." Brown, surprised at what Sandy had
told her and thinking that it was all so strange, explained
to Sandy about the appointment she had with Ted the fol-

lowing day and said that they had been planning to get together all week.

"Well, you better call tonight to see if he can make that appointment," Sandy had told her. Brown then offered to pick Sandy up for lunch, but she declined. "No, it's just not worth it. Every time I go out he interrogates me."

Although she liked Ted Binion, Barbara Brown had witnessed his abusive side. On one occasion she had seen Sandy Murphy in a hysterical state, crying and running down the street after she and Binion had gotten into an argument. Brown related that on another occasion, when she was visiting Binion's home, the three of them were sitting in the living room when their conversation turned to talk of physical abuse.

"Every woman needs a beating once a month, ain't that right, babe?" Brown quoted Sandy as saying.

"And you got yours already," Brown quoted Binion's response.

When Buczek contacted Kathy Rose, she explained to him the circumstances of Sandy Murphy's visit to her at her office on the afternoon of September 17. Sandy had said that she wanted to deposit a check into one of Binion's accounts and stated that she had stayed up all night with him. Rose said that Sandy had not come to her office in the past. Buczek noted that Rose worked for Jack Binion, head of Horseshoe Gaming, Inc., on south Industrial Road, which included the operations of his casinos in other states, particularly Louisiana and Mississippi. Jack was no longer affiliated with the Horseshoe Hotel and Casino downtown. That was now solely owned and operated by Ted's sister, Becky. It seemed strange that Sandy Murphy would be having contact with that office, except for the fact that Kathy Rose had worked as Ted's personal secretary for a considerable time prior to Becky's takeover. Investigators began to suspect that Sandy had gone to see Kathy to try and establish an alibi for herself, to have a witness who

had seen and talked to her in the hours before it was discovered that Ted was dead.

According to Kathy, Sandy had called the office again
the next day wanting to speak to Jack, who was executor
of Ted's last will and testament, to make him an offer. "She
said she knew where some things were buried in Pahrump,"
Rose explained. "She would tell Jack where they were buried, and they could split whatever they found."

Rose said that Sandy had not told her who had buried
the items, what they consisted of, or where they were. Jack,
however, had wanted no part of the offer and had turned
her down. Buczek didn't know if Sandy had called Rose
regarding Binion's buried silver on Highway 160, or if she
had been referring to items that she believed were buried
on Ted's ranch. The timing seemed a bit odd, however,
since Sandy had made the phone call only hours before
Tabish, Mattsen, and Milot were arrested in Pahrump digging up Binion's silver.

As he continued running down leads, Buczek soon
learned that Ted Binion had placed a telephone call to one
of his attorneys, James J. Brown, at 11:50 a.m. on September 16, shortly before Rick Tabish and Binion's ranch hand,
Roy Price, had shown up at his home. Brown wasn't home
when Binion had called, but he had spoken to Brown's
wife, Laura, and left a message for Brown.

"Just tell Jimmy to take Sandy out of the will and put
Bonnie in," Binion had said. "You know, Bonnie gets it
all."

"Is Sandy gone?" Laura Brown had asked him.

"No, but she might as well be," Binion had said.

Approximately ten minutes later James Brown, Binion's
friend for more than 40 years, received the message and
called Binion wanting to know what was going on.

"Take Sandy out of the will if she doesn't kill me tonight," Brown quoted Binion as saying. "If I'm dead you'll
know what happened."

Although somewhat taken aback by Binion's statement

and instructions, neither Brown nor his wife knew what to make of it. Binion hadn't sounded like he was high on drugs but, in fact, seemed quite lucid. Brown decided to simply comply with Binion's instructions and did not press the issue. Brown explained that neither he nor his wife had notified the police about Binion's phone call after learning of Ted's death because neither of them knew whether or not a homicide had been committed. He said, however, that when he had spoken to Binion he had not sounded suicidal and the directive to remove Sandy from the will had been clear.

When questioned, Brown said that he had drafted a number of wills for Ted over the years. He also said that Binion had a cohabitation agreement with Murphy that had been drafted by another attorney. Changing Binion's will was nothing new. Older versions had included illegitimate children as well as a number of his prior girlfriends as beneficiaries to portions of his vast estate, and it was par for the course for Binion to add and delete people from time to time. The version of the will that Binion had wanted changed had a handwritten entry on the bottom of it that read, "Sandy Murphy, one million dollars." The entry, however, had since been crossed out.

CHAPTER 9

Ted Binion was known around town as "the rock 'n' roll cowboy," primarily because of his wild lifestyle and for trying to follow in the footsteps of his legendary cowboy father, and that was how he was remembered, at least in part, at his funeral at Christ the King Catholic Church on Tuesday, September 22, 1998. Held in the early afternoon, the church on South Torrey Pines Drive held a crowd of an estimated 700 to 800 people who had come to mourn the passing of a man whom Las Vegas would long remember. The Mass began with the playing of the song, "The End" by the Doors, which had been selected by Binion's daughter, Bonnie. An unusual selection for a funeral, the lyrics talk about insane children and a son who wants to kill his father; a photo of a young, long-haired Ted Binion was passed out to the mourners. A pair of boots, a cowboy hat, spurs, and a rope lariat lay across Binion's coffin, and a horseshoe-shaped floral arrangement stood alongside it.

In addition to many of Binion's friends and family members who were in attendance, there were a number of pimps, loan sharks, and politicians there as well. Ted Binion's ranch hands were there, as were many casino workers and too many gamblers to count. Among the recognizable faces that turned out to bid Ted farewell were former federal Judge Harry Claiborne, a longtime friend of the family; Las Vegas Mayor and gubernatorial candidate Jan Jones; Jackie Gaughan, owner of the Plaza hotel and casino; Bob Stupak, the person who was in part responsible for the metamorphosis of the old Vegas World into the eyesore, visible from nearly anywhere in the valley, known as the Stratosphere Tower; and state Senator Bob Coffin. Showing up late and among the last to enter the church was Sandy Murphy, escorted arm-in-arm by her two attorneys, Oscar

Goodman and David Chesnoff. As heads turned, among those gazing at Murphy and her entourage were Horseshoe security officers John Boylan and Donald Kershaw. It was noted that upon her arrival she appeared emotionless, apparently in full control. The tears, sobbing, and hysterics she displayed when she reported finding Binion's body were now notably absent.

Father Bill Kenny, who had known Ted Binion from the time that both of them were children, presided over the Mass and commented that Ted marched to a different drummer than most everyone else. The priest said that Ted would have been pleased to know that so many people had turned out to bid him farewell. "This shows that Ted was a most affable person and that he was a friend to so many people of all different backgrounds."

Harry Claiborne, 81, had the honor of delivering the eulogy, just as he had at the funeral of Binion's mother, Teddy Jane, a few years earlier. He recalled Ted Binion as a likeable, good person despite his shortcomings, and shared some memories of his longtime friend.

"Ted was a great conversationalist and had one of the highest intellects of anyone I've ever known," Claiborne said. "He had a big heart and a compassion for others. There were hundreds and hundreds of cases of him reaching out to help people, and some he barely knew." Claiborne even remarked about the loss of Binion's gaming license because of his association with reputed mob figures like Herbie Blitzstein.

"He was cheated out of that license," Claiborne said, "and getting it back became an obsession to him . . . I will maintain until the day I join him, he was entitled to [that license] he should have had and which he was cheated from . . . The gaming board frowned upon a friendship of his, and I told him it would hurt his chances for the license if he continued this association. He looked at me in awe when I said that, and told me that his friend was an old man with no friends and that he couldn't turn him away from his door if he came to see him . . . Ted was complex and he was intense. He had faults like all of us had, some to a higher degree and some to a lesser degree, but on balance his good points far outweighed the bad . . . none of us are as bad as maybe our public perception . . . his compassion for others may have been his undoing . . . I can truthfully say that Ted Binion was the most unforgettable character I ever knew . . . Father Kenny said that Ted marched to a different drummer than the rest of us, but I would add that Ted was about a mile and a half ahead of the drummer."

"He was a good friend and a good guy," Bob Stupak said after the service. "I'm going to miss him."

Following the hour-and-forty-minute Mass, John Boylan and Donald Kershaw noted that Sandy Murphy was one of the first to leave the church. They also noticed that her demeanor had changed completely from when she had arrived. She began to shake and sob, but to Boylan and Kershaw the gestures did not seem real. Although the emotions that she now displayed fell short of the hysterics that she had shown when she reported finding Binion's body, the guards felt that she was either acting or greatly exaggerating her current emotions.

Following the funeral services, Ted Binion's body was entombed in Bunkers Eden Vale Mausoleum.

It didn't take long for Detective James Buczek to discover why Sandy Murphy had arrived late for Ted Binion's funeral service. She had been delayed at the offices of the Nevada State Gaming Control Board with another of her attorneys, Bill Knudson, demanding to speak to an agent. She and Knudson were allowed to speak with Deputy Chief Paul Markling. Her apparent desire to talk to gaming agents surprised Markling because she had, in the past, refused to speak to them regarding her relationship with Ted Binion and had even invoked her rights against self-incrimination at one of the public hearings held regarding Binion's gaming license. Nonetheless, Markling wanted to hear what she had to say.

The information that Sandy provided to Markling included details of Binion's relationship with the rest of the Binion family, the alleged theft of the Pahrump silver, a shooting incident at Ted's house that had occurred on June 4, 1997, and threats that had allegedly been made against Ted and herself. She also played a tape recording for Markling which, she said, included the voice of Nick Behnen, Becky Binion-Behnen's husband, speaking in a threatening manner.

According to details contained in the Gaming Control Board report taken by Markling, Sandy indicated that she wanted to talk about the shooting incident at Binion's home. Indicating that Nick and Becky's son, Benny Behnen, were involved, she said that the incident began when three boys appeared at the house and attempted to get inside. Sandy identified the "boys" as Chancelor "Chance" LeSueur, Avery Church, and Jimmy Walker. Sandy said that Nick Behnen had called the house and was told by her that Ted was not at home. It was a short time later that the three "boys" showed up at the Palomino Lane residence.

According to Sandy's statement, Chance LeSueur indicated that they were friends of Ted's nephew, Benny, and demanded to be allowed in. Sandy told him that Ted was not at home and explained that she had been told not to allow anyone inside when Ted wasn't there. Chance wouldn't take no for an answer and continued to beat on the door. Frightened, Sandy said that she grabbed one of the many guns inside the house and threatened to use it if they didn't leave. Reluctantly, they left the premises. However, they returned about a week later at which time, according to Sandy, they said that Nick Behnen had sent them the previous week. They allegedly told Sandy that Nick had known that Ted had not been at home at that time, and had instructed them to kill her and wait for Ted to return, at which time they were to kill him, too. They indicated that they were afraid of Nick, according to Sandy, and that Nick had told them that Ted had more than $200,000 in the house.

As she continued, Sandy's statement became even more strange. She said that Nick and Benny had found out that Chance, Avery, and Jimmy had told Sandy and Ted about their plan and that Nick and Benny had eventually come to the house to talk to Ted. They met in the garage, she said, with Ted holding a shotgun. Both Benny and Nick appeared, to Sandy, to be intoxicated and became engaged in a "screaming match" with Ted. She said that Ted cocked the shotgun and told them to "get the hell out of here." Sandy had learned that Nick and Benny had kidnapped Chance LeSueur and were holding him. Markling's impression of the alleged kidnapping was that it was being used as a tactic to scare Chance, Avery, and Jimmy, if it had in fact even happened. Sandy said nothing to indicate any other details of the meeting in the garage or how it had turned out.

Sandy told Markling about the tape that she had taken off of her telephone answering machine that, she claimed, had several messages on it from Nick. She turned the tape over to Markling. Most of the calls consisted of a male voice that identified himself as "Nick," asking Ted to call him back or to pick up the phone. It sounded like the caller believed that Ted was at home but was just not answering. Three of the calls, however, consisted of conversations between the caller and one or two other people. According to Sandy, the voices were those of Nick, Benny, and Chance, while Chance was allegedly being held against his will. Aside from the voice of the primary caller, the other voices were either barely audible or were unintelligible, and appeared to be from a conversation going on in the background while the primary voice was trying to raise Ted Binion.

Sandy claimed that the taped conversations occurred just days prior to the drive-by shooting at Binion's home, and she alleged that the shooting was done or arranged by Nick and Benny Behnen.

Sandy also told Markling that "Teddy started using drugs again" after losing his gaming license. She said that the only thing that Ted really cared about in life was his gaming license. He had become extremely depressed after losing it, she said.

"Teddy did this on his own," Sandy said, indicating that Ted had committed suicide. "He was very, very depressed."

Sandy stated that Ted had hated his sister, Becky, and most of the rest of his family. She also stated that the Binions had done nothing to help Ted in any way. She stated that someone, whom she believed to be Nick Behnen, called her on the night of September 21 while she was staying at the Desert Inn and had threatened her by saying something like, "I'm going to see that you fucking fry, bitch." She stated that Nick was heavily involved in running the Horseshoe, and that the Behnen family, particularly Becky, are "treacherous" and "low-lifes."

As she neared the end of her statement to Markling, Sandy, who had been very upset throughout the meeting and had cried on and off, said that Rick Tabish had been given specific instructions by Ted to dig up the silver, to liquidate it, and put the money into a trust account for Bonnie. She said that Ted didn't want to just give Bonnie the silver or the cash because he didn't want his former wife to get the money and because he felt that his daughter was not a good money manager. She indicated that Ted felt that Rick Tabish was the only person that he could trust to handle the job. She also stated that she was being mistreated by just about everybody, especially the Behnens and the press, and that she was being kept from going inside "her" house. She said that she had to sell some diamonds to get enough money to live on. As she finished giving her statement to Markling, Sandy said that Rick Tabish was her "best friend in the whole world."

Buczek didn't quite know what to make of Sandy's

statement to Paul Markling. Other than the initial interview that she had given to Detective Mitchell at the hospital on the evening of Binion's death, Sandy Murphy had refused to talk to the police, yet she had willingly initiated contact with the Gaming Control Board and had done so on the day of Ted's funeral. The information that she had provided to Markling appeared, on the surface at least, to be insignificant to Metro's ongoing suspicious death investigation involving Ted Binion, and left Buczek and the other investigators wondering what her motive for the meeting could have been. The only motive that seemed reasonable to them was that she was attempting to avert attention away from herself and Tabish, but in her apparent stupidity she had only placed more attention on herself and Tabish.

The information that Sandy had provided to Markling had been of an inconclusive nature and had appeared to be little more than an attempt to disparage Ted's sister and her husband, and to throw mounting police suspicion off of herself and Tabish and onto Becky and Nick. The tape recordings proved nothing, and her remarks about the Behnens boiled down to little more than her word against theirs. Nonetheless, being the dutiful detective that he is, Buczek decided that it would be a good idea to follow up on the drive-by shooting incident by studying the police reports taken at the time of the shooting.

Buczek read that Detective Phil Miller from the Admin Detail had responded to Binion's residence after receiving a report from patrol officers of a "shooting into an occupied structure." According to the initial report, Miller had observed numerous pellet holes in a 1997 Ford Explorer bearing Nevada license plate 839 HKJ, parked in the driveway, and another pellet that had penetrated the front door and had lodged in a picture on the north wall of the residence. From examining the holes, Miller suspected that the shots had been fired from a shotgun firing double-0 buck shells. After taking the initial report, he turned the investigation over to Detectives Paul Page and John Hannon.

Page and Hannon were met by Sandy Murphy and invited into the house where Ted Binion joined them for the interview regarding the incident. According to what Sandy had told these two detectives, the incident involving the three "boys" had occurred on May 7, 1997, nearly a month before the shooting incident. When she heard the knock, she said, she walked to the door but did not open it. Instead she peered out the window next to the door and observed two white male adults, ages approximately 20–25, standing at the door. She said that she recognized one of the young men as Chance LeSueur, who said that he wanted to speak to Binion, but she could not see the other individual from her position near the door. She said that she knew LeSueur because she had met him on a previous occasion, but that she had nonetheless refused to allow him inside the house. After realizing that she was not going to let them inside, LeSueur and the other young man knocked, kicked, and banged on the door, finally giving up. They walked over to a white Jeep Cherokee where they joined two other young men, one of whom she thought she recognized as Benny Behnen, and left. Sandy was reluctant to name Benny as a suspect at that time because she was not positive that it was him that she had seen.

Sandy did say that she felt that Benny Behnen was jealous of her, perhaps because of her relationship with his uncle—Benny and Ted had been close before Sandy had come into Ted's life—and he had been threatening her for some time. She told the detectives that he had even called her at her parents' house in California and had threatened her and her father. She said that she thought that this shooting incident had been prompted by someone thinking that Binion would be receiving his gaming license back and that she was sure that it was a "relative" who was involved in the incident.

Similarly, Binion told the detectives that he thought a relative of his, whom he would not name, had spread the word that he had $275,000 in cash stored beneath his bed, which he said was not true. Binion also told Page and Hannon that he called Chance LeSueur on June 2, 1997, and told him that he was having a barbecue at his house and wanted him to bring his friends over. He said that they had in fact come over and he proceeded to get them drunk in order to question them about who had come to his house on May 7, and why. He said that he also questioned them regarding what they knew about the money in the bedroom and where they received the information about it. Although Binion was evasive concerning what he had learned regarding the names of those involved and their intent, he did tell the detectives that he thought they had come there on May 7 to kill Murphy and take the money. He later told the detectives that he thought the same people were there to kill him as well. After talking to the detectives for some time, Binion stopped the interview and said that he didn't want to talk about the incident any further without first conferring with his attorney, Richard Wright.

Murphy and Binion's interview with Page and Hannon was continued later at Wright's office, and was tape-recorded with Wright present. At that time Binion provided the detectives with the names of those whom he considered suspects being somehow involved in the shooting incident: Benny Behnen, Chance LeSueur, Avery Church, Lennie Duvall, and Jimmy Walker.

Later, Page and Hannon conducted an interview with each of the suspects named by Binion, and without exception each of them denied any knowledge of the shooting incident. Benny Behnen, however, told the detectives that he thought that Binion had shot up his own vehicle. He said that he had heard that Binion was upset with his daughter, Bonnie. Benny further stated that Binion had fired guns at his residence in the past, usually when he had been drinking.

Although they had found no record of incident reports being filed under Binion's address for the previous three years, with the exception of the June 4, 1997, drive-by incident, Page and Hannon nonetheless interviewed several of Binion's neighbors. One of the neighbors, Caroline Lacayo, told the detectives that in the past she had heard gunfire coming from Binion's back yard, the last time being about a year earlier. She said that she had heard the gunshots on June 4, but did not see anyone when she peered out the window. She said that she had seen Binion a few days later and had asked him if he was the one shooting off guns at his home. He told her that he had not fired any guns, and said that if she heard any shots being fired in the future she should call the police.

After checking with the residents of Palomino Lane, the detectives spoke with neighbors who live behind Binion on an adjacent street. They said they thought they'd heard gunshots coming from the area of Binion's house on occasion, and one neighbor told the detectives that Binion liked to practice target-shooting in his back yard. Yet another neighbor, who lived directly behind Binion, told the detectives that she had heard gunfire coming from the back yard and had also heard Binion threatening Murphy. According to the neighbor, she once heard a female screaming, "Don't hit me again," and "Don't shoot me." She said she recognized the voice as Sandy Murphy's. She said that it was a recurring event, prompting her to think that Binion was chasing Sandy around the yard with a gun and threatening her with it. The neighbor said she believed that Binion would someday kill Murphy, and that it was because of Binion that she and her husband were planning to sell their house and move.

It was all pretty dramatic stuff, Buczek concluded, and provided considerable insight into Binion and Murphy's relationship, as well as Binion's feelings and relationships with his relatives. But he doubted that he would be able to tie it all together to fit into a scenario explaining Binion's death unless something more substantial surfaced. Despite Binion's own suspicions about who was involved in the drive-by shooting and why, in Buczek's mind the evidence and suspicion continued to mount against Murphy and Tabish and not toward the Behnens, as he felt that Sandy would have him believe.

As a result Buczek began to look more closely at a possible romantic relationship between Sandy Murphy and Rick Tabish. His reasoning was based on the personal note from her that Nye County detectives had found inside Tabish's briefcase when they arrested him, the fact that Sandy had posted bail for Tabish and Milot, and the fact that they had been sharing the same lawyer, William Knudson, until recently. Buczek also learned that members of the Binion family had been informed that Tabish and Murphy had been seen together at an expensive Beverly Hills hotel about a week prior to Binion's death. Buczek wanted to locate Sandy to obtain more information about the possible relationship, but he had been unable to find her. Buczek and the investigators for Metro conceded that even if they determined that a romantic relationship between Murphy and Tabish existed, it wouldn't necessarily upgrade the investigation into a homicide case.

When word got back to Rick Tabish that investigators were looking at a possible romantic link between himself and Murphy, he denied it to a reporter from a Missoula, Montana, newspaper. He said that he knew Sandy through Ted Binion, and it was Binion who had encouraged a friendship between them. He alleged that the so-called romantic relationship was a result of Becky Binion-Behnen's attempts to make Sandy Murphy look bad.

"She's a good girl," Tabish was quoted as saying to the reporter. "I like her. But there's nothing to this but bad blood in the Binion family."

In the meantime, now more than ever unconvinced that Binion's death was the result of an accidental overdose of drugs or a suicide, the Binion estate put up a $25,000 reward for information that would lead to the arrest and conviction of the person or persons responsible for Ted Binion's death.

CHAPTER 10

As in any investigation of great intensity, one question leads to another as detectives run down leads in their attempts learn the truth. One such question for Detective Buczek and his fellow detectives was that of the romantic relationship that they were beginning to believe existed between Sandy Murphy and Rick Tabish. Because of information that was being funneled to the Binion family and Ted Binion's estate, in part through the efforts of private investigator Tom Dillard, the trail soon led Buczek to the posh hotels and lifestyles of Beverly Hills, California.

As he followed the trail to Southern California, Buczek learned that on September 11, 1998, the Friday prior to Ted Binion's death, a "Mr. and Mrs. Rick Tabish" checked into the Peninsula Hotel on Little Santa Monica Boulevard in Beverly Hills. The woman calling herself "Mrs. Tabish" registered the couple into the hotel and signed the guest registration card "S. M. Tabish." Upon checking in she had requested a room with a Jacuzzi, and ordered a bottle of Barbaresco wine and two dozen long-stem red roses. She told the clerk that the wine and the roses were a surprise for her "husband." When Buczek checked the guest registration card, he compared the signature of "S. M. Tabish" to other signatures of Sandra Murphy's that he had obtained, and it was his opinion that they matched.

Upon interviewing the hotel's employees, Buczek learned that the couple he now believed were in fact Murphy and Tabish had rented a cabana the following day. They also rented one for the next day, and ordered massages in their room for that evening. When he examined the charge slips for the cabana rentals and the massages, Buczek noted that "S. M. Tabish" had again signed them.

Assisted by Detective Les Zoeller of the Beverly Hills

Police Department, Buczek was able to interview the cabana and spa supervisor of the Peninsula Hotel. From that, he determined that Sandy Murphy was indeed the person that she had served during the couple's stay at the hotel. The hotel supervisor positively identified Sandra Murphy as the person she knew as "Mrs. Tabish" from a photo that Detective Zoeller had shown her.

Similarly, Zoeller contacted the masseuse who had performed the massages on "Mr. and Mrs. Tabish." After showing her photos of the couple she positively identified both Murphy and Tabish as the persons who had received massages at the hotel.

With the romantic link between Sandy Murphy and Rick Tabish now more firmly established, Buczek sought out other possible witnesses who might be able to corroborate the new information. One of the people he contacted was Sandy's friend, Linda Carroll. According to Carroll, Sandy had confided in her that she had gone to Beverly Hills with Rick Tabish and that the two of them had stayed at the Peninsula Hotel. Carroll had also seen a photograph of Sandy and Tabish posing together in what she termed an affectionate pose.

In Buczek's mind there was no longer any doubt that Sandy Murphy and Rick Tabish were romantically involved with each other at a time when Sandy was still living with Ted Binion. It also appeared to him that Sandy was spending Ted Binion's money to pay for their weekend tryst. Upon further investigation, Buczek also learned that Binion had become even more suspicious that Sandy was cheating on him than investigators had originally thought.

Buczek discovered that Binion had sought the assistance of a surveillance expert on Saturday, September 12, 1998, only five days before his death, the weekend that Sandy and Rick were in Beverly Hills together. Binion, Buczek learned, had previously hired Brad Parry to install a video surveillance system at Binion's Palomino Lane home. The surveillance system consisted of eight cameras situated on the exterior of the house, each connected to a television monitor in Binion's den and another in his bedroom, and the entire system was connected to a video recorder.

Binion had seen a truck parked outside his home recently, and was concerned that Sandy may have had contact with the truck's owner or driver. When he tried to view the surveillance tapes, he discovered that there was something wrong with the system and had called Parry because he had installed it and was familiar with how it operated. The buttons were all jammed, like someone had deliberately pressed them all down at once, and they had become stuck in that position. Binion asked Parry to see if he could get the recorder to play the tape but he, too, was unable to do so. He told Binion that he would have to take it into the shop for repairs.

Buczek recalled that when technicians had processed Binion's home following his death, they had found that several wires had been disconnected from the security system making the system inoperable. He considered that the fact that Parry had been in the process of removing the system from Binion's home at that time might serve to explain why the technicians had found several of the wires removed. It didn't, however, explain the damage that had been done to the recorder.

Binion, Buczek learned, had asked Parry if he could install a hidden recording device on Sandy's telephone, so that he could monitor all of her calls. Parry told him that he could, and indicated that he would need to buy the equipment.

Parry returned to Binion's home on Tuesday, September 15, to finish disconnecting the surveillance recorder so that he could take it to his shop for repairs. Sandy had returned from her trip to California by this time, and was home when Parry arrived. She made it known to him that she was aware that he and Binion had been attempting to view the surveillance tapes, and she indicated to him that she knew what was on them but did not say what they contained.

When Sandy had returned from her trip to Beverly Hills, Binion, suspecting that Sandy had been cheating on him, had confronted her about where she had been all weekend. She had told Binion that she had been in California visiting relatives, but he had not believed her.

While inside Binion's home, Parry noted that someone, presumably Sandy or someone she had hired, had installed audio recording devices that would allow her to monitor all of the phone call activity at Binion's home so that she could listen in on Binion's calls to learn what he may have discovered about her and her activities. The tape recorders that were connected to the recording devices were found in Sandy's bedroom. Parry removed the surveillance recorder and took it with him.

As a result, the surveillance system was out of commission for the next several days, including the day that Binion died. With the system now useless, there were no surveillance tapes for the police to use in determining who came and went at Binion's home the night before Binion died or on the day of his death, and they were left wondering whether the recorder had been deliberately damaged to prevent its use on the days in question.

After reviewing what he had so far, Buczek decided to do a follow-up inquiry with Binion's maid, Mary. He wanted to further explore the information that he had learned from John Rieker, who had indicated that Binion thought that Sandy Murphy had been stealing from him. When he questioned Mary, she recalled that in June or July 1998, Binion had been concerned about a bag of silver that had gone missing. The bag had contained approximately one thousand coins. Binion believed that Sandy had stolen the coins from him and had expressed his belief to Mary. Although she wasn't sure where Binion had kept the silver, she presumed that it was in his safe. She told Buczek that Binion had told her that he had given the safe's combination to Sandy.

*   *   *

As Detective Buczek continued putting the pieces of this real-life jigsaw puzzle together, he soon learned of the comfortable lifestyle with which Ted Binion had provided Sandy Murphy during the course of their relationship. Buczek learned that Kathy Rose had provided private investigator Tom Dillard with a statement that outlined Sandy Murphy's spending habits and other information.

According to the statement Rose had provided to Dillard, Binion had given Sandy a Bank of America MasterCard with a $10,000 credit limit to use for her daily expenses. When Buczek obtained Sandy's credit card bills, which normally were paid by Kathy Rose through one of Binion's checking accounts after he sent her all of the monthly bills, he noted that from January to August 1998 Sandy Murphy's average monthly credit card charges amounted to approximately $5,100. Binion also provided her with a cellular telephone, and had purchased a black 1997 Mercedes for her, following a fight in which he had allegedly beaten Sandy.

One of Binion's longtime friends, Tom Martinet, told the investigator that he and his wife had observed Sandy Murphy after the beating she had sustained at Binion's hands, which allegedly had occurred on or about October 9, 1996. Martinet said that he had seen defensive wounds on her forearms, an abrasion on Sandy's forehead, and a bare spot on the back of her head where her hair had apparently been pulled out. While in Ted Binion's presence, Sandy related in response to Martinet's inquiry that Binion had beaten her.

With all of his other problems, the last thing he needed was to have Sandy file domestic abuse charges against him. As an apparent attempt to reconcile with Sandy, Ted offered to buy her a new Mercedes. It was in his best interest to make up with her the best way he knew how and that was by providing her with material goods.

They soon located a black Mercedes at Fletcher Jones

Imports on South Rancho Drive not far from Binion's home, and he paid for it with a check for $97,300. Martinet and his wife went with Sandy to pick up the new car at the dealership but, because of Sandy's license revocation for problems she had encountered in California previously, she was not allowed to drive the car home and it was instead driven for her.

As Buczek and Tom Dillard continued to interview Binion's friends, a picture of a very avaricious Sandy Murphy began to emerge. Ted's sister, Becky, told investigators that Sandy was very materialistic, and that on a number of occasions Sandy had told her that she was only dating Ted because of his wealth.

Another of Binion's friends, Sid Lewis, a gaming executive who had known Binion for many years, told the investigators that he had been present at Binion's home on a number of occasions when Sandy had asked Binion to make investments for her. Yet another friend, Steve Morris, a Horseshoe Casino employee, told Tom Dillard that Binion had confided in him, and quoted Binion as having said that, despite all the things he had bought for her, "I'll never marry the bitch. The other bitch got enough from me. Another one ain't going to get my money like the other one did!"

The version of Binion's last will and testament that was drafted by his attorney and friend James J. Brown and executed on May 16, 1996, did not include Sandy Murphy. She was only added later as a partial beneficiary, which Binion revoked in his conversation with Brown on the day prior to his death. The May 16, 1996, will made specific bequests to six individuals, with the remainder of his estate going to his daughter, Bonnie, upon his death. Buczek made a note to locate the codicil to Binion's will that had listed Sandy as a beneficiary.

In January 1997, Buczek discovered, Binion had hired attorney Tom Standish to draft a cohabitation agreement between himself and Murphy, and which Binion intended to use to prevent Sandy from claiming an entitlement to palimony should they ever split up. The agreement basically stated that if they did go their separate ways, each would keep their own separate property. The agreement provided that Sandy would be able to keep the Mercedes and the profits from specific Rio Hotel and Casino stock if it was sold. Sandy and her attorney at that time, Glen Lerner, had signed the agreement.

Meanwhile, Buczek recalled that Sandy Murphy had been asking questions shortly after Binion's death regarding how to file a claim for a $1 million life insurance policy that she believed had been issued to Binion through the Horseshoe naming her as beneficiary. He learned from Harry Claiborne, who had also served as an attorney for Binion for many years, that the Horseshoe Hotel and Casino did in fact provide for a $1 million life insurance policy for many of its executives. Ted Binion had a policy and had listed his nieces and nephews as beneficiaries.

However, Buczek learned from Ron Faiss, the former controller at the Horseshoe, who for thirty years—up until Binion had lost his gaming license—had managed many of Binion's financial dealings, that at a point sometime between January and June 1998, Binion had asked for a change-of-beneficiary form from the insurance company. At that time Binion had indicated that he wanted to make Sandy Murphy the beneficiary and Faiss said that the forms had been delivered to Binion through Kathy Rose. However, Faiss said, Binion had not followed up after he had sent the forms. Sandy had called Faiss shortly after Binion's death asking for his help and saying that she was meant to be Binion's beneficiary. Faiss said that he had told her that only Binion would have been authorized to make changes to his life insurance policy, and he hadn't done so. Faiss also related that he did not like Sandy, but did not provide specifics as to why.

Harry Claiborne told Buczek that he had seen Binion

with the insurance forms and offered to complete them for
him. Binion had declined his offer.

Buczek reflected on how Sandy had called James Brown
the morning after Binion's death and expressed concern
about possibly not "getting the house," and how she had
also phoned Richard Wright that morning wanting to know
how she could file the claim on Binion's life insurance
policy. Murphy, it seemed, was more of a gold digger than
a bereaved woman who had just lost the man she claimed
to love. Buczek decided to delve deeper into Rick Tabish's
background.

CHAPTER 11

As he prepared to probe into Rick Tabish's activities, Detective Buczek considered what he already knew about Tabish: his business, MRT Transport, Incorporated, in which his wife, Mary Jo, was listed as the corporation's secretary/treasurer; his failed business ventures and need to quickly raise capital; his criminal history in the state of Montana; and how he had come to know Ted Binion. Buczek knew that lust for another man's woman, as well as greed and a desperate need to obtain money could be deadly ingredients. People had been killed for far lesser reasons. Despite the fact that Rick Tabish had denied stealing Binion's silver in Pahrump after essentially being caught red-handed with it, not to mention all of the other facets of the case that had been uncovered so far, Buczek was still reluctant to call Ted Binion's death a homicide. Before he could do that he needed more incriminating evidence. It was along those lines that Buczek, as well as private investigator Tom Dillard, decided to turn to Tabish's friends and business associates to see what they could learn.

Buczek interviewed Charles Skinner, a friend of Rick's, who had met Tabish through Kyle Washington of Missoula, Montana. Washington, said Skinner, was a childhood friend of Tabish's and had become a mutual friend of both Tabish and Skinner. Skinner said that he had met Tabish in late 1995 or early 1996 at Piero's restaurant, which was owned by Skinner's stepfather. He said that after he had become acquainted with him, Tabish had stayed at his house while in Las Vegas on business.

While Tabish was still living in Montana, Skinner told Buczek, he was merely a "meat and potatoes" blue-collar worker. He explained that he knew about Telepro, Tabish's telemarketing business in Missoula, which marketed long-distance phone services, and that the business had failed. Tabish had lost money on that venture. As a result, by 1998, Tabish, whom Skinner characterized as friendly and likeable, was spending a lot of time in Las Vegas attempting to make new business connections, and he had been successful at meeting a number of influential business people—including Ted Binion—while socializing at Piero's.

Earlier in 1998, Kyle Washington had interested and persuaded a number of people, including Skinner and his stepfather, to invest in a gold mining stock venture called Delgratia Mining located in Vancouver, British Columbia. Although it wasn't clear whether Tabish had participated in the sale of his friend's stock or not, he had given it his endorsement and claimed that he had invested $500,000 of his own money in it. The venture had failed, and the investors lost their money. Buczek, however, was unable to determine if Tabish had actually invested the money, or whether his involvement had gone beyond merely endorsing it.

Skinner continued: he began to see changes in Tabish over time. He would no longer be the "meat and potatoes" person that he had known before. Tabish, he said, had transformed into a man almost obsessed with obtaining money, and had become preoccupied with expensive "toys." According to Skinner, Tabish at one point had leased his own airplane and hired a full-time pilot.

Sometime in the early part of 1998, Tabish told Skinner that he had befriended Ted Binion and related to Skinner information regarding a large collection of silver that Binion had stored inside the vault at the Horseshoe. Tabish had told Skinner that Binion was interested in selling the silver and Tabish was going to act as the broker for its sale.

After learning of Tabish's purported statements about Binion's silver, private investigator Tom Dillard spoke with Binion's friend, Sid Lewis, about the collection. According to Lewis, Binion had said that he needed to move the silver out of the Horseshoe because his sister had taken over the hotel/casino, but he had indicated to Lewis that he had no intention of selling it due to the depressed silver market.

Meanwhile, as he checked on the validity of the claims being made, Buczek again spoke to Steve Morris, Binion's friend and former Horseshoe employee. Morris basically echoed Lewis's statement by saying that Binion had no intention of selling his silver. However, according to Morris, he did want to obtain an independent appraisal of its value.

It was in early 1998, Buczek learned, that Tabish had contacted William Marin, an independent business promoter who lived in Beverly Hills, about brokering Ted Binion's silver. Marin, in turn, had contacted Mark Goldberg, the owner of Superior Stamp and Coin in Beverly Hills, to negotiate a potential referral fee based upon a percentage of Goldberg's profits if he sold Binion's silver. When contacted by Buczek, Goldberg stated that he was under the impression that Sandy Murphy and Rick Tabish would get a portion of the finder's fee that was to be paid to Marin if the deal went through.

As such, Goldberg traveled to Las Vegas to conduct the appraisal of Binion's silver. Horseshoe security guard John Boylan was present in the vault when the appraisal was conducted, as were Rick Tabish and Sandy Murphy. Boylan recalled that Tabish and Murphy seemed to be "very friendly" with each other, and he had observed eye contact between them which suggested that their relationship consisted of more than friendship. Boylan also heard one of the appraisers assure Sandy that his company could generate a sales document that would indicate that the sales price of the silver was *less* than the actual negotiated sale price. Goldberg estimated that Binion's silver was worth between $5 million and $7 million.

Shortly after Goldberg had completed his appraisal, Binion called and told him that he did not want to sell the silver after all. Goldberg expressed his disappointment over

Binion's decision, and afterward sent him an invoice in the amount of $31,000 for his services. Upon receiving it, Binion became upset over the amount of the bill, and Sandy Murphy called Goldberg and told him so. When Goldberg expressed his disappointment to Sandy over Binion's decision not to sell the silver, she said that she felt the same way and that "we had wanted the deal, too." Goldberg later stated that he understood that she had been referring to herself and Tabish. Goldberg encouraged Sandy to "work on Ted," and in the meantime he would consider reducing the amount of his bill. A short time later Rick Tabish also called Goldberg and stated that "we are still working on the deal." As with Murphy's statement, Goldberg said that he understood "we" to mean Sandy Murphy and Rick Tabish.

Tabish had formed a Nevada corporation under the name of MRT Transportation of Nevada, Incorporated, on October 6, 1997. Soon afterward, he obtained checking accounts for the company at Bank West of Nevada, and by December 19, 1997, he had obtained a loan of $200,000 on a revolving line of credit secured by the assets of all of Tabish's businesses as well as by signed personal guarantees of both Tabish and his wife, Mary Jo. The loan's date of maturity was June 19, 1998.

As he delved into Tabish's finances, Buczek learned that Tabish had been unable to meet the loan's maturity date and had teetered on the brink of defaulting. However, Tabish managed to convince the bank to extend the loan's maturity date to September 19, 1998—two days after Ted Binion's death, and the same day that Tabish, David Mattsen, and Michael Milot were arrested in Pahrump after removing Binion's silver. It now seemed more obvious than ever that Tabish's financial situation had been in dire straits for some time, both before and leading up to the time of Ted Binion's demise.

*   *   *

By this point in the investigation word had spread via the media that investigators looking into the suspicious death of Ted Binion were scrutinizing Rick Tabish and Sandy Murphy. Michael Wells, an attorney in California, recognized Tabish's name and called investigators regarding an alleged incident that involved a man named Leo Casey. Wells said that he worked for Rubber Technology, Incorporated, a company that had expressed interest in purchasing one of Tabish's companies. It was during a meeting with Tabish that Leo Casey's name had come up. According to Wells, Tabish had bragged to him not to worry, that they would not hear from Casey again. "He told me that he had taken Leo Casey and beaten the hell out of him with a phone book." Wells said that the beating had continued until Casey had signed a confession of some sort, after which Casey had left town.

Shortly after Wells called the authorities in Nevada, Leo Casey began talking about having been abducted by Tabish and other men, taken into the desert, tortured and forced to turn over his rights to a sand mining operation in Jean, Nevada.

When Buczek tracked down Casey's whereabouts in California, Casey was at first reluctant to talk to him. He expressed fear of Tabish and said that he was hiding from him and another man, Steve Wadkins. After considerable effort, Buczek convinced Casey to provide him with a formal statement regarding the allegations that he had been making.

Casey explained that over the years he had maintained part ownership of the Jean sand pit. His involvement in the pit's day-to-day business operations soon brought him into contact with Steve Wadkins, president of All Star Transit Mix, a concrete company that purchased significant amounts of sand from the Jean pit, and Rick Tabish, whose MRT Transport hauled the sand. It wasn't unusual for them to talk about their personal lives with each other, he said.

Casey told Buczek that Rick Tabish had told him about his newfound friend, Ted Binion.

"Tabish said that Binion had a lot of money and that he [Tabish] was going to get some of it," Casey said.

According to Casey, Tabish also talked about murdering Ted Binion and stealing his large collection of silver and rare coins. Tabish purportedly told Casey that Binion was using drugs, and described how he would kill him.

"I'll overdose him and no one will know the difference," Casey quoted Tabish as having told him. "He uses another drug that knocks him out, that's when I can pump him up with the other drugs."

Casey said that Tabish also talked to him about Sandy Murphy, and bragged that he was "laying the pipe" to her, saying that he was "fucking Sandra Murphy and she was really loving it." Casey also said that Tabish explained to him how his relationship with Sandy would simplify matters for stealing Binion's silver. After obtaining Binion's silver, said Casey, Tabish planned to sell it to a coin collector in California. Tabish also had indicated that he would ask John Joseph to help him sell some of the silver, particularly the silver bars, through Joseph's banking connections.

Joseph, president of the Jean sand pit, as well as Dakota West, Incorporated, and Pacific Western Aggregate Corporation—all of which were tied to the Jean sand pit and did business regularly with Rick Tabish's MRT Transport—had agreed to participate in a scheme that involved Leo Casey.

If Tabish's prior revelations hadn't been sufficient reason to scare Casey out of the state, his account of what happened next surely had been.

Unable to recall the exact date, Casey related that sometime between July 25 and July 27, 1998, John Joseph had summoned him to his office. Casey said that Joseph asked him to take Steve Wadkins and Rick Tabish to the Jean sand pit so that they could inspect the serial numbers of the equipment that Joseph desired to sell to Tabish.

On July 28, Casey said that he again drove to the Jean sand pit with Wadkins and Tabish. After they got out of the car, Casey said, Tabish and Wadkins grabbed his arms and twisted them behind his back, and told him that "they were in control now." Sixty-two-year-old Casey was easily rendered helpless. While they held him immobile they had placed a pair of thumb cuffs on him.

Had these been the same thumb cuffs that Sandy Murphy had told Binion's maid, Mary, that she was going to loan to a friend to collect a debt? Buczek pondered the likelihood.

After they had him restrained, Tabish and Wadkins accused Casey of embezzling money from John Joseph's companies. They began cursing at him and calling him names, saying that he was a "no good sonofabitch." At one point, according to Casey, in their attempts to elicit a confession that Casey had embezzled money as well as equipment from Joseph, Wadkins began to shove a gun into his mouth and, at other times, in his ears, threatening to kill him. At another point he inserted the blade of a knife beneath Casey's fingernails. Forcing Casey to stand against the front of an old diesel tank, Tabish repeatedly beat Casey on his face and body with a telephone book, which wouldn't leave signs of a beating.

In addition to wanting the confession from Casey, they were attempting to get him to sign a document that would transfer Casey's ownership and interest in the sand pit, as well as that of the equipment, over to Joseph. Casey resisted, and Tabish and Wadkins continued to beat him.

"Rick took the phone book, the Yellow Pages, and began violently beating me on my head from one side to the other and on top of my head," Casey said.

While Casey continued to refuse to sign the confession and transfer document, Tabish at one point directed Wadkins to start up a front loader that was located nearby and to dig a hole in which they could bury Casey after killing him. After digging Casey's intended "grave," they dragged him over to its edge and allegedly threatened to bury him alive.

"They drug me over to the hole and told me they were going to throw me in it and take the loader and bury me," Casey stated. At that point, Casey said, he finally relented and agreed to sign whatever they wanted him to sign.

After Casey had agreed to sign the documents, Tabish and Wadkins forced him back into the vehicle. Casey, still restrained by the thumb cuffs, sat quietly in the front passenger seat as Wadkins continued to hold a gun on him from the back seat. During the trip back to town Tabish, using his cellular phone, called Joseph and instructed him to meet them on the street in front of Tabish's business, also located on Las Vegas Boulevard South. When they arrived at MRT Transportation, Joseph was there, waiting. As he approached the car, Casey attempted to get into the back seat, but Joseph told him to stay in the front and got in back with Wadkins, who continued holding a gun to Casey's head.

From MRT's offices, Tabish, Wadkins, and Joseph drove Casey to the offices of All Star Transit Mix, located on East Lone Mountain Road in North Las Vegas. When they arrived they removed the thumb cuffs from Casey's thumbs, and he was escorted inside to the offices where he signed a handwritten document that essentially agreed to their demands.

Afterwards, Tabish, Wadkins, and Joseph drove Casey to the law offices of Hutchison and Steffen where he could sign formal legal documents. Attorney Mark Hutchison, unaware of the events that had transpired involving Casey's torture, drafted a three-page document entitled "Asset Transfer Agreement" which both Casey and Joseph signed in the presence of a notary.

After Casey had signed the documents, Tabish and Wadkins warned Casey "not to meddle in our business" and "to leave town." They threatened that if he did not heed their warning, Casey's family and friends would suffer the consequences. Casey quoted them as saying that they would "either cut their heads off or blow their goddamn heads off and they'd take my daughters or girlfriend or ex-wife and fuck 'em to death and blow their heads off." Casey said that he had believed every word they said to him, and had done as he was told and, after withdrawing $250,000 from the bank, left town the next day without contacting the police.

"I was going to be killed if I didn't," Casey said. "If I came back to town or meddled in their business in any way, I'd be killed . . . they put the fear of hell in me."

When he conducted a follow-up inquiry regarding Casey's allegations, Buczek talked with Joe Booher, 69, an employee of the Jean sand pit who lived in a trailer on the pit property with his wife, Sandra, who, it turned out, was Leo Casey's ex-wife.

Did everyone associated with this case know each other in one way or another? Buczek wondered. It was certainly beginning to look that way.

Booher recounted how he saw three men arrive at the sand pit on July 28, 1998, and how he later heard a piece of heavy equipment being started up. He said that he had also seen Tabish and Wadkins assist Casey into a car, and that they had waved at him as they drove off "like everything was okay." He said that he had later seen a hole that he had never seen before at the sand pit, and a front-end loader nearby.

"It [the hole] was just as long as the front-end loader was long," Booher said.

Booher's wife, Sandra, who worked as a secretary at the sand pit, echoed her husband's statement and said that she, too, had seen the freshly dug hole and said that it had looked somewhat like a grave to her.

Buczek also subsequently spoke with William "Willie" Alder, a truck driver foreman for MRT Transportation. Alder stated that he was present at the Jean sand pit on July

28, and that he had observed Casey, Rick Tabish, and a third individual whom he could not identify, drive up in Casey's car. Tabish had told him that they were there to look at some equipment. Alder said that he had not seen the hole that had allegedly been dug, and stated that he doubted that Joe Booher would have been able to hear any equipment start up. Booher was hard of hearing and his trailer was located about a half-mile from the site where Casey claimed that he was tortured. He hadn't, however, witnessed the violence that allegedly had been inflicted on Casey.

Alder, Buczek also learned, had assisted in the moving of Binion's silver from the Horseshoe to Binion's home. He said that Tabish and Murphy had also been present that day. Alder further stated that he had been instructed to stop what he was doing on September 18, 1998, and to pick up an excavator that was to be transported to Pahrump to remove Binion's silver from the underground vault. He said that the job of removing Binion's silver that day was not a secret.

Tabish, Buczek reasoned, had informed his employees of what he was doing that day, perhaps to bolster or add credence to his claims that he was to remove the silver on Binion's behalf and at Binion's request.

As he continued putting his case together, Buczek also spoke with Troy Morrison, who worked at the Jean sand pit as a rock crusher. Morrison said that after the alleged incident involving Casey, Tabish had described to him how he had hit Casey with a phone book, and had laughingly stated that Casey's "strong" toupee had remained attached to his head throughout the ordeal.

"He said that he had Leo Casey up against a diesel tank and was whacking him over the head with a telephone book," Morrison said. "He said that Casey was having trouble with his toupee staying on, but it stayed on."

Morrison said that Tabish had told him that Casey had not paid him for the jobs in which he had hauled sand away from the pit, and he had blamed Casey, without elaborating, for another of his failed business ventures. Morrison also stated that Tabish had pointed out to him a shallow hole, about two feet deep and eight feet long, which he had said was to have been Leo Casey's grave.

"He told Leo that's where he was going next if he didn't tell him where the stuff was," Morrison said, apparently referring to the missing equipment for which Tabish was holding Casey responsible.

In the aftermath of Casey's ordeal in the desert with Tabish and Wadkins, when asked if he was able to produce any documents that outlined his prior agreements with Joseph, papers that could show that he was not embezzling money and equipment, Casey said that he could not. He stated that his agreements with Joseph had been stored inside the garage of his house. However, at some point those documents, and nothing else, had been mysteriously stolen.

Shortly after Buczek learned of the startling allegations involving Leo Casey, the Clark County District Attorney's office assigned investigator Mike Karstedt to follow up on the services that attorney Mark Hutchison provided to John Joseph and Leo Casey on July 28 and, particularly, the interactions that he'd had with them.

Karstedt, who had worked for twenty-six years as a police officer prior to going to work for the district attorney's office, subsequently learned that lawyer Jim Randle, a partner in Hutchison's firm, had received a telephone call during the early morning hours from either John Joseph himself or from someone representing Joseph. During the phone call, Randle had been informed that Leo Casey had been stealing money from the company. The caller had urged that Randle clear his schedule because Joseph and Steve Wadkins were brining Casey in to the firm's offices to sign a confession, as well as other documents, and that time was short because Casey was planning to leave town. Randle, however, had been unable to rearrange his schedule and as a result attorney Mark Huchison had agreed to meet with them instead.

It was later that day, Huchison said, sometime in the afternoon, that John Joseph, Steve Wadkins, Leo Casey, and another individual later identified by Casey as Rick Tabish, arrived at Huchison's offices. Although he had not observed any bruises, blood, or any other evidence of foul play on Casey, Huchison said that he had noted that Casey was shaking and appeared to have been very upset.

Huchison explained that he was instructed to draw up a transfer agreement ceding Casey's interest in the Jean sand pit to John Joseph. Although Huchison had no discussion with Casey, he said that Joseph had described to him an elaborate embezzlement scheme that allegedly involved Casey. He stated that neither Tabish's name nor the names of any of his companies appeared on the asset transfer agreement or on Casey's signed admission.

A short time later, after conferring with Karstedt about what he'd learned, Detective Buczek obtained a document entitled, "MRT Contracting, Incorporated, Investor's Summary." Attorney William H. Knudson, MRT's attorney, had drawn it up. According to the document, MRT was attempting to attract investors to bring $500,000 into the company in return for a promissory note that would provide the investors with eighteen percent interest on their investment. The funds were to purchase the option rights to a fifty-year lease of the Jean sand pit and North Wash Plant from John Joseph's companies. A portion of the document contained the following information:

"The extremely favorable terms offered to MRT are a result of Dakota West and Pacific Western Aggregate Corporation's desire to sell said business in order to mitigate economic losses incurred from company mismanagement as well as losses in excess of $500,000 suffered as a result of embezzlement by a former corporate officer and manager.

"Following Dakota West's and Pacific Western Aggregate Corporation's discovery of misconduct, Dakota West and Pacific Western Aggregate Corporation hired MRT [Contracting's] co-owner and president, Mr. Rick Tabish, to run its sand and gravel operations. Mr. Tabish, who owns and operates MRT Transportation of Nevada, Incorporated, also holds the exclusive contract with Dakota West and Pacific Western Aggregate Corporation for the transport of its sand to the Las Vegas market."

Included with the document were four letters of commitment from Las Vegas companies, including one which had been written by Steve Wadkins on behalf of All Star Transit Mix. The commitment letters were dated July 21 and July 22, 1998, prior to Leo Casey's purported torture in the desert.

Buczek later learned through copies of Steve Wadkins's cellular telephone records, particularly those that pertained to July 28, 1998, that Wadkins had called the Huchison and Steffan law office twice on that date: once at 12:18 p.m. and again at 12:31 p.m., presumably to finalize the arrangements surrounding their plan to bring in Leo Casey. That occasion had been only one of several times that Buczek would obtain the cellular telephone records of those involved in this case.

Based on the aforementioned solicitation for investors, it now seemed that Leo Casey had been forced to turn over his share of the Jean sand pit so that Rick Tabish could buy into it from John Joseph for a half-million dollars. A half-million dollars was a small price to pay, comparatively speaking, for the potential financial returns of the long-term deal with Joseph. A deal like that had the potential to solve Tabish's financial woes. But Tabish didn't have that kind of money, and it seemed doubtful that he could obtain it through his solicitation for investors. With that thought in mind, a half-million dollars seemed to the investigators to be a pretty good motive for murder. With Ted Binion out of the way and his silver liquidated, they suspected that Tabish could have easily gotten the money for the sand pit investment and still would have had at least ten times the amount he needed left over.

CHAPTER 12

As time moved forward, so did Detective James Buczek's investigation into Ted Binion's death. Although by now Buczek felt that Binion had been murdered for his wealth, he still could not officially label his case a homicide investigation. He still needed more evidence before he could bring murder charges against Sandy Murphy and Rick Tabish, and he pushed onward in that vein. Every day seemed to bring revelations that pointed toward that conclusion, and nearly every day he found that he had a new avenue to investigate.

One such avenue took him back to Binion's home where, on September 28, 1998, a locksmith drilled open the safe located inside Binion's garage. According to what Buczek was being told at that time, the safe was where Binion had kept a collection of old coins and currency valued at $300,000 or more. James Brown, attorney for Binion's estate, was present when the safe was opened.

Brown observed what he believed was probably Ted Binion's handwriting and hand printing on the inside of the safe's door. The message was a threat or warning to anyone who might steal the safe's contents. However, someone hadn't paid any heed. The safe was empty, cleaned out except for a single dime.

Buczek immediately recalled how Binion's vault in Pahrump had been completely cleaned out as well, with only a single silver dollar left behind. Was the thief trying to convey some kind of message? he wondered. Or was the thief leaving the single coins as a signature of sorts? No one knew the answer, of course, except for the thief or thieves.

*　　*　　*

Initially, after Ted Binion's death, many aspects involved in the processing of the inside of his house were not examined closely enough, in part because the circumstances of Binion's death had not been immediately determined and it was only remotely suspected to have been caused by foul play. However, because of the direction the case was taking, it was decided that yet another examination of the house's interior be conducted. This time Buczek was present, as were several Metro criminalists, private investigator Tom Dillard, and James Brown. Mary Montoya-Gascoigne was also brought along this time because of her familiarity with the contents of the home and the fact that she was the last person, aside from Binion's killers, known to have been inside the house prior to his death.

In the southeast den, where Binion's body had been discovered, Buczek and Mary examined the numerous spots on the floor that had been observed by Dr. Lary Simms. The spots began at the threshold of the den and led up to the mattress where Binion's body was found. Mary pointed out that the spots were not there on the day prior to Binion's death. Believing that the spots consisted of gastric fluids from Binion's body, the same opinion held by Dr. Simms, Buczek directed crime scene analyst Jessie Sams to remove samples of the carpeting that contained the stains.

Buczek also observed several flannel pillowcases located near the television in the den. Mary told him that the pillowcases had not been there on September 16, the day before Binion's death, and that they were normally kept in the linen closet. Mary reiterated at that time that Binion never slept on the floor, even on a mattress or in sleeping bags. He *always* slept in his bed, she said. Buczek recalled that Binion's ex-wife, Doris, had made a similar statement.

Mary pointed out that a coin collection, encased in plastic, was missing from a shelf near the television where Binion had always kept it. She also pointed out where she had last seen Binion's will, now missing, with the handwritten entry "Sandy Murphy—one million dollars" scratched out.

When they examined Binion's bedroom, located on the northeast side of the house, they discovered a somewhat significant point that had been overlooked earlier. Mary pointed out that Binion's bed was made differently from the way in which she had normally made it. She stated that someone must have used the bed after she had made it up on September 16, and that whoever had used it had re-made it. Binion never made his own bed, she said, and Sandy Murphy rarely made hers. Jessie Sams removed and bagged as potential evidence two pillows, a throw pillow, and a regular pillow in a white case, found on Binion's bed. Both contained stains of an unknown nature.

When Sams removed the mattress from Ted Binion's bed, she and Buczek observed a pair of shoe or boot impressions on the top of the box springs. Buczek believed that someone lifting the heavy mattress in their search for Binion's valuables had made the prints. Metro's shoe impressions examiner, Edward Guenther, told Buczek that it was his opinion, based on the tread design, that the impressions were made by hiking or work boots.

When they examined the dressing room area of Ted's bedroom, Mary pointed out a chair situated beneath the attic opening. The chair, she said, was normally kept under a desk in Binion's bedroom, and that is where she last had seen it on September 16. She pointed out, however, that she had seen the chair underneath the attic opening on another occasion, approximately two weeks before Binion's death.

When Buczek reviewed the photographs that were taken by crime scene analyst Mike Perkins on the day Binion's body was discovered, he noted that the same chair was located near the desk in Binion's bedroom. Someone, he reasoned, had moved it to gain access to the attic sometime afterward, but had failed to return it to its original location.

Next, Mary pointed out the fact that numerous gaming

chips issued by the Horseshoe Casino were missing from the nightstand on the right side of Binion's bed, as was petty cash that he kept inside a cigar box on the nightstand. She also noted that a brown wooden box that contained silver dollars was missing from Binion's bedroom closet, and a wooden lockbox that Binion kept beneath the dresser in the hallway had been broken open and appeared to have been gone through. Also missing were two gold watches that Binion normally kept on top of the desk in his bedroom.

When they examined the living room, Mary opened a wooden box that Binion always kept on the coffee table. The box, she said, had contained Binion's checkbook and other paperwork. All of the items, she said, were now missing, as was a pound of marijuana that Binion had kept in the house. However, the owner of a vacant lot directly behind Binion's home subsequently told Tom Dillard that she had found a checkbook bearing Ted Binion's name, along with a bullet cartridge, in her lot on September 24.

Before leaving Binion's house, Buczek searched through Sandy Murphy's bedroom closet. He soon found a book among her things entitled, *Lovers, Killers, Husbands and Wives*, by Martin Blinder, M.D. Buczek noted that the author had documented several actual court cases that involved "crimes of passion," one in which a mother had killed her children by putting barbiturates in their milk. After the children had lapsed into a coma, she had smothered them to death.

As he continued to piece together the details of the relationship between Sandy Murphy and Rick Tabish, Buczek located a former roommate who said that he and Tabish had shared an apartment at The Meridian, located just off The Strip, for most of 1998. During that period the roommate said that he had observed Tabish and Murphy to be affectionate toward each other.

Buczek also learned that Tabish frequented an athletic

club, the Las Vegas Sporting House, during this same period. When he checked the establishment's records, he found that Sandy Murphy was listed as a member under Ted Binion's membership. When he checked further, Buczek found that Sandy also had a second membership under Rick Tabish's corporate account. He found that Tabish had added Murphy in July 1998, even though Murphy was not an employee of any of Tabish's companies.

Convinced that Murphy and Tabish had developed a very close romantic relationship, Buczek obtained Murphy's cellular telephone records with Alltel Communications from Tom Dillard. Because Binion had been paying Murphy's bills, including her cellular telephone bill, Dillard had access to the records. And because he was a private detective working for the Binion estate, he didn't need a court order. By examining Murphy's bill, Dillard was able to determine the numbers to which she had made outgoing calls.

The records showed frequent daily telephone contact between Murphy's and Tabish's telephones that appeared to begin in April 1998 and continued up until the day Ted Binion died, including, it was learned after investigators obtained Tabish's cellular bills, one call that Murphy received from Tabish seven minutes before reporting Ted Binion's death.

Buczek also noted that the account inquiry portion of Murphy's phone records indicated that Sandy Murphy had called an Alltel account representative on July 28, 1998, at 7:13 p.m. in which she had requested that the telephone call description or details portion be removed from her future phone bills. She had further instructed the representative that ". . . no information is to be given to anyone except the account holder—not even her secretary."

Throughout the investigation Buczek tried to locate Sandy Murphy's friend, Linda Carroll, but she remained evasive and refused to meet with him to provide a formal statement.

Up until this point she had only spoken to him about Murphy and Tabish's tryst at the Peninsula Hotel in Beverly Hills. However, Buczek learned that Carroll had remained in contact with one of Binion's attorneys, Richard Wright, and had spoken with him on several occasions.

Among the things that Carroll had told Wright was that she had enjoyed a close personal friendship with Sandy Murphy. On one occasion, she said, Sandy had confided in her regarding her relationship with Binion. Carroll related that Sandy always tried to control Ted's life, and one of the ways that she attempted this was by recording and listening to his telephone calls. Sandy also claimed to have handled Ted Binion's banking for him.

According to what Carroll told Wright, Sandy was very concerned about her financial well-being and continuously complained to Binion that he had not included her in his will. On more than one occasion Sandy had berated Binion in front of his friends for not providing for her in his estate plan. Binion's typical response to her was, "Don't worry about it, you'll be taken care of if something happens to me." According to Carroll, Sandy had confided to her that she was supposed to receive $3 million and Binion's house and its contents in the event of his death and that she had taken the will to an attorney to ensure that it was in fact valid.

However, when Buczek finally located the codicil to Binion's will that was executed on July 9, 1998, he found that Binion had deleted specific previous bequests and had it changed to bequeath $300,000 to Sandy Murphy, as well as his Palomino Lane home and all of its contents.

Carroll told Wright that she had observed Murphy and Tabish growing closer over time. She also said that Tabish did not attempt to hide his ill will for Binion and that he once stated in her presence that ". . . he hated Ted and wanted Ted dead." Later, Carroll said that Murphy had told her, "Rick is okay. We did something together that would turn your stomach and land us in jail."

Carroll related to Wright that she was aware of Tabish's financial difficulties, and described them as significant. Before Binion's death, she said, Tabish was desperately involved in a search for investors to obtain funding for his failing businesses.

On one occasion, according to Carroll's account, Murphy confided to her that she was having an affair with Tabish, which was nothing that she hadn't already figured out. Sandy told Carroll that she had purchased clothing for him at Neiman Marcus, and had paid for the items with the credit card that Binion provided her.

When he followed up on that lead, Buczek learned that Sandy Murphy had purchased a pair of men's Gucci jeans, size 36" × 34", at the Neiman Marcus store in the Fashion Show Mall on The Strip on July 27, 1998. According to Brian Hall, a salesperson in the men's department, Sandy had charged the jeans to her MasterCard and had them gift-wrapped in a butterfly design wrapping. Hall recalled the transaction because he was the salesperson who had assisted her. He reviewed the store documents and provided the account number that the jeans had been charged to and, sure enough, it was the credit card that Binion provided for her every day use. However, Buczek recalled that Binion's pants size was 36" × 31", not 36" × 34". It appeared that Carroll's lead had checked out, and Buczek concluded that the pants must have been for Tabish.

Brian Hall stated that he had again waited on Sandy Murphy, who had been accompanied by another female, on August 3, 1998. This time, still using Ted Binion's MasterCard, Murphy had purchased a pair of black Armani slacks for $240, a Wilke-Rodriguez knit shirt for $85, and an Armani woven top for $445. As she had done before, she had the items gift-wrapped in butterfly design packaging. Hall said that he overheard Murphy say to her friend that she was going to surprise someone, a male whose name he did not catch, by placing the package of clothing on the bed.

*   *   *

Buczek subsequently learned that the trip that Sandy Murphy and Rick Tabish had made to Beverly Hills in September had not been their first. Through the assistance of detectives in Beverly Hills, Buczek learned that they had checked into the Beverly Hills Hotel, another very exclusive and expensive establishment, on Saturday, August 8, 1998. Similar to their trip in September, the hotel's guest registration records had been signed by a "Ms. S. Tabish." They had rented a single room with a deluxe king-size bed. That evening Tabish and Murphy had drinks in the hotel's Polo Lounge. The charge slip indicated that they had ordered a Coors Light and a glass of merlot wine.

The next morning, according to the hotel's records, a telephone call had been placed from their room to Ted Binion's residence in Las Vegas. Although it was not known or determined what was said during the call or whether it had been Tabish or Murphy who had made it, it was an important link or factor in establishing the caller's connection with Ted Binion and helped solidify the identification process by showing that they were indeed in Beverly Hills and had made, or at least had attempted to make, contact with Ted. They also had rented a poolside cabana for the day, which this time was signed by "Sandy Murphy (a.k.a. Tabish)." The poolside café server positively identified the couple as Sandy Murphy and Rick Tabish after being shown photographs.

If there had been any doubt in Buczek's mind that Murphy and Tabish were romantically involved prior to Ted Binion's death, that doubt had now been irrevocably erased. He was satisfied that he and his fellow detectives had uncovered sufficient evidence to prove that such a relationship existed. Now all he had to do was tie them to Ted Binion's death. Given enough time, he felt confident that he could.

Although Sandra Murphy and Rick Tabish refused to talk with the Metro investigators on the advice of their attorneys, Buczek and his colleagues escalated their investigation over the next several weeks. Apparently feeling that she needed a change of legal counsel due to the increased heat and prodding from the cops, Murphy met with famed criminal defense attorney Oscar Goodman. Goodman, who would soon be elected mayor of Las Vegas, gained fame and notoriety for representing various reputed mobsters over the years, including Anthony "Tony the Ant" Spilotro. On October 8, 1998, Goodman and his partner, David Chesnoff, agreed to provide legal counsel to Murphy and to defend her in court in the event that she was charged with any crimes associated with Binion's death.

Buczek learned that by July or August 1998, paychecks for Tabish's MRT Transport began to bounce, and he found evidence that suggested that Tabish had begun to liquidate some of his companies' heavy equipment to help cover the checks. Buczek examined bank account records for Tabish's companies and found that in September 1998 alone more than $130,000 of MRT's checks had been returned by the bank because of insufficient funds.

Buczek recalled that Tabish, while free on bail following his arrest for stealing Binion's silver, had negotiated the sale of MRT Transportation to Rubber Technologies International, also known as RTI, a corporation located in California. Buczek also remembered that it had been RTI's attorney, Michael Wells, who had alerted Nevada authorities about the Leo Casey incident. As part of the deal that he had negotiated, RTI was to obtain MRT's mining rights to the Jean sand pit, which Tabish had acquired from John Joseph following the alleged Casey incident.

Fred Schmidt, RTI's chief financial officer, soon began scrutinizing MRT's accounting records, and realized that he'd been had. He learned that MRT's line of credit at Bank West had been depleted, and that more than $100,000 in checks was still outstanding at the time of the deal. He also learned that MRT was in deep trouble with the Internal Revenue Service for back employee withholding taxes for portions of 1997 and 1998. Creditors were also beginning to foreclose on Tabish's other businesses, including those that were located in Montana.

It was now evident to Buczek that Tabish had considerably exaggerated the value of his assets and had under-reported MRT's liabilities to RTI. Buczek was now convinced that, because of his poor financial condition prior to Ted Binion's death, Tabish had attempted to resolve his financial problems by stealing Binion's silver. When that attempt had failed, he turned to negotiations with RTI.

CHAPTER 13

On Thursday, November 5, 1998, Sandra Murphy's attorneys, Oscar Goodman and David Chesnoff, filed a challenge in Clark County District Court to Binion estate attorney James Brown's October petition that sought to exclude Murphy from Ted Binion's will. Murphy's challenge claimed that Brown's changes to Binion's will were not in accordance with a Nevada state law that says "no will in writing shall be revoked unless by burning, tearing, or canceling or obliterating the same, with the intention of revoking it, by the person who wrote the will or by some person in his presence or direction." Murphy's challenge also sought to remove Brown from the fight over the will due to the fact that he and his wife might be witnesses to "Binion's state of mind concerning his alleged decision to remove Murphy . . . Mr. Binion's capacity to make such a change would certainly be affected by his mental condition."

Murphy's lawyers also stated that the alleged telephone call that Binion made to James Brown the day before his death, instructing Brown to remove Murphy from his will, was contrary to his prior and repeated assurances that Murphy, as well as others to whom he had made promises, would receive their share of his estate.

"I guess Mr. Brown's now a witness, not a lawyer," said Murphy's attorney, David Chesnoff. "The position we take is that Teddy loved and lived with this woman and intended for her to receive a portion of his estate, and we will litigate that if necessary. There's a very large estate here and Sandy is not asking for more than Teddy intended her to have."

A hearing on the matter was held the following day before District Judge Myron Leavitt. After reviewing Brown's petition and Murphy's challenge, Judge Leavitt ruled that the $300,000 Murphy claimed Binion left her would be held in an interest-bearing account until such time that the matter could be resolved in court. Leavitt also ordered that 24-hour security be provided at Binion's Palomino Lane home to protect the house and its contents until it could be determined whether, in fact, Sandy Murphy was entitled to them.

Because it was by now common knowledge that investigators were looking at Binion's death as a possible homicide and that, consequently, Murphy and Tabish were being closely scrutinized as potential suspects, members of their camp were quick to point out that people should not think that Murphy had a motive to kill Binion simply because she stood to inherit part of his estate or benefit from his life insurance policy. Those close to Murphy indicated that Binion was worth more to her alive than dead, and that anything she stood to gain from his death amounted to only pennies on the dollar of his overall wealth.

It was also pointed out that Binion's will had named his daughter, Bonnie, as beneficiary of most of his estate, and that Binion had left nothing for his sister, Becky, or for his brother, Jack.

"Decedent intended by his directions to James J. Brown that decedent's daughter, Bonnie Leigh Binion, take all of decedent's estate and that Sandra Murphy receive nothing from decedent's estate," read a portion of Brown's petition.

Also, because of the arrangement that Ted had made with his sister over the transfer of his portion of the Horseshoe, the value of his estate would be increased by approximately $9 million when Becky paid the obligation of the legal agreement she had made with Ted.

As Metro detectives James Buczek and Tom Thowsen continued to escalate their investigation into Ted Binion's death, the question of valuable coins and old U.S. currency, minted and printed prior to the Civil War, came into play. Although they didn't know a precise value of the unaccounted-for coins and currency, the detectives knew they were quite valuable and one of Binion's friends had indicated that they were worth in excess of $500,000. The friend also said that Binion had always kept the collection inside his safe at his home.

Within days of Binion's death, Buczek learned, Sandy Murphy had taken a number of bags of silver coins into Oscar Goodman and David Chesnoff's law offices. It was said that she had removed the coins from Binion's home because of her fear that James Brown and Binion's estate were removing items from the house which, she felt, she was entitled to under the terms of the will as contents of the house. Murphy purportedly showed the coins to Goodman and Chesnoff, and had told them that Binion had given her the collection before his death. Expecting a legal battle over the estate, and knowing that she was being focused on as a possible suspect in Binion's death, Sandy purportedly wanted the lawyers to accept the coins as payment for her legal fees. Goodman pointed out that, as Murphy's attorney, he wanted to make certain that her best interests were looked out for.

"They haven't even given this poor lady time to grieve," Goodman said. "She lived with Teddy as his significant other for years and apparently made him very happy. She's getting a raw deal." Goodman added that if foul play were an element in Binion's death, his client was not involved.

"You can be assured that my office would not be representing her," Goodman told a local reporter, "since we have a very close relationship with the Binion family, if we felt that she had engaged in anything that was improper . . . all we know is that Teddy loved her and she loved Teddy. And we just want to see that she's treated fairly . . . with any situation, if you look into it, you always find oddities because human nature is that way. And this has been looked at very closely, so you see more oddities than you would normally see."

Goodman and Chesnoff reportedly took possession of

the coins at that time and told Murphy that they would have to have them inventoried before they could accept them for legal fees. However, a few days later, before the inventory could be completed, Murphy retrieved the coins, and then they disappeared.

As Buczek attempted to trace the movement of the coins he believed were in Murphy's possession, he eventually learned that prior to taking them to Goodman and Chesnoff's offices she had taken them to the home of attorney William Knudson, where she was staying on a temporary basis.

When Knudson was questioned about the coins, he stated that he knew that there were items of value that Sandy had removed from Binion's home on September 18, 1998, but would not confirm or deny that the coins were among them. He also would not reveal whether he had knowledge of Sandy bringing the coins to his home, but there was nothing uncovered during the investigation that indicated Knudson had such knowledge or had acted improperly. He stated that his own lawyer had advised him to use caution when talking about the case regarding matters that could become public if the district attorney's office pursued the alleged criminal aspects of the investigation.

James Brown, meanwhile, spoke out on the subject of the missing coins and currency. Brown stated that he believed Sandy and her friends had removed a number of items from the house on the afternoon of September 18 while he was out attempting to get a court order permitting him temporary possession of the house. He stated that there were several people with her, including Tanya Cropp and Linda Carroll, and that her car was parked inside the garage at the time.

"I'm sure they took things that day without my knowledge," Brown said in a public statement. "They were in there for about two hours with her car parked in the garage. There were four or five different people there, and I wasn't physically there all of the time . . . I'm sure we will pursue this."

A spokesman for the district attorney's office said that authorities did not believe and had no reason to believe that there was any impropriety on the part of Oscar Goodman and David Chesnoff with regard to the coins and that neither Goodman nor Chesnoff would knowingly put themselves into a position to possess stolen property.

After they had returned the coins to Murphy, Goodman and Chesnoff were eventually paid for their services by check. She had reportedly sold her black two-seater Mercedes for cash, and Buczek subsequently learned that an elderly Irish businessman, William Fuller, whom Murphy had met at a restaurant, had loaned her $125,000 to help pay the lawyers. Fuller, an immigrant in his eighties was, it turned out, something of a legend in Irish show business. He had owned several ballrooms in Ireland, had worked with promoter Bill Graham on several projects, and had been responsible for bringing Irish bands to Las Vegas. Fuller, reportedly worth millions, had also made part of his fortune in the mining industry. There was no indication that Fuller and Murphy had known each other prior to their meeting at the restaurant. However, they had apparently become good friends in a relatively short time and it wasn't long before they were seen dining together around town on a somewhat regular basis. They had also reportedly attended church together. Sandy, claiming to be a strict Catholic, did not take communion at Mass; she said she wasn't entitled to receive the Eucharist because she did not go to confession regularly.

Meanwhile, additional background information on Sandra Murphy revealed that before moving to Las Vegas from California, she used to associate with celebrities in Los Angeles including former Lakers basketball player Magic Johnson. She had also been seen in the company of Dennis Rodman in Las Vegas. On one such occasion, she took Rodman out for a night on the town in Benny Binion's

Rolls Royce limousine. It was no wonder, then, Buczek
concluded, that she had been able to develop an association
with Mr. Fuller.

Before long Buczek and the other investigators stepped up
their interactions with the district attorney's office. They
began talking about the possibility of convening a grand
jury to hear testimony from witnesses who might have significant details they could share about what they knew or
things that they had been told regarding Ted Binion's death.
It would provide them an opportunity to question under
oath the people they had talked to previously, which is
sometimes more persuasive. It could also possibly lead to
other witnesses coming forward whom the investigators
previously had not known about.

On Tuesday, December 8, 1998, a high-priority meeting
was held at the district attorney's office behind closed
doors. Present were Clark County District Attorney Stewart
Bell; Bill Koot, chief of the D.A.'s office's Major Violators
Unit; Clark County Coroner Ron Flud; Binion estate attorney Richard Wright; private investigator Tom Dillard; and
detectives Jim Buczek, Tom Thowsen, and Lt. Wayne Petersen, members of Metro's homicide unit. Although specifics of the ninety-minute meeting were not revealed, Bell
told reporters that it was held to allow detectives to bring
everyone up to date on their progress in the investigation,
and for the district attorney's office to provide the investigators with information on the type of evidence they would
need to bring the case before a grand jury.

"Obviously, there are some suspicious circumstances
that necessitate them continuing to investigate," Bell said.
"It's a quantum leap from suspicious circumstances to evidence of a crime."

The case took a very unusual turn when investigators
learned that Rick Tabish sought and was granted a meeting
with Binion's sister, Becky, on Wednesday, December 16,

1998. According to what they had learned, Tabish's friend, Charles Skinner, had attempted to persuade Becky to meet with Tabish. Becky did not immediately agree to the meeting because she naturally was concerned about having a possible killer in her house. She subsequently contacted FBI Agent John Plunkett and told him what was being requested of her, and Plunkett agreed to have two FBI agents nearby secretly monitoring the proceedings. With that arrangement, she had agreed.

During their two-hour meeting, Tabish acknowledged that he had stayed with Sandy Murphy at the Peninsula Hotel in Beverly Hills, but at the same time denied he was having a romantic relationship with her. At one point when Nick apparently made disparaging and derogatory comments about Murphy, Tabish defended her. The investigators considered his defense of Murphy somewhat unusual for someone who had denied and continued to deny being romantically involved with her. At another point in the meeting Tabish admitted that he had called Sandy at 3:47 p.m. on September 17, but only to check on how she was doing. That particular call, Buczek remembered, had been the one that Tabish had made just seven minutes prior to Sandy calling for emergency assistance to deal with Binion.

Tabish also described the scene in the den where Binion's body was found, and made an attempt to get Becky to agree that Ted always slept on the floor in a sleeping bag. Becky later said that she knew this was not true, that Ted had told people he knew that one of the best ways to incapacitate someone was to wrap them up inside a sleeping bag. At another point in their conversation, according to Becky, Tabish had commented about seeing Ted with his pants clumped on the floor.

"You were there that day?" Becky had asked.

Tabish hadn't answered her question, but attempted to change the subject.

Tabish also talked to Becky and her husband about Ted's drug usage. He said that Ted had told him that he

"would take Xanax and be clean from drugs forever."
When she asked Tabish how he explained all of the heroin
found in Ted's stomach, he responded that the heroin had
accumulated there because Ted "always licked the knife
that he used to cut heroin."

"I could tell he had talked to Ted for hours," Becky said.
"He knew intimate details about Ted that only someone
who had spent long hours with him would know."

At another point in the meeting Tabish denied having
anything to do with Ted's death, and claimed that he was
not worried about being indicted for murder because he had
an alibi with credible people who he claimed he was with
at 12:30 p.m. on September 17. He also stated that, "Sandy
would never roll over on me." Before the meeting concluded, Tabish assured Becky and her husband that he
would contact the FBI and tell them what he had just related.

"Here was a person who could possibly have something
to do with the death of my brother," Becky said after the
meeting. "It was a really strange feeling being in a room
with him." She also said that she did not believe everything
that Tabish had said at the meeting.

When word of the meeting between Tabish and the Behnens was made public, a number of people associated with
the case spoke out about it.

"This is absolutely shocking news to me," said family
friend Harry Claiborne. "I can't conceive of him going to
Becky when Becky was the first person who began pointing
the finger at him."

Tom Dillard agreed. "Desperate people do desperate
things," he said.

Although Tabish called Becky again just before Christmas to say that he was still going to contact the FBI, records show that he never did.

On Friday, December 18, 1998, a week before Christmas,
Clark County District Court Judge Myron Leavitt sided

Murder victim Lonnie "Ted" Binion.
LAS VEGAS METRO POLICE

Mug shots of Sandra Murphy *(right)* and Richard "Rick" Tabish *(below)* following their arrests for Binion's murder.
LAS VEGAS METRO POLICE

Welcome to Fabulous Las Vegas—a sign located on the south end of the Strip. PHOTO BY THE AUTHOR

Binion's Horseshoe Hotel and Casino, located downtown on the Fremont Street Experience. PHOTO BY THE AUTHOR

Statue of Lester "Benny" Binion outside the Horseshoe Hotel and Casino. PHOTO BY THE AUTHOR

The Binion family home on Bonanza Road, where Ted Binion grew up. One of Benny Binion's rivals once planned to bomb it from an airplane. PHOTO BY THE AUTHOR

Ted Binion's gated Palomino Lane home, valued at approximately $900,000. PHOTO BY THE AUTHOR

Cheetah's Topless Club, one of Ted Binion's favorite haunts. This is where he met Sandra Murphy. PHOTO BY THE AUTHOR

All Star Transit Mix in North Las Vegas. Steve Wadkins worked there and Rick Tabish conducted a significant amount of business there. PHOTO BY THE AUTHOR

The building at Bella Vista Apartments where Tabish and Murphy lived after Binion's death. They occupied the unit in the lower right of the photo, around the corner from the garage. PHOTO BY THE AUTHOR

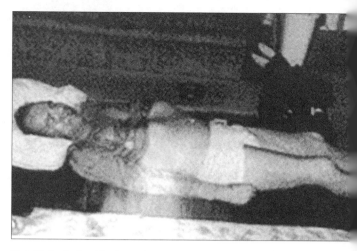

Ted Binion's dead body, as paramedics found it when they arrived. The killers staged it in a mortuary pose. LAS VEGAS METRO POLICE

The entrance to Ted Binion's 125-acre ranch in Pahrump, Nevada. Note the large horseshoe on the gate. PHOTO BY THE AUTHOR

View of Binion's ranch looking northeast, away from Pahrump.
PHOTO BY THE AUTHOR

Site of the excavated vault in Pahrump, located one-and-a-half miles from
Ted Binion's ranch. There, Tabish, Milot, and Mattsen attempted to steal
Binion's silver. PHOTO BY THE AUTHOR

Detective James Buczek, lead investigator of the Ted Binion case for the Las Vegas Metropolitan Police Department. PHOTO BY THE AUTHOR with Sandra Murphy's lawyers and dismissed James Brown's petition to exclude Murphy from Ted Binion's will. Leavitt ruled that the telephone conversation between Ted Binion and James Brown was not legally binding. For the changes to the will to be legally binding, Brown would have had to change the will prior to Binion's death. His decision essentially paved the way for Murphy to receive the inheritance that she was claiming. However, Binion's estate remained in possession of the Palomino Lane home for the time being. Murphy, despite wanting to move back into the home, was not allowed access. She was unable to retrieve even her personal belongings at this point.

Harry Claiborne, representing Binion's estate, indicated that the estate would appeal Leavitt's decision, and would also pursue civil litigation against Murphy to reclaim the valuable coin and currency collection that the estate believed Murphy removed from Binion's home following his death.

A few days after Judge Leavitt's decision on Binion's will, Chief Deputy District Attorney David Roger was assigned to begin evaluating the evidence so far obtained in connection with Ted Binion's death. One of the prosecutors in the Major Violators Unit, Roger had been provided with the case file during the somewhat secret meeting that was held in the district attorney's office on December 8, and he'd been relieved of all other cases so that his time could be spent working solely on the Binion case. The purpose of getting Roger involved at this point, according to District Attorney Stewart Bell, was to assist the police detectives with ideas that could possibly help the investigation. Bringing Roger in at this point and announcing it publicly also showed potential witnesses that rather than winding down, the district attorney's office was escalating the effort to resolve the mystery of Binion's death.

*   *   *

To leave no stone unturned, so to speak, Detective Buczek continued to peer into Rick Tabish's and Sandra Murphy's activities shortly after Binion's death. It was along those lines that he learned of a trip to Montana that they had made together in October, in which they had met up with Tabish's friend, Kurt Gratzer.

The meeting with Gratzer occurred, Buczek learned, at the Cutting Crew hair salon in Missoula. Michael Barger, Tabish's and Gratzer's hair stylist, recounted how Tabish had told him about his affair with Sandy Murphy in graphic sexual detail on that particular day.

"There was a flair of braggadocio," Barger recounted. "He had a good time with her. He talked about having sex with her. He seemed fascinated with the aspects of sex."

He also recalled how Murphy, on the other hand, had described their relationship as a loving one. He said that Murphy told him how they had to sneak away from Tabish's wife to have sex: they would leave Tabish's home and drive out to the country to make love in the car.

"Sandy would allude more to a relationship of permanence and beyond . . . almost with the infatuation of a schoolgirl," Barger said. "She seemed smitten with Rick. It seemed genuine." Barger said he thought that Sandy believed that Rick would leave his wife and children for her.

Barger was under the impression that Tabish and Murphy had made the trip to Montana to attend the birthday party for one of Tabish's two children. He said that he had cut, colored, and styled Sandy's hair in preparation for her attendance at the party. There were two other reasons, he believed, that they had made the trip to Montana. "One, so they could be together," Barger said. "And two, to give the appearance of having it [a business relationship] out in the open. How could anybody believe he was having sex with her when he was bringing her to his home?"

Barger also related how Kurt Gratzer had told him in August 1998, during a haircut, that Tabish had wanted him to kill someone in Nevada. "He said, 'I got to get away from him because he wants me to go to Vegas to kill some guy,' " Barger quoted Gratzer. "He gave the impression that he wanted to distance himself from Rick ... [But] he seemed nervous, shifty. He didn't want to elaborate." Barger said that he didn't push Gratzer for more details.

After talking with Gratzer for a while at the salon that day in August, Tabish asked Gratzer to meet him later at his telemarketing office.

Buczek later learned that when the trio met and walked upstairs to Tabish's office after leaving the hair salon, Tabish laughed and bragged about what he had "accomplished," presumably in Las Vegas. After entering the office, Tabish asked Gratzer questions regarding what type of explosive device he would need to blow up a medium-sized building. Although Buczek was unable to learn which building Tabish was considering blowing up, he learned that Tabish had asked Gratzer whether or not a rocket launcher would do the job. Gratzer had indicated that he would do some research on the subject and would let Tabish know what he learned.

As the sketchy details of the Montana trip continued to trickle in, Buczek learned that Gratzer, described as somewhat "goofy," had subsequently called an acquaintance, Detective Ronald Rey, who worked at the sheriff's office in Canon City, Colorado, to ask about how he might obtain hand grenades or rocket launchers. It wasn't clear at this point why Gratzer had called Rey, but Rey declined to help him locate or obtain any weapons whatsoever. However, Rey confirmed the details of his conversations with Gratzer when he spoke with Buczek.

Tabish warned Gratzer not to tell anyone about the meeting they'd had and to avoid talking to either him or Murphy on the telephone about anything that they'd discussed. Tabish had promised to give Gratzer some money for his help, but left Missoula without paying him. This prompted Gratzer to visit Tabish's wife, Mary Jo. Shortly thereafter, Tabish called Gratzer and warned him to stay away from

Mary Jo and not to talk to her about anything. Tabish also told him that he would get the money to him, and instructed Gratzer to call him daily. Afterward, Tabish asked his accountant to prepare a check in the amount of $2,000, made payable to Kurt Gratzer.

Buczek recalled that on Friday, October 23, 1998, shortly after the trip to Montana, an article in the Las Vegas *Sun* was published which revealed that investigators were scrutinizing Tabish's and Murphy's cellular telephone records. It was in that article that a reporter revealed the telephone call Murphy received from Tabish at 3:47 p.m. on September 17, seven minutes before her hysterical call to summon emergency medical personnel to Binion's home.

Shortly after the article appeared, Buczek learned, Tabish had called Kurt Gratzer and asked him to do some research regarding whether it was possible for someone to intercept cellular telephone calls. He also wanted to know whether the geographical location at which a cellular customer placed a call or received one could be determined. Gratzer later advised Tabish that cellular calls could not be intercepted and that the location of cellular calls could only be traced to a ten-mile radius. Tabish, Buczek learned, was ecstatic about that.

Meanwhile, in the midst of all the denials that were still being made by Tabish and Murphy—and their attorneys—that a romantic relationship existed between them, the two were seen together on October 11, 1998, on a Delta Airlines flight from Salt Lake City, Utah, to Las Vegas. When Buczek traced their movements he learned that they were apparently on the return flight home from Montana. Flight attendant Denise Wieser indicated in her statement that she recognized them from newspaper photos. Wieser said that they were sitting together in first class, and she recalled Murphy nuzzling Tabish's neck with her hand on his leg.

"They looked very cozy," Wieser said. "They were leaning into one another and at one point it looked like she was possibly kissing his neck." Wieser said that she saw Tabish and Murphy leave the plane together after it landed.

Recalling that Tabish had said that he was on his way to the airport on September 17 when he learned of Ted Binion's death, Buczek did some sleuthing and learned that Tabish normally used Northwest Travel in Missoula to make arrangements for him. When he checked with the agency, he learned that Tabish had no flight reservations to return from Montana anytime soon. Similarly, local airlines reported that Tabish had no reservations leaving Las Vegas, either. It was possible that Tabish had found that all flights to Missoula were booked and was planning on traveling standby, in which case there would be no reservation. Delta Airlines also indicated that it was possible that Tabish was planning to use an unused ticket that was dated September 11, 1998. The results of his efforts left Buczek without an answer as to Tabish's statement regarding his travel plans the day Binion died, and he could only wonder whether Tabish had been telling the truth or not.

Before the year ended, Buczek learned that Sandy Murphy had told a number of people that she was severing her relationship with Ted Binion. She also had "predicted" Ted Binion's death to several people. While Buczek didn't consider this information to be a turning point, what he learned from the witnesses he tracked down, or from those who came forward on their own, turned out to confirm much of what he already suspected.

One of the people Sandy talked to was Christopher Hendrick, a salesperson at Neiman Marcus in the Fashion Show Mall. Hendrick knew Sandy as a client, a regular customer, and recalled that she came into the store on or about September 7, 1998, and appeared either drunk or high on cocaine. In a rambling monologue, Sandy told Hendrick that her relationship with Ted Binion was deteriorating. She said that she was no longer sleeping in the same bed with Binion, and that the two of them were no longer having sexual relations with each other. She confided in Hendrick that a break-up was imminent, and that she was going to see an attorney about obtaining a legal separation as well as a settlement from Binion. She also said that she had a wealthy boyfriend who was pursuing a relationship with her.

Sandy related to Hendrick that she was "scared," but did not elaborate why. She stated that she was going to try to obtain some money from Binion before telling him about her plans for a legal separation, and that her attorney had told her that she could probably get $2 million as a settlement. "I'm not worried about money," Sandy said. "I still have four million dollars in the bank."

That last statement caused many, including the investigators, to take pause and wonder if she had been referring to Binion's silver hoard buried in the desert.

While she was at the store, Sandy ordered a number of clothing items from Hendrick, including a fur coat as well as some bedding items. The bill came to about $7,000. Two days later Hendrick called Ted Binion's home to say that the order was ready to be picked up or delivered. Although Binion was calm and coherent during their conversation, Hendrick said that he had just laughed when told of Sandy's purchases.

"Sandy is not going to be able to afford the clothes," Binion told him, laughing. He then instructed Hendrick not to ship the clothes to Sandy.

A short time later Deanna Perry, a manicurist who worked at the Neiman Marcus beauty salon, contacted investigators. She was concerned because Sandy Murphy had predicted Ted Binion's death to her about a week before it occurred. Sergeant Ken Hefner, who had been assigned to work on the case with detectives Buczek and Thowsen, went to the Fashion Show Mall and interviewed her.

Perry told Hefner that Sandy Murphy showed up at the salon on Thursday, September 10, 1998, with a female friend, and they spent much of the day there. Sandy had introduced herself to Perry as "Sandy Binion."

Perry said that while she was giving Sandy a manicure

and a pedicure, Sandy kept complaining about Binion, who she referred to as her "husband." Sandy described her relationship with Binion as "rocky." She said that he was abusing heroin and Xanax, and that he would die soon of an overdose. Perry said that Sandy had remarked about having a rich boyfriend on the side, and that her new boyfriend was going to dig up Binion's buried silver after he died.

When Perry asked her why she didn't just leave Binion, Sandy explained that if she did she wouldn't get $3 million and the house on Palomino Lane. Sandy stated that she would just have to "hang in there" in order to get the money and the house, and that she would "stay with him" because she would have more by staying than she would have by leaving him. Perry said that she understood "more" to mean more money.

At another point that day, Perry said she observed Sandy and her friend trying on different outfits and discussing upcoming social events such as Andre Agassi's annual "Grand Slam for Children" benefit at the MGM Grand Garden Arena. Perry said she heard Sandy imply that she had a way of ending her relationship with Binion without having to leave him. She became alarmed, Perry said, when she heard Sandy tell her friend that Ted was "going to die of a heroin overdose within the next three weeks!"

Sandy's friend had asked her if she was going to bring "Richard" to the Agassi event, Perry recalled, and Sandy had laughed at the inquiry. She responded that "Richard" would indeed be at the event, but with his wife. Sandy said it would be inappropriate for her and "Richard" to attend the event together within such a short time of Ted Binion's death. However, Sandy told her friend, she thought it would be acceptable if she and "Richard" attended the opening of Steve Wynn's Bellagio Hotel on October 15, 1998.

It seemed overwhelmingly cold-blooded to make the remarks that Sandy purportedly had about going to social events *after* Binion's death while Binion had still been alive.

Sergeant Hefner later determined that the female friend who had accompanied Sandy to the Neiman Marcus beauty salon that day had been Linda Carroll.

Hefner's interview with Deanna Perry led him to hairstylist Michelle Gilliam, who later said that she had been present during a portion of the conversations between Perry and Murphy. Gilliam said that her station was in close proximity to Perry's station where Sandy had received the manicure and pedicure. Gilliam recalled hearing that Murphy predicted Ted Binion would die of a drug overdose in a matter of a few weeks, and remembered part of the conversation in which Sandy had revealed that she was having a "secret love affair" with another man.

On another of Sandy's visits to the salon in October, after Binion's death, Gilliam recalled how Sandy had shown up dressed "undercover" in jeans and a T-shirt, with a baseball cap pulled low over her eyes. She was somewhat surprised because Sandy wasn't wearing her usual designer suits and dresses. Gilliam described Sandy during that visit as visibly upset, and she was complaining that Binion's family was "threatening to take it all away." She explained that they were attempting to prevent her from obtaining the assets left to her in Binion's will, and expressed astonishment that they were taking such a hard line with her. She added that just about everyone knew that her relationship with Ted Binion was merely a "financial arrangement." She had, in fact, told Becky on a previous occasion that she was only with Binion because he was rich. Gilliam stated that Murphy had not shown any emotion when she referred to Ted Binion.

"She said that she couldn't even get to her articles of clothing," Gilliam stated. She said that Sandy was there that particular day to have her hair styled, and she was carrying three cellular telephones with her. Sandy explained to Gilliam that she was using three because she "... never knew who might be listening to her."

Gilliam overheard one of Sandy's calls in which she had used codes and referred to the party whom she had phoned as "Bear." The investigators learned later that Sandy was known to have referred to Ted Binion as her "Teddy Ruxpin Bear" when he was alive.

Upon learning of Hefner's revealing interviews at the beauty salon, Detective Buczek later paid the establishment a visit and also spoke to the witnesses. Many of the same details were repeated for him. However, Buczek also spoke to the salon's manager, Sheldon Cornette.

Cornette provided Buczek with salon records that confirmed that Sandy Murphy had been a customer on September 10, 1998. He also recalled how Sandy had appeared to be intoxicated upon her arrival, and characterized her as being very loud while she was in the salon. After she left, Cornette said that Deanna Perry commented to him that she would not be surprised if Ted Binion was "gone soon."

While at the salon, Buczek also spoke with Georgia Gastone, a hair stylist who occupied a stall next to Michelle Gilliam's. According to her, when Sandy arrived that day she was carrying an open bottle of wine and appeared to be under the influence of alcohol. Gastone related how she had overheard portions of Sandy's conversation with Deanna Perry and Michelle Gilliam in which Sandy had spoken of her relationship with Binion. She said that Sandy had explained that she would be able to "get more money if Binion passed away."

Gastone said that she had heard Sandy talk about her "other" boyfriend, whom she had characterized as Ted Binion's "best friend." She said that she heard Murphy state that her boyfriend possessed the combinations to all of Ted Binion's safes. After Murphy had left the salon, Perry had also said to Gastone that she would not be surprised if Ted Binion died of an overdose within a few weeks.

In the weeks prior to Ted Binion's death, Buczek

learned, Rick Tabish had also told people that Binion was using a lot of drugs and that he was on a path of destruction. One of the people Tabish had spoken to was his friend, Charles Skinner. In July or August 1998—Skinner couldn't remember which month—Tabish had related details of Binion's drug usage and predicted, "he's going to kill himself. . . ."

Similarly, Sandy Murphy had told Binion's friend and former Horseshoe employee Steve Morris that Binion was ingesting a large amount of drugs and that he was "going to kill himself."

When Buczek followed up with Morris regarding Binion's state of mind prior to his death, Morris indicated that he had spoken with Binion four or five times a week, usually by telephone, and had never noticed any signs that Binion was in a poor state of mind. "He was never, never despondent," Morris said.

A short time before Binion's death, Binion told Morris that he was interested in purchasing property near the Fiesta Hotel and the Texas Hotel. They also spoke of his investments in Rio Hotel stock, and Binion had seemed optimistic about the future.

Binion's friend, Sid Lewis, echoed similar statements regarding Binion's frame of mind prior to his death. Lewis said that he had visited him at home in August 1998, and did not observe any signs that Ted was suicidal or out of control in any manner. He said that at one point during his visit he witnessed Sandy Murphy throw a temper tantrum, and after she left the room Binion shared his feelings with him about Sandy.

"I don't know why I put up with this bullshit," Lewis quoted Binion as saying. "I'm getting rid of that bitch."

By this point in the investigation it was very clear to Buczek and the other investigators that Binion was of a sound frame of mind in the days leading up to his death. It was also very clear what his intentions were regarding

Sandy Murphy. He had been planning to break off his relationship with her. But now they were concluding that Sandy Murphy and her lover, Rick Tabish, had gotten rid of Ted first.

CHAPTER 14

As the investigation into Ted Binion's death continued to make progress, 1998 made the transition into a new year and still no charges had been brought against anyone. Binion's death was still officially being called "undetermined," but by now Clark County Coroner Ron Flud indicated that his office was in a holding pattern waiting to see where the investigation led and what evidence might be presented to give him cause to change the designation to something more specific.

Before 1998 ended, Clark County District Court Judge Myron Leavitt accepted an appointment to the Nevada Supreme Court and passed the gavel to Chief District Judge Lee Gates, who would oversee Ted Binion's massive estate. One of the first things Gates did in the new year was to order Sandy Murphy, Rick Tabish, Michael Milot, and David Mattsen to appear in court before him on Thursday, February 4, 1999, to answer the estate lawyers' questions, under oath, regarding the items missing from Binion's home, including the rare coins and currency. He set the date far enough ahead on his calendar so that everyone could be rounded up and properly served with subpoenas.

Gates based his decision to call them into court on a sworn affidavit filed by Ted Binion's brother, Jack, who had been named executor, on behalf of the estate. Jack had raised a number of questions in his affidavit about the suspicious activities of Murphy and Tabish both before and after his brother's death.

"Based on the information available to me at this time," Binion wrote in his 10-page affidavit, "Ted believed Murphy was having an affair, and intended to sever his emotional and financial relationship with her . . . The circumstances surrounding Murphy, Tabish, Milot and Mattsen make it highly probable that they either converted Ted's property or have knowledge regarding the whereabouts of Ted's property that is missing."

The affidavit also stated that an unknown person drafted a check on Ted Binion's bank account on September 15, 1998, two days before his death, to the amount of $3,772 made payable to Neiman Marcus. The affidavit indicated that the estate suspected that the check was to pay for the "purchase of clothes for Tabish."

The affidavit also requested permission for the estate to take a deposition from Murphy's friend, Linda Carroll, who was believed to be in Los Angeles and was possibly going under an assumed identity. The estate believed that Carroll could provide information about the items missing from Binion's home. Judge Gates granted the estate permission to take the deposition. Now all the investigators had to do was find her.

Jack Binion's affidavit also alleged that a $20,000 bundle of $100 bills, 100 gold coins valued at $35,000, a bag of diamonds, other coin collections, and two gold pocket watches were taken from Binion's home. He also alleged that Sandy Murphy had used one of Ted Binion's credit cards on September 19, 1998, to obtain $3,000 cash, and, after the card had been canceled, she had attempted to obtain an additional $5,000 from the same card. Binion's affidavit also indicated that he believed Murphy and Tabish were now living together.

When Tom Dillard arrived at MRT Transportation's offices on Wednesday, January 13, to serve the subpoenas ordering Tabish and Murphy to court the following month, he found them there together and noted it in his report. On the same day shortly after news of Jack Binion's affidavit was made public, Sandy Murphy contacted Neiman Marcus clerks and demanded that they provide her with a receipt for the purchases that she had made on September 16, 1998. She explained to the clerks that she had purchased a dress on that date and had used a post-dated check that Binion

had given her to pay for it. She indicated that she needed
a copy of the transaction receipt so that she could show the
court what was purchased, since she had been accused of
". . . buying men's clothing for a boyfriend . . ."

The next day, January 14, Christopher Hendrick, who
no longer worked at Neiman Marcus, received a telephone
call from Sandy Murphy. Hendrick, who now worked at
Versace in the Forum Shops inside Caesars Palace, reported
that Murphy had expressed her dismay at him for having
cooperated with investigators. She purportedly told Hendrick that she knew that he had told investigators that she
had a secret boyfriend and that she had been hiding money
from Ted Binion.

"I thought you were my friend," Hendrick quoted Murphy as having said to him.

Hendrick said that Murphy had asked him to meet with
her attorneys so that ". . . we can just get this taken care of
and you don't have to be involved." Hendrick said that he
told her that he did not want to meet with her attorneys,
after which she provided him with one of her cellular telephone numbers so that he could call her if he changed his
mind.

That same day Sandy Murphy placed a telephone call to
Sprint Telephone Company and requested that the telephone bills for service at 2408 Palomino Lane be sent to
9555 Las Vegas Boulevard South. Detective Buczek noted
that the address was that of MRT Transportation, which
had been sold to RTI, Incorporated, but was still being operated under the MRT name.

Also on January 14, Detective Buczek applied for and
was granted a warrant to search Ted Binion's residence
again. Search warrants had not previously been needed because Binion's estate had given its permission to search the
home on prior occasions. However, because of the ruling
in which the house had been awarded—but not yet released—to Sandy Murphy, a search warrant became necessary to keep things legal.

When Buczek executed the warrant, accompanied by Chief Deputy District Attorney David Roger, he examined the northeast bedroom that had been occupied by Sandy Murphy. During the course of the investigation Buczek had learned that Linda Carroll had told attorney Richard Wright that Sandy had hidden a bag of silver behind the television in her bedroom. When he looked Buczek found a large bag of silver coins that had obviously been hidden there. Also, in the dressing area of the walk-in closet, Detective Tom Thowsen discovered an empty plastic case of the type normally used to protect silver dollars.

Later, during the process of probate proceedings in which attorney James Brown had been authorized to gather Binion's assets and obtain appraisals for the value of certain items, the bag of coins found in Murphy's bedroom was opened in the presence of an independent appraiser, Oscar Schwartz. When Brown removed the contents of the bag, he and Schwartz discovered a pair of thumb cuffs and a knife among the coins. Brown, recalling the alleged incident involving Leo Casey, immediately contacted the authorities.

Meanwhile, as the February 4 court date drew closer, the attorneys for Murphy and Tabish responded to Judge Gates's order and indicated that they would contest it.

"I think it's a twisted version of events to paint a picture that suits their interests," said Tabish's lawyer, Louis Palazzo, making reference to Binion's estate. "It's riddled with a host of inaccuracies . . . an absolute distortion . . . We didn't have an opportunity to be heard by the judge. We'll file the appropriate response."

Similarly, Murphy's lawyers, Oscar Goodman and David Chesnoff, indicated that they would "fight tooth and nail" the attempts being made by the estate to take away what was rightfully Murphy's.

"Teddy Binion intended for her to have the house and the contents, and we're going to make sure Teddy Binion's wishes are fulfilled," Chesnoff said.

Goodman and Chesnoff were legally allowed one challenge, and they used it the following week to remove Judge Lee Gates from the case. Neither lawyer offered an explanation for their actions. Afterward, District Judge Michael Cherry was assigned to oversee the proceedings.

On Friday, January 22, 1999, Goodman and Chesnoff, along with another attorney, R. Gardner Jolley, filed an 11-page motion that essentially accused Binion's estate of being more concerned with attempting to use Sandy Murphy's testimony, scheduled for February 4, to connect her with Binion's death than they were about learning what actually happened to the valuables missing from Binion's home, and accused the estate and the district attorney's office of abusing the discovery process.

"The representatives of the estate are nothing more than a stalking horse for the police and district attorney's office with whom they have met on several occasions regarding the investigation of Ted Binion's death," the attorneys wrote in their motion. "Therefore, it is the belief . . . that the information sought is not to determine whether Murphy has property in her possession belonging to the estate, but instead to seek evidence in support of future criminal allegations against Murphy."

The motion was obviously an attempt to halt the estate's case. The attorneys' argument was that they had not been afforded the opportunity to argue in front of the judge against the hearing in which Murphy was being forced to testify. Their motion also sought to quash the deposition of Linda Carroll in California.

Murphy's attorneys argued that she would take the Fifth Amendment if she were forced to testify about items missing from Binion's home unless she was granted immunity from criminal prosecution. Bill Koot of the district attorney's office, however, said that his office had no authority to provide immunity from prosecution in the probate case, and had no plans to offer her immunity in any subsequent criminal prosecution.

"She will assert whatever privileges that are available to her," Goodman told Judge Cherry.

Cherry, however, denied the attorneys' request, and said that his primary concern was to assist the estate in obtaining a complete accounting of Binion's assets.

"I want her to come forward," Cherry said. "If she takes the Fifth Amendment, then we'll go from there."

It was pointed out that if Murphy refused to testify, she would be putting herself at risk of losing her inheritance. "Apparently she's begging for what we call an immunity bath," estate attorney Richard Wright said. "That happens when someone who has something to hide wants to be the first one to go before authorities to be cleansed and protected."

"I'm not begging for anything," Goodman retorted. "I'm trying to protect a client against . . . greed and aggression. Knowing the kind of power these people exert and the pressure they can bring, I'm not going to let her be anybody's sacrificial lamb."

Meanwhile, on Tuesday, January 26, 1999, District Judge Gene Porter authorized the installation of a trap-and-trace device, as well as a pin register device, on Rick Tabish's cellular telephone, which was being used by Sandy Murphy. He also authorized the installation of the same devices on Tabish's business phones at MRT Transportation.

In the days that followed, numerous calls were made from the phone, and many incoming calls were recorded on the voice mail. However, Buczek noted that beginning on February 1, there was little activity. The only calls that registered were outgoing calls made to the voice mail number.

The reason for the decrease became apparent when Chief Deputy District Attorney David Roger received several telephone calls on Wednesday, February 3, 1999, from Oscar Goodman and David Chesnoff. The two attorneys were making inquiries about the warrant that had been executed at Binion's residence, but Roger couldn't tell them anything except that the search warrant application had been sealed by order of the court. During one of the conversations, Chesnoff asked Roger straight out whether there was a wiretap on Sandy Murphy's phone. Roger told him that he could neither confirm nor deny that such a possibility existed.

Although Oscar Goodman announced that Sandy Murphy would be willing to testify on February 4 about the items missing from Binion's home, he said it would be against his legal advice for her to do so. As a result, he asked Judge Cherry for additional time so that he could work out the apparent conflict between his advice to Sandy and her apparent willingness to testify. Describing the apparent conflict as a "mild disagreement," Goodman was adamant that he wanted Sandy to take the Fifth Amendment on the witness stand.

"She's a wounded caribou being chased by an angry pack of wolves," Goodman alleged when he asked for more time. He also indicated that he would withdraw as Murphy's counsel if he could not work out their differences regarding strategy.

Judge Cherry gave Goodman one week for him to come to terms with Murphy, and ordered Murphy to appear in court on Thursday, February 11, 1999.

Afterward, attorney Richard Wright called Goodman's request for a delay an "old legal ploy" as an attempt to create an impression that Sandy desired to cooperate with the court.

"I'd be happy to have her testimony next week," Wright told reporters after the hearing. "But I fully expect her to take the Fifth Amendment then. I don't believe that she can testify truthfully without providing answers that will incriminate her . . . If she testifies fully, completely, and truthfully to help us resolve this mystery, that thump you hear in the courtroom will be me falling off my chair."

"Mr. Wright should confine these arguments to the courtroom," Chesnoff retorted. "When did he figure out this alleged ploy, an hour later? Why didn't he raise it with the judge? Mr. Wright presumes that the Fifth Amendment is only used by the guilty. It's to protect the innocent from being persecuted."

In the meantime Rick Tabish showed up in District Court on February 4 as planned, as did Michael Milot and David Mattsen. After providing the court with his name and address, Tabish was asked a number of questions that ranged from whether he'd had a sexual affair with Sandra Murphy to whether he had knowledge about any of the missing items. He was also asked whether he had taken the pair of thumb cuffs that were previously missing from Binion's home, whether he was a felon, and what his activities were on the day of Binion's death. However, the court didn't get any answers from him. On the advice of his attorney, Louis Palazzo, Tabish took the Fifth Amendment—ninety-eight times! David Mattsen and Michael Milot also asserted their Fifth Amendment rights and refused to answer the estate attorneys' questions.

Sandra Murphy showed up at Clark County District Court on February 11, as ordered. As was her style, she was dressed to the nines in designer clothing by Versace. After being sworn in she was asked many of the same questions as Rick Tabish and, like him refused to answer, and asserted her Fifth Amendment rights against self-incrimination more than 200 times as her attorney, Oscar Goodman, stood by her side.

In response to charges by Murphy's attorneys that the estate was merely trying to persecute her, Harry Claiborne, on behalf of Binion's estate, said that the estate would not have to have taken on its own investigation if Murphy had cooperated with the police from the outset. Representing Bonnie Binion's interest, Claiborne said that Bonnie had asked his help in uncovering the facts surrounding her father's death, and insisted that she had a right to know how her father had died.

Moments before Sandy Murphy entered Judge Cherry's courtroom, a Clark County grand jury was convened in another area of the courthouse to begin probing for answers

166	**GARY C. KING**

to why and how Ted Binion had died. Many people who knew Murphy and Tabish were subpoenaed to testify, including Tanya Cropp and Linda Carroll. David Roger was named to oversee the grand jury proceedings, which District Attorney Stewart Bell described as an investigative tool that could help the police sort out the circumstances behind Binion's death.

"We are not at all in a position to determine whether or not charges might be initiated," Bell said of the grand jury proceedings. "Ted Binion died as a result of an overdose of narcotics. How he happened to overdose on narcotics remains a mystery."

"We are using the grand jury as an investigative tool to question witnesses," David Roger added. "We have not submitted a proposed indictment."

As the grand jury and courtroom proceedings were underway, Detective Buczek learned that Sandy Murphy had ordered telephone service on January 28, 1999, for an apartment located at 251 S. Green Valley Parkway, #5014, in Henderson, just south of Las Vegas. He also obtained records from Nevada Power Company that showed that electric service had been ordered for that same apartment at the Bella Vista complex and was being billed to MRT Leasing of Nevada and Richard Tabish. It now seemed clearer than ever that Tabish and Murphy were living together.

Buczek took the new information and prepared an affidavit for a search warrant for the Henderson apartment and MRT Transportation's business office, as well as for Tabish's residence and MRT's offices in Missoula. Buczek and his partner were looking to find Tabish's business records dating from 1997 to the present, men's clothing items that they believed were purchased for Tabish by Sandy at Neiman Marcus, computer disks that may have been downloaded from a business or personal computer, audio and video items, and a pair of work boots. They were also looking for anything that would tend to firmly establish a romantic relationship between Tabish and Murphy, and hoping to catch them together during the early morning hours at the apartment they believed they were sharing. On February 18, 1999, District Court Judge Gene Porter authorized the searches.

The next morning at approximately 7:00 a.m. the search warrants were executed. Buczek and his partner, Thowsen, executed the Nevada warrants, and Ken Hefner executed the Montana warrants.

When Buczek knocked on the door to the two-bedroom, $1,000-a-month luxury apartment and announced that they had a warrant to search the premises, Sandy Murphy refused to answer the door. She insisted, through the closed door, that she be allowed to speak with her attorneys before letting the detectives inside. Buczek calmly explained that he would have to force open the door if she didn't allow them in. At that point Sandy, clad in muu-muu–type pajamas, reluctantly opened the door.

Upon entering the apartment, Buczek immediately recognized Rick Tabish, who was seated on a sofa in the living room. With Sandy and Rick looking like they had just been awakened, Buczek was satisfied that he had found at least part of what he was looking for, namely a firm link to a romantic relationship between the two.

"I would think that is the best evidence one could get of a relationship," David Roger said of Buczek's discovery. "A man and a woman together in the same apartment at seven in the morning. We find that very intriguing ... We're trying to find out what happened to Ted Binion, and we'll leave no stone unturned."

Apparently the news media found it intriguing as well. Shortly after Buczek and his partner entered the apartment, several trucks from a number of local television stations showed up and began focusing their attention on the apartment door. A short time later Oscar Goodman arrived to provide legal counsel and moral support for his client.

Tabish and Murphy were allowed to remain in the apart-

ment while the search was being conducted. Oscar Goodman was also allowed to observe the detectives perform
their work.

Buczek found photos of Rick Tabish's children on a
nightstand next to the bed in the master bedroom. When he
looked in the spare bedroom, he saw women's shoes, so
many that they wouldn't have fit inside the closet even if
Sandy had tried to store them there. For a brief moment,
the sight of all those shoes brought back memories of Im-
elda Marcos, the former First Lady of the Philippines, who
also had a love of footwear.

As they pressed on with their search, Buczek and Thowsen recovered all of the men's clothing items that Sandy
Murphy had purchased at Neiman Marcus including a pair
of Gucci jeans, a pair of black Armani pants, and a black
velour Armani shirt. They also found a pair of shoes with
soles similar to those found on work boots. However, cri-
minalist and shoe print expert Edward Guenther later determined that the shoes did not match the impressions that
they had found months earlier on Ted Binion's box springs.

During the search Buczek also seized a Horseshoe Club
money clip with the name "Ted" engraved on it, and cuff
links with engravings that suggested they had belonged to
Ted Binion. They also took a Kodak disposable camera,
and a computer disk that was attached to a credit report.

Buczek had set the computer disk aside so that the criminalists who were working with him could properly package it. However, when the criminalists went to package the
disk, it was missing. When Buczek asked Sandy Murphy
what had happened to it, she admitted that she had hidden
it and claimed that it contained attorney–client privileged
material. Buczek nonetheless retrieved the disk from Murphy after she was advised of the potential legal ramifica-
tions if she failed to cooperate with the execution of the
search warrant. Buczek also found two micro-cassette tapes
that Oscar Goodman claimed were attorney–client privileged material. The tapes were nonetheless taken and pack-

aged, with a notation that they were not to be examined by the police because of the privilege claim.

Interestingly, when Buczek searched Tabish's briefcase, he found a map of Ted Binion's ranch in Pahrump. Buczek considered the map significant because of Sandy's previous claims that she knew where Ted Binion had hidden some of his assets, presumably on the ranch. He recalled how Sandy had previously called Kathy Rose asking to speak to Jack Binion regarding money and valuables that she knew were buried on the property, and how she had offered to split whatever was recovered with Binion. He also recalled how Tom Dillard had spoken to one of Binion's Pahrump neighbors who had reported seeing a man and a woman using a backhoe to dig on the property after Binion's death. Although the neighbor had been unable to identify Tabish and Murphy as the people he had seen, Buczek felt that the discovery of the map shed new light on the possibility that it might have been Tabish and Murphy using the backhoe.

In Montana, Sergeant Hefner seized numerous business documents that related to Rick Tabish's businesses. Included in the seized items was a canceled check made payable to David Lee Mattsen in the amount of $436.49, dated November 5, 1998, and drawn on one of MRT's accounts. A payroll schedule also showed Mattsen's weekly salary payment, even though there was no evidence that Mattsen had ever put in a single day's work for any of Tabish's companies.

After the searches at all of the locations had been concluded, Murphy's and Tabish's lawyers downplayed the fact that Murphy and Tabish were found together inside the apartment at 7:00 a.m. Louis Palazzo and Oscar Goodman were quick to point out to reporters that Murphy and Tabish were very close friends, but said that the fact that they obviously cared for one another was not in and of itself a crime.

"The more pertinent question is, was there a romantic relationship prior to Ted Binion's death?" Palazzo said. "I have not seen any evidence of a romantic relationship during that period of time. To explore a relationship at this point is an attempt to bootstrap an argument to create a murder case." Palazzo also pointed out that even if a romantic relationship existed at this point, it meant nothing as far as the case was concerned.

"There is no question that they are looking to each other for support to get through the intensity of the investigation," Goodman said. "As far as I know, that is the extent of it."

Meanwhile, Sandy Murphy went back to court to try to gain permission to move back into the Palomino Lane residence. David Chesnoff argued before Judge Cherry that there was no reason for her not to be able to move back into the house that had been previously awarded to her. He accused the estate of treating her like a "leper," and indicated that there was insufficient reason for the suspicions centering on her as having been involved in Binion's death. He compared Binion's death to the drug-related deaths of prominent individuals, including John Belushi, Lenny Bruce, and Jim Morrison, among others.

Attorney Bruce Judd for the estate, on the other hand, argued the seriousness of all the unsolved issues that possibly would not be resolved in Sandy's favor and recommended that caution be used in any decision regarding Murphy being allowed back into the house. He also wryly brought up the matter of her having a place to live.

"She apparently has a place to stay," Judd said.

Cherry agreed with the estate, saying that he did not feel comfortable allowing Murphy to move back into the house until the questions regarding Binion's missing assets had been resolved. He did say, however, that he would reconsider the issue at a hearing set for May 7 and deferred an official ruling until then.

CHAPTER 15

As Buczek continued his probe he learned that Binion had received a call from a long time friend of his, Jay Kerr, late on the morning of September 16, 1998. Kerr told Buczek that he had known Binion for twenty-five years or longer, and that he had enjoyed a very candid relationship with him. On that particular morning, Binion had confided to Kerr that he was disappointed in himself because he had begun using heroin again. Kerr said that Binion had stopped using the drug for a while.

"But sure enough, as soon as I do it [stop using it]," Kerr quoted Binion, "I run into a guy that can get me some good dope and he's on his way over here now."

Kerr told Buczek that Binion had described the man bringing him the heroin as "a young, sharp guy." Those words immediately rang a bell in Buczek's mind. He recalled that James Brown had stated previously that Binion had described Rick Tabish to him as "a young, sharp guy." Buczek, of course, had no way of knowing whether Binion had been referring to Tabish when he had spoken to Kerr. But it had been on that particular day, September 16, that Tabish had been at Binion's home with Murphy, along with Binion's ranch hand, Roy Price. Buczek recalled how Price had said that Binion had pointed toward Murphy and Tabish and said, "They got me the best shit I have had in a long time." Although it seemed possible that Tabish had supplied Binion with heroin that day, Buczek couldn't be certain with the sketchy information he had and he realized that it was a question in his mind that might never be answered.

Kerr also told Buczek that he had spoken again with Ted Binion by telephone later in the evening on September 16. He stated that he had not noticed anything unusual about Ted during their conversation, and that Binion's thought processes seemed clear enough to him. Kerr said that he had not sensed that Binion was depressed at all, much less suicidal.

Buczek also learned that Ted Binion's nephew, Key Fechser, had called Binion on September 16. Fechser, who had been provided with tickets to the premier of Oscar Goodman's movie, *Mob Law*, had offered the tickets to Binion, who had declined them. Fechser heard Binion offer the tickets to Sandy Murphy, who had been nearby at the time of his call, but she declined his offer as well. When Sandy apparently had left the room, Fechser said that Binion had stated to him that he was "getting rid" of her, and that he was "writing Sandy out of the will." Aside from expressing negative feelings about Sandy, Ted had sounded fine.

A day earlier, Buczek had learned that Binion had summoned Kevin Page to his home at approximately 10:00 a.m. Page worked as vice president and senior portfolio manager for First Security Bank. When Page arrived, Binion and Sandy Murphy were at home together. Page said that Binion had asked him to come to his home so that he could give him a check for $1,000,000 to open an investment account. He also wrote Page a second check for $40,000, and asked Page to cash it and bring him two bundles of $100 bills for him. Page said that he cashed the check for Binion and brought him the money later in the day.

Buczek also learned that Binion had been visited on September 15 by a reporter from the *Las Vegas Review-Journal*, who had talked to Binion about writing a book and possibly a movie script about the life of Binion's father. The reporter later wrote that Binion had been excited on the day of his visit, and had invited him to "bring the family" and visit him at his ranch in Pahrump.

Binion's state of mind, Buczek concluded, certainly didn't appear to have been one of someone who had been contemplating suicide. Quite the contrary. Virtually everyone Buczek had interviewed regarding Binion's final days had said that he seemed in good spirits, was not depressed or despondent, and had been making plans for the future.

In the meantime, Buczek learned that Rick Tabish's creditors had received court authorization to repossess the tractor, belly dump truck, and excavator that had been used in the removal of Binion's silver from the vault in Pahrump. After the creditors had provided their consent for investigators to search the equipment, District Attorney Investigator Mike Karstedt and crime scene analyst Joe Szukiewiez recovered a pair of handcuffs in the tractor-trailer. Recalling the abrasions that were noted on Binion's wrists, Buczek could only wonder whether the handcuffs had been used to restrain him on the day of his death. Again, it was a question that he knew might never be fully answered.

According to information from David Mattsen's wife, Thressa, Rick Tabish had interviewed ranch manager David Mattsen on August 24, 1998, for the position of truck driver for MRT Transportation. Afterward, Mattsen told his wife that he had been hired to work for MRT. Thressa said that she had driven her husband to MRT's offices on a few occasions in August and September.

Buczek learned that Mattsen had also told another individual, Bill Browning, that he had been hired to work for MRT to "head the fleet of trucks and drivers." Mattsen had also told Browning that he was sometimes required to drive the trucks. Browning had observed that Mattsen was driving a new pickup truck, and Mattsen had told him that it was part of MRT's benefit package.

Mattsen also told Browning that he and his wife had purchased a new home, saying that he had financed the down payment by using their savings and by cashing in their 401k-retirement account.

Larry Baker, another acquaintance of Mattsen's, told authorities that Mattsen had bragged to him about going to work for Rick Tabish. According to Baker's statement, Mattsen had told him that Tabish had agreed to pay him $1500 per week.

In reality, Buczek learned, Mattsen was being paid $436 per week. However, according to the information he was getting, including from Mattsen's wife, Mattsen never worked a day as a truck driver for the company. Thressa Mattsen said that her husband never went to work, but stayed at home and watched television. Also, MRT employee Willie Alder told authorities that he never met David Mattsen and had never assigned any work to him.

So why was Mattsen being paid by Tabish? Was it for his help in removing Binion's silver from the vault? Buczek could only wonder. However, to try to get some answers, Buczek filed an affidavit for a warrant to search Mattsen's home in Pahrump, which the court promptly approved.

The primary purpose for the surprise raid on Mattsen's home was to retrieve financial records and anything else that might establish a relationship between Mattsen, Tabish, and Murphy.

On Tuesday, March 9, 1999, Buczek executed the search warrant at Mattsen's home, located at 1520 Appaloosa Lane in Pahrump. Mattsen was present when the search was conducted, and he expressed his displeasure over it.

During the search, Buczek and crime scene analysts seized a total of seven firearms, including a Colt AR-15 rifle. One of the others was a Smith & Wesson .38 revolver that was registered to Ted Binion's attorney, James Brown. Brown later told the investigators that he had given the gun to Binion as a gift.

Recalling Mattsen's status as a convicted felon for armed robbery and sexual intercourse with a minor, Buczek knew that he was possibly in violation of the law and seized the weapons as potential evidence.

The search also turned up several newspaper articles regarding Mattsen's arrest for the attempted theft of Binion's silver, as well as articles about Mattsen's refusal to testify under oath at the probate proceedings regarding Ted Binion's estate. Buczek recalled that Mattsen had even refused to answer whether he had known Ted Binion after having worked as his ranch manager.

In one area of Mattsen's home the investigators found Mattsen's financial records for 1997 and 1998. When Buczek reviewed them, he saw that Mattsen's average income was roughly $350 every two weeks in 1997. However, in 1998 his income increased to approximately $500 every two weeks, and in November of that year he began receiving paychecks from MRT in the amount of $436 per week after MRT was sold to RTI. When he searched through Mattsen's personal papers, Buczek found a W-2 form that Mattsen had received from MRT, which listed his 1998 income as approximately $4,000, which did not appear to match bi-weekly amounts for a full-time employee. He also found a notice from MRT dated February 12, 1999, that advised workers that their employment with the company had been terminated because creditors had filed an involuntary bankruptcy petition against the company. Buczek also found a bill dated October 1998 that listed a child support debt for $15,000 that Mattsen owed.

Perhaps the most interesting item seized during the raid was Thressa Mattsen's daily diary for 1998. Buczek noted the following entries:

August 24, 1998—"Tomorrow David meets Rick Tabish to see about a job with him."
August 25, 1998—"David came home excited about working for Rick."
September 6, 1998—"Lord all the reports about Ted are bad. David heard a tape where he [Ted] talks about killing him [David]. Help Ted. He's sick."
(According to Thressa Mattsen's statements to authorities, "Rick" refers to Rick Tabish, and "Ted" refers to Ted Binion, and so forth.)

September 8, 1998—"David picked up his truck from Rick, it's real nice."

September 16, 1998—"Got up at 7:30, David left a note not to make him breakfast. He was gone until 11 o'clock. David talked to Rick, fed the animals, got dressed up and left for Vegas. Everything with him and Rick is hush, hush and secret. I don't know Lord. Reveal to me what he's up to and if it's not right sever that relationship with Rick. Ted's acting crazy and release him from the drugs."

September 17, 1998—"Ted died today."

October 3, 1998—(This entry was made after Mattsen's release from jail on bail for the attempted silver theft.) "Lord if Rick and Sandy are on the up and up please let me know cuz I feel they're using David."

October 4, 1998—"Now Sandy's telling him she's bringing some money. Lord if that money is not from you, please keep it away . . . David went at 8:30 to meet Sandy at Smith's [supermarket]. I'm really concerned about them."

Mattsen, by his own later admission in court proceedings, had received $600 from Sandy Murphy.

As he continued reading the diary, Buczek noted that David Mattsen had received his final paycheck from the Ted Binion ranch on October 9, 1998, and Mrs. Mattsen's diary entry for October 21, 1998, indicated that Mattsen had filed for unemployment insurance benefits. His period of unemployment was short-lived, however. He began receiving payments from MRT in November. Other diary entries included:

November 8, 1998—"Thank you for David's job with Rick."

November 16, 1998—"I seen Sandy she's all dressed up, changed her hair and all. I didn't feel good talking to her. I felt real strong that she had something to do

with Ted's death. It hurts me to think that someone hurt
him."
November 19, 1998—"Lord he [David] is so lazy. He
just sets on the couch all day watching TV."

Buczek noted that Thressa's entry for November 19,
1998, was an indication that Mattsen was not performing
work for MRT even though he was collecting paychecks
from the company. Buczek also noted that some, if not all,
of the weapons seized at Mattsen's home might have belonged to Ted Binion. If that turned out to be the case,
Binion's estate would have to decide whether they wanted
to file theft charges against him or not. Also, because ex-
felons are prohibited by law from possessing weapons, it
was possible that Mattsen could face seven additional fel-
onies, one for each of the weapons found at his home.

Meanwhile, the search was on to locate Murphy's friend,
Linda Carroll. Her attorney, Chet Bennett, had previously
spoken with Clark County investigators and had made arrangements to accompany her to Las Vegas to provide a
statement to authorities on two separate occasions. However, both Bennett and Carroll had canceled both appoint-
ments.

Because she had refused to come forward and talk to
the grand jury and investigators voluntarily, prosecutors
convinced Judge Porter to request that a California court
order Carroll to appear before the Clark County Grand Jury.
However, law enforcement officers in California were unable to locate her to serve her with the proper process papers. As a last resort, a material witness warrant was issued
for her arrest, and her attorney was duly informed of that
development. Nonetheless, despite diligent efforts by law
enforcement officers to locate her, Carroll remained a fugitive.

In their attempts to find her, Las Vegas police released
a photo of her taken from her Clark County work card when

she had worked locally, in Las Vegas. *America's Most Wanted* presented a television piece on her, asking for anyone knowing her whereabouts to come forward and contact authorities. Information regarding her arrest warrant was also placed in the National Crime Information Center, which police regularly use to obtain information about suspects and others. By utilizing the NCIC, if police officers from another jurisdiction stopped her, they could enter her name into their computer and would see the information about the outstanding warrant from Las Vegas.

Las Vegas investigators particularly wanted to talk to Carroll because of information that she had been sharing with others about the Binion case. Carroll had apparently told one of her neighbors, who in turn passed the information along to a private investigator, that Binion had been murdered; "murder, straight away," the neighbor had quoted her as saying.

"She told me straight out that if she testified against whoever," the neighbor had said, "these people would kill her. If the cops got hold of her and they put her under protective custody, these people would kill her. That's exactly what she said. Over and over and over. That's what she was worried about."

In the meantime, the investigators were unable to verify if Carroll did make the statements and all Buczek could do was wait and hope that the police could locate her or that she would come forward on her own.

CHAPTER 16

On Monday, March 15, 1999, nearly six months after Ted Binion's death, Clark County Coroner Ron Flud called a rare news conference and announced that he was changing the classification of Binion's death from "undetermined" to "homicide." According to the coroner and Prosecutor David Roger, someone else had overdosed Binion. It was not being considered an accident. Although Flud would not comment on specifics as to why he had changed the classification of Binion's death, police sources indicated that it had been changed because investigators believed that the death scene had been staged and because so many witnesses had provided statements that appeared to implicate Tabish and Murphy in Binion's death.

It was generally believed and theorized by those in law enforcement circles that Binion had been subdued and forcefully overdosed by one or more people near the entrance to the den, and then later dragged to the spot where he was found when paramedics arrived. Investigators had found spots of what they believed were gastric fluids that Binion had purged near the entrance to the den, and the fact that the spots traversed nearly a straight line to the point where his body was found lent credence to the theory. It was possible, according to investigators, that Binion had purged heavily while wrapped in a sheet, blanket, or something similar, and that the liquids had leaked onto the floor as his body was being moved. Similar investigations involving drug overdoses, whether intentional or accidental, have shown that subjects or victims nearly always purged, or vomited, heavily, which is the body's natural response to rid itself of the damaging materials.

Based on the estimated time of Binion's death, it was noted, there had been sufficient time for rigor mortis to set in prior to the paramedics' arrival. However, when paramedics arrived the only rigor mortis they observed was in the area of Binion's jaw. This fact suggested to the detectives that the effects of rigor mortis had been eradicated by the mere act of moving his body. Considering the amounts of heroin, Xanax, and Valium found inside Binion's stomach at the time of the autopsy, it seemed nearly inconceivable to the detectives that there would be no signs of purging on Binion's body. It was widely believed among law enforcement personnel that someone with those amounts of drugs in his stomach would have purged significantly, and the fact that there was no vomit suggested that someone had cleaned his body before the paramedics were called.

Prior to the classification of the manner of Binion's death being changed, David Roger had provided images of the marks on Binion's body to an outside forensic science laboratory for further evaluation. The images examined included Binion's chest, and right and left wrists.

The independent examination concluded that the small round red mark on Binion's chest was compatible with the button of his shirt having been compressed with considerable force against his chest. A larger and darker partial circle with an approximate diameter of seventeen millimeters was noted in relatively close proximity to the smaller red mark, and the examiner suggested that it could have been caused if the button believed to have made the smaller mark had been moved and compressed, possibly through a layer of fabric from Binion's shirt. It was also possible that the larger mark had been made by an object larger than the button. In fact, according to the forensic scientist who had conducted the analysis, the larger mark on Binion's chest was compatible with the diameter of the muzzle end of a firearm. It was a possibility that could not be ruled out, especially since paramedics had not performed a sternum rub when they had arrived, and there was little else to sug-

gest how Binion might have received the obvious, somewhat fresh wound.

The linear series of abrasions found on Binion's right
wrist, as well as the abrasions on his left wrist, were examined, along with the possibility that they had been made
by the use of handcuffs. However, the non-uniform spacing
of the lines on the right wrist was not considered compatible with the use of handcuffs. Similarly, it was not possible
to associate the marks on Binion's left wrist with handcuffs,
although the forensic scientist wrote that he could not positively exclude that possibility, either. The marks on the
right suggested that it was more likely a wristwatch band
had made them. The only problem with that theory, the
detectives found upon follow-up, was that Binion was not
known to wear a wristwatch. In fact, James Brown stated
that in all the years that he had known Ted Binion he had
never observed him wearing one.

Reporters asked coroner Ron Flud about the considerable
amount of heroin found inside Binion's stomach.

"You tell me," Flud said. "How do you inhale [heroin
smoke] and get it into your stomach?"

Another theory that required further consideration surrounding the day of Binion's death was the likelihood that
at least some of the drugs had been force-fed to him by the
time gardener Tom Loveday arrived. Sandy Murphy had
already instructed the maid not to come to work that day,
and it was one theory that she and Tabish had forgotten
that it was the gardener's day to take care of the grounds
and had failed to call to tell him not to come in. When
Loveday had knocked on the door and checked the other
doors and windows, it seemed possible that his activities
had taken Murphy and Tabish by surprise. At that point,
according to this theory, Murphy and Tabish, possibly in a
panic, may have smothered him by placing a hand over his
mouth, or with a pillow. A pillow with an unknown sub-

stance on it had, after all, been found in Binion's bedroom.
If the death had occurred in that manner, Murphy and Tabish would have had no choice but to remain inside the
house until Loveday left at approximately 1:00 p.m. It was
all theory and conjecture on the part of the investigators at
this point, and proving the events as theorized would be
the real trick.

If the gardener theory turned out to be correct, Tabish
would have had his vehicle parked in the garage, out of
sight of Loveday, which would have given him and Murphy
easy access to remove the $20,000 cash, the silver coin
collection, and other valuables that were missing from the
house, including the contents of the safe in the garage.

On the other hand, if Tabish had left prior to Loveday's
arrival, leaving Murphy inside with a dead or dying Ted
Binion, he would have had easy access to the house through
the garage later, upon his return after Loveday's departure.
If that were the case—which also seemed possible because
of witnesses who had seen him at other locations up until
about 12:30 p.m.—he would still have been able to carry
out the theft of the valuables and move Binion's body to
the location where paramedics found him. But if this theory
was correct, either Ted Binion was already dead by the time
Tabish departed, or Sandra Murphy was left there alone to
finish the job of killing him. There was evidence of cellular
telephone calls between Tabish and Murphy that day between 1–1:30 p.m., which would have coincided with Tom
Loveday's departure from Binion's residence and could
possibly be construed as a go-ahead or an all-clear signal
to return to Binion's home.

Because real estate agent Barbara Brown had called to
speak with Binion at 12:04 p.m., at which time Sandra Murphy had attempted to persuade her that Binion couldn't talk,
that he didn't want to be seen, and that she had a big mess
to clean up, it seemed reasonable that the cleaning up of
the "mess" had begun around noon and continued until after

Loveday left for the day. It also seemed reasonable that Binion's body had been dragged or otherwise moved from the den's entry area and placed flat on its back on the mattress in front of the couch in the den, which is near the door to the garage. But because of the linear trail of what investigators believe were Binion's bodily fluids that led from the den's entry to the location where his body was placed, it seemed evident that the clean-up of the "mess" had not been thorough.

If this line of reasoning were correct, Murphy and Tabish would have to have left the house sometime after 1:30 p.m., after Loveday had left, to go to Horseshoe Gaming's offices, where Sandy spoke with Kathy Rose and stayed for only a few minutes. The exact time they had left the house would be difficult, if not impossible, to establish precisely. If they had left shortly after 1:30 p.m., it certainly wouldn't have taken an hour or more to drive to the Horseshoe's offices, but only a few minutes.

Sandy had told Rose and others that she, Tabish, and attorney William Knudson were going to have lunch that afternoon at Z' Tejas Grill. However, it seemed likely that this could not have been true. It was 3 p.m. when Murphy left Rose's office, and given the time it would take to drive to Z' Tejas Grill, order and eat lunch, and arrive back at Binion's home in time to receive the call from Rick Tabish, then place the call to summon paramedics seven minutes later, it would have been virtually impossible to accomplish within that time frame. It seemed that she was either lying about the lunch date, or had eaten lunch prior to going to Rose's office and had lied about where she was going afterward.

Another point requiring further consideration was the fact that Sandy had possibly left her keys and sunglasses on the floor in the den. That's where they were found when the paramedics and the police arrived. If she had in fact left them on the floor at the time that she had left the residence, it would mean that she had to ride to and from

Horseshoe Gaming's offices with Rick Tabish or someone else. It would also mean that she would likely have been locked out of the house upon their return. If that were in fact true, then either Rick or Sandy would likely have to have used the white chair to stand on to gain entry to the house through Sandy's open bathroom window.

The investigators also considered another theory about the white chair. Tom Loveday had said in his earlier statement that the bathroom window was open the day he worked the grounds, but there was no chair beneath the window while he was there. It was possible, the investigators theorized, that Binion had ordered Murphy out of the house as part of his plan to break off his relationship with her, and that either she or Tabish, or both, had used the chair to get back inside the house to kill Binion. The details surrounding that day were so confusing, and, since neither Murphy nor Tabish would talk to the detectives, all they could do was theorize about the possibilities. Because there were no eyewitnesses who would give them a statement as to what really happened to Ted Binion, they were not able at this point to prove who was responsible for his death.

Meanwhile, as the search for Linda Carroll continued, Detective Buczek learned of additional statements that Carroll had purportedly made to attorney Richard Wright during the times when they were communicating with each other, prior to her sudden disappearance. Apparently Sandy Murphy had made attempts to influence Carroll's recollection of certain events. On one occasion, Carroll told Wright, Murphy had reminded her that Ted Binion frequently slept on a mattress and on sleeping bags on the floor. Carroll, however, said that she knew that what Murphy had said was untrue.

On another occasion, Carroll and Murphy had discussed the reports that were appearing in the newspapers about Ted Binion having a large quantity of heroin in his stomach.

Murphy had attempted to explain to Carroll that Ted had the drug in his stomach because he always licked the aluminum foil that he used to smoke it. Carroll hadn't believed that statement, either, and said she had found it comical that Sandy had expected her to believe it.

According to Carroll, Sandy Murphy had also told her that she was going to receive the house on Palomino Lane, three hundred thousand dollars, three million dollars from a savings account, and an additional one million dollars from Binion's life insurance policy. Carroll also said that Murphy claimed that she was going to be paid a large sum of money for the literary rights to "her story."

In their efforts to find Linda Carroll, the Las Vegas Metropolitan Police Department enlisted the help of the FBI's Criminal Apprehension Team. It was generally believed that she was hiding out in Southern California. Her residence was listed in Orange County, but she hadn't been at her home when several attempts to serve her with papers to appear in court were made. Her neighbors had not seen her, either. According to David Roger, police believed Carroll was hiding out because she genuinely feared for her life. Roger told newspaper reporters that witnesses had been "intimidated" during the police investigation, but he did not say by whom.

Similarly, private investigator Tom Dillard stated that Carroll had told him several weeks earlier, before she went into hiding, that she had been threatened and feared for her life. At that time Dillard had attempted to persuade her to give him a tape-recorded statement.

"She has told us things that certainly suggest she has more information," Dillard said.

According to Dillard, she had told him that she felt that Rick Tabish was responsible for Binion's death, and she feared retaliation.

For some reason, after talking to Dillard, Carroll had called Sandy's attorney, David Chesnoff. While Buczek and the other investigators didn't know the reason for the

call to Chesnoff, whether it was out of loyalty to Murphy
or fear of Tabish, or both, they learned that she had also
called attorney Richard Wright afterward and complained
that Chesnoff had been rude to her. Although investigators
did not know what she had said to Chesnoff or, for that
matter, what Chesnoff had said to her, she informed Wright
that she had been told that if she were truly Murphy's
friend, she would ". . . suck it up and keep her mouth shut!"

A short time later, she had told Wright, Sandy Murphy
called her and had left a message on her answering machine
accusing her of lying "for the reward," which had by this
time been increased to $100,000. Carroll had said that she
had not been aware that a reward was even being offered
at that time. She also told Wright that she had kept a copy
of the tape-recorded message left by Sandy and had given
it to her son for safekeeping. She also stated that Murphy
had warned her that she should not talk to anyone about
the case except Murphy's attorneys.

"She seemed genuinely fearful to me," Wright said.

In her conversations with Wright, Carroll also revealed
that she had met with Tabish's attorney, Louis Palazzo.
According to what Carroll had told Wright, Palazzo had
purportedly wanted her to sign an affidavit stating that attorney James Brown had not acted professionally when he
was at Binion's home the day that Murphy, Carroll, and
Tanya Cropp were there. He also purportedly had wanted
her to state in the affidavit that Murphy and Tabish did not
have a sexual relationship, and that Tabish had stated, "I'm
going to Pahrump to save the silver," presumably to convey
the meaning that he was saving it from being looted by
Binion's estate. However, Carroll told Wright that she had
refused to sign the affidavit because not all of the allegations were accurate.

She also told Wright about a computer disk that Murphy
possessed. The disk, according to Carroll, held information
concerning Murphy's story about Binion's death. Carroll
explained that she had accompanied Murphy to a printing

shop that also rents computers by the hour so that Murphy could view the information on the disk. However, Murphy had not been successful in operating the computer and the printer.

In the meantime, after an exhaustive search for Linda Carroll's whereabouts, her attorney, Chet Bennett, announced that she would testify before the Clark County Grand Jury. "I'm going to produce my client," Bennett said. "I'm trying to get it resolved. I don't want to see her handcuffed, and I don't want to see her in jail . . . I want everybody to understand that this warrant does not indicate that she's done anything wrong."

"I'll be awaiting for her arrival, but I won't be holding my breath," David Roger said upon learning of Carroll's intention to testify. "She's made plans to come to meet with me on two prior occasions, and I was stood up both of those times."

Detective Buczek learned that Linda Carroll and her attorney stayed at the Frontier Hotel on The Strip upon their arrival in Las Vegas. Just before it was time for her to testify, she arrived at the courthouse with her attorney in a white limousine. Interestingly, at about the same time, Harry Claiborne and another attorney observed Sandy Murphy and Rick Tabish driving around in the vicinity of the grand jury hearing room in a black Mercedes. Whether it was a coincidence that they were in the area at the same time as Carroll or whether they had an ulterior motive for being there was not known. Nonetheless, Claiborne and the other attorney reported what they had observed to the investigators.

Carroll's appearance before the grand jury lasted approximately four hours. In response to questioning, she acknowledged that she had spent time with Tabish and Murphy at their apartment two weeks earlier. Her testimony, according to David Roger, was riddled with denials and allegations of memory loss. Judging by the expressions on Roger's face after he left the grand jury room, Carroll's testimony had fallen way short of his expectations. He was clearly upset and frustrated.

"I've known Roger a long time, and I've never seen him that upset," Tom Dillard said afterward. "I don't know what she said inside the grand jury room, but in my opinion something didn't go right . . . She has flatly stated [in the past] that Ted Binion was murdered and that she feared she would be killed if she testified against those responsible for his death. The truth will come out. We will continue to investigate, and all information will be turned over to the district attorney's office."

After providing her testimony, Carroll indicated to reporters outside the courthouse that she had sympathy for Sandra Murphy and did not know how Ted Binion died. She said that it was her belief that he was extremely addicted to heroin and prescription drugs. She said that she had answered the questions to the best of her ability, and was happy that it was over so that she could get on with her life.

Roger indicated that her statements to the grand jury had apparently differed from the statements she had previously made to Tom Dillard, Richard Wright, and one of her neighbors. He would be comparing the statements she made, and would look for inconsistencies.

"We are leaving no stone unturned," Roger said, repeating one of his favorite phrases. "We are continuing to investigate the case until we find out what happened to Ted Binion."

Following Carroll's grand jury testimony, Detective Buczek examined the Frontier Hotel's billing records and found that Carroll had placed a call to Sandy Murphy and/or Rick Tabish prior to the grand jury proceedings. Similarly, Buczek learned that Chet Bennett had placed a call to either Sandy or Rick the following day. Unfortunately, it was not known what was discussed during those phone calls.

*   *   *

In the meantime Rick Tabish, upset over the recent search of his home in Montana, sought to have the affidavit to obtain the search warrant unsealed, claiming that the right to privacy afforded him by the Constitution entitled him to review the information contained in the affidavit. Tabish and his attorney in Montana, Wade Dahood of Anaconda, argued that the warrant was illegal because of the lack of probable cause to search his home. Upon learning of the motion to unseal the 45-page affidavit, which Montana's 4th Judicial District Court had agreed to seal at David Roger's request, Roger and James Buczek boarded a plane and headed for Montana in an attempt to prevent their investigation from being compromised.

CHAPTER 17

When David Roger and James Buczek arrived in Montana, the post-winter chill that still filled the air contrasted greatly with the arid desert they had left behind. They had gone over their game plan on the flight to Missoula. By the time they walked up the courthouse steps, they knew exactly what Roger would present to the judge.

Upon entering District Judge David Harkin's chambers, they reiterated their concerns for the safety of certain individuals if the sealed affidavit were to be opened and made public. Roger also argued that the integrity of their investigation into Ted Binion's death would be compromised. In addition, Roger said that there was an element of "witnesses being hounded."

Tabish's attorney, Wade Dahood, was quick to argue that under Montana law the affidavit should not be allowed to be sealed.

"Your home cannot be invaded unless there is probable cause for the invasion," Dahood argued. "They've got to give you a copy of the search warrant application so that you can challenge the search."

Judge Harkin did not agree.

"Mr. Tabish's argument that no provision under Montana law authorizes this court to deny him access to the affidavit is incorrect," Harkin wrote in his ruling. "Montana's own grand jury provisions are consistent with Nevada's provisions . . . Tabish's concern is valid [only] if no indictment is ever issued against him by the Nevada grand jury. . . ."

Rather than outright deny Tabish's petition to have the affidavit unsealed, Harkin met him halfway and ruled that the petition would be stayed for six months to give the grand jury in Nevada time to finish its investigation into

Binion's murder. For the time being the affidavit would remain sealed.

Two days after Roger and Buczek returned victorious from Montana, the unexpected occurred. Missoula attorneys Brian Tipp and Rich Buley arrived in Las Vegas, accompanied by Tabish's friend, Kurt Gratzer, whom they represented. When Roger and Buczek met with them, Tipp and Buley explained that Gratzer had significant information concerning Ted Binion's death, and wanted to cooperate fully with the investigation. Gratzer's attorneys had a request, however. They wanted to cut a deal in return for Gratzer's information. Gratzer, who they said feared Rick Tabish, wanted immunity from prosecution, and law enforcement assistance in relocating. After receiving an offer of proof and assurances that Gratzer did not, himself, murder Ted Binion, Roger agreed to the conditions and a meeting was set for the following day. As it turned out, the information that Gratzer provided against Murphy and Tabish that day would turn out to be among the most damning that authorities had received.

Buczek was present in David Roger's office when Gratzer arrived with Tipp and Buley. Roger presented Gratzer and his attorneys with an immunity agreement, but Gratzer had two more conditions. First, he wanted Roger to attempt to persuade Montana authorities to release him from probation so that he could relocate without leaving a paper trail, as he didn't want Tabish to be able to find him. Second, he wanted the state of Nevada to make a commitment that it would not seek the death penalty against Tabish if Tabish was prosecuted. Roger agreed to do what he could for Gratzer with regard to his first condition, but asserted that he could not assure that he would be successful. He flatly declined Gratzer's second condition and told him that he was not in a position to determine whether Nevada would seek the death penalty against Tabish. Nonetheless, after additional discussion about the issues, Gratzer agreed

to cooperate fully and the court granted him an order of
immunity.

In his tape-recorded statement to Roger and Buczek,
Gratzer explained how he had grown up with Tabish and had
attended elementary school with him. After high school,
Gratzer joined the army and was trained as a Ranger. Following his discharge, he returned to Missoula and went to
work for the telemarketing business owned by Tabish.

It was in late August or early September 1998, said
Gratzer, that Tabish had summoned him to his office. At
that time Tabish told him that he knew a casino owner in
Las Vegas named Ted. Tabish told him that Ted was
wealthy and kept a large sum of money, silver, and jewels
inside his house. Tabish also told Gratzer that Ted had a
girlfriend named Sandy, and explained that Ted was physically abusive toward her. He said that Sandy was named
as the beneficiary of a life insurance policy of Ted's that
was valued at $875,000. Gratzer said that Tabish told him
that Sandy was "one of the pigs that he fucks," and that
"she is in his back pocket and she'll do whatever he wants
her to do."

According to Gratzer's account of the meeting, Tabish
explained how Ted had hired him to build a vault outside
of Las Vegas in which he wanted to store his silver collection. Tabish complained that Ted still owed him $13,000
for building the vault, but had refused to pay him. Tabish
described Ted as arrogant, and quoted him as having said,
"I'm not going to pay you. You make too much money
anyway, Rick." After quoting Ted, Tabish asked Gratzer to
murder Ted Binion for him.

In return for committing the murder, Tabish promised to
pay Gratzer a portion of the proceeds from Ted's life insurance policy. He also promised that he would provide
Gratzer with a 1999 Pontiac Trans Am. All in all, Gratzer
said, Tabish promised to pay him anywhere from $100,000
to $3 million for Binion's murder.

Tabish told Gratzer that he would profit from Ted's

death as well. He said that he would get all of the money, silver, and valuables that Ted had stored in his home, and that he would excavate the vault in Pahrump and steal *all* of the silver. Tabish explained that if he was caught during the theft or afterward, he would tell the authorities that Ted had asked him to secure the silver so that his brother, Jack, would not get it. In the end, Tabish said that he would get *all* of Ted's assets, including those that Sandy might inherit.

Gratzer said that he had not known "Ted's" last name, but related that he and Tabish had discussed a number of ways in which to carry out the murder. He said that Tabish told him that Ted owned a ranch outside Las Vegas, and suggested that Gratzer act as a sniper and shoot Ted through a window of the ranch house. Gratzer said that he had rejected that plan because of the risk of missing his intended target.

Another plan called for Tabish to drive Gratzer to Ted's home to meet Ted. Tabish had told Gratzer that Ted was a person who was interested in the military and would be intrigued by hearing of Gratzer's military background. Tabish explained that Ted had a substantial gun collection that he proudly kept on display in his house, and speculated that Ted would show him the collection. Gratzer, said Tabish, could grab one of the guns and shoot Ted in the head. Tabish further stated that he and Gratzer could dispose of Ted's body by wrapping it in carpet and placing it in a rock crusher. Gratzer, however, said that he had declined this idea as well.

According to Gratzer, after dismissing another plot in which he or Tabish would drop out of a helicopter and attack Binion, Tabish also discussed the possibility of staging a suicide by overdosing Ted with drugs. Tabish apparently thought, mistakenly, that Ted's life insurance benefits to Sandy might increase if Ted's death was determined to be a suicide. However, Buczek and Roger believed that Tabish was confused when he discussed this issue with Gratzer and instead had been thinking of a double indemnity clause for an accidental death. Buczek recalled that

Tabish had told a number of people at the crime scene that he did not believe that Ted Binion was suicidal, which suggested to Buczek that Tabish's apparent confusion over the supposed insurance policy had been cleared up by the time of Binion's death.

At any rate, during his discussion with Gratzer about making Ted's death look like a drug overdose, Tabish had explained that Ted was a heroin addict who took the drug by placing it on aluminum foil, heating it with a flame and inhaling the smoke. He also told Gratzer that Ted abused the anti-anxiety drug, Xanax, and discussed the idea of forcing Ted to take a lethal mixture of heroin and Xanax. Tabish had wondered aloud how he could force Ted to take the drugs, and Gratzer suggested forcing a tube down his throat. Tabish asked Gratzer if he could find out how much of each drug would comprise a lethal dose.

Gratzer said that he called Jon Berman, a friend and pharmacist in Missoula, and posed the questions about lethal drug doses. Berman, according to Gratzer, said that he didn't know how much Xanax it would take for it to be lethal, but assured Gratzer that he would do some research and try to answer his question.

At one point during the meeting between Tabish and Gratzer, Tabish had placed a telephone call to Ted Binion's house so that Gratzer could hear Ted's voice. When Ted's answering machine picked up the call, Gratzer listened in so that he could hear Binion's tape-recorded message.

During Gratzer's meeting with Tabish, Sandy Murphy called Tabish three times. During one of the calls she complained that Ted was in the bathroom smoking heroin. After that particular phone call, Tabish had said to Gratzer, "The guy's a piece of shit," and stated that he "didn't want the guy around anymore." Gratzer said that in the days after the meeting, Tabish called him numerous times to discuss the various murder scenarios.

As Gratzer continued his statement, he said that he had spoken to his friend and physical workout partner, Timothy

Boileau, prior to Ted's murder. Gratzer said that he told Boileau, who works as a juvenile transportation officer at the Missoula City Jail, that Tabish had offered him $100,000 to kill a guy in Las Vegas. Gratzer and Boileau then discussed various ways in which to kill a person.

At one point, during another meeting Gratzer had with Tabish in Montana after Ted Binion's death, Gratzer had pressed Tabish for details of how he was able to force Ted Binion to ingest a potentially lethal dose of heroin. Although Tabish had refused to answer the question directly, as he drove off he roared with laughter and yelled out the window, "Xanax!"

As the interview concluded, when asked if he had read newspaper articles about the case after Ted Binion's death, Gratzer responded that he had, but insisted that the information he provided to Roger and Buczek was based on his meetings and discussions with Rick Tabish, not on media accounts of what happened.

Buczek and Roger agreed that it was quite a statement. Although they felt that Gratzer had been truthful, it was decided that James Buczek and Tom Thowsen would fly to Missoula to try and corroborate the information that he had provided. It was a difficult time for the two detectives because the Binion case was not the only one they were working on. Because of a serious back-up within the homicide division due in part to Las Vegas's ever-burgeoning population growth and the corresponding increase in crime, the two detectives found themselves rotating between the new cases that were coming on board and the Ted Binion case. With dedication and personal sacrifices, however, they found the time to make yet another trip to Montana.

Buczek and Thowsen first interviewed pharmacist Jon Berman. Berman told them that at some point between March and September 1998 he had received a telephone call from Kurt Gratzer in which Gratzer had made inquiries regarding how much of a particular drug would be needed to kill a person. Berman could not recall the name of the

drug Gratzer had asked him about, nor could he be more
specific regarding the time frame in which Gratzer had
called him.

Berman said that one of the substances that Gratzer had
asked him about was an opiate, and he said that he told
Gratzer that he could not provide the information he wanted
because a lethal amount of an opiate would depend upon a
number of factors such as the method of absorption into
the bloodstream, the individual's weight, and the person's
tolerance for the particular drug. He said that the second
medication that Gratzer had asked him to look up was not
in his manual, but he told Gratzer that he could research it
at the library if he wanted him to.

"Gratzer said, 'Don't worry about it,' " Berman said, and
then Gratzer had hung up the phone abruptly. He said that
Gratzer was always asking him "strange questions," and
indicated that the latest round of inquiry had not seemed
all that unusual. However, Gratzer had not called him again.

Buczek asked Berman if he would look in his pharmacy
manual to determine if it contained information regarding
lethal amounts of Xanax, but the manual did not contain
that information. It appeared from Berman's statement that
Gratzer had been truthful with them. Buczek and Thowsen
thanked Berman for his help and left.

Next, Buczek and Thowsen contacted Timothy Boileau.
Boileau stated that he and Gratzer had been workout part-
ners at Gold's Gym during the summer and early fall of
1998, and that they sometimes socialized together. One evening prior to Ted Binion's murder, while at Gratzer's apartment, Gratzer told Boileau that Rick Tabish wanted to kill
someone in Las Vegas and had offered Gratzer $100,000
to commit the murder. Boileau said that Gratzer had described the intended victim as a heroin addict.

"He said a lot of things that night," Boileau related, including that he was worried about becoming a "fall-guy"
for Tabish. Gratzer had told him that he was worried that
Tabish might try to pin the murder on him and that was

why he had begun to tell people about his discussions with Tabish about murdering Ted Binion. Boileau said that he and Gratzer also talked of various ways that a person's life could be taken, including using a firearm and martial arts chokeholds.

"At one point Kurt said, 'Do you want to be a part of it?' " Boileau quoted. "I stated to Kurt that he had to be out of his mind."

A few days after his discussion with Gratzer, Boileau said that he had read about Ted Binion's death in the local Missoula newspaper. He said that he told his parents about his conversation with Gratzer and was considering talking to the police, but it was their opinion that it could be dangerous for him to speak to the police about it at that time. Boileau, therefore, had decided against reporting what Gratzer had related to him.

Following the discussion with Boileau, Buczek was approached by an individual in a public restroom who told him that he should speak to Mike Church, the owner of Church's Jewelry Store, before he left Missoula. Buczek and Thowsen immediately went to see Church, who acknowledged that he knew Kurt Gratzer. Church told the detectives that Gratzer had approached him prior to Ted Binion's death and had asked him how he could sell a large amount of silver coins. Gratzer would later deny that he'd had such a conversation with Church. Although the information from Church was sketchy, it was yet another avenue that would require further investigation to determine whether some of Binion's silver had made its way to Montana.

Before they left for home, Buczek and Thowsen met with Terry Sweeney, a convenience store owner who met Kurt Gratzer outside the Missoula YMCA on September 18, 1998, the day after Ted Binion's death. During the interview, Sweeney stated that he and Gratzer had gone to college together, but had never really known each other or socialized as students.

Sweeney said that he and Gratzer talked for a while that

day, and reminisced about friends that they had in common, mostly from college. During their conversation, Sweeney told Gratzer that he was going to the Testicle Festival, an annual weekend event about an hour from Missoula. He said that he invited Gratzer to ride along with him, and Gratzer had accepted. On their way to the festival they talked about school for a while, and then Gratzer moved on to another subject that had disturbed him.

According to Sweeney, Gratzer talked about a guy named Rick Tabish who had asked Gratzer to help him kill a man in Las Vegas. Sweeney, shocked by the revelation, asked Gratzer if he would ever do such a thing, and Gratzer had told him that he probably would never go through with Tabish's plan. Because he wanted someone to know what he'd been told in the event that something happened to him, Sweeney said that he had told his father what Gratzer had revealed to him. He said that after he had learned about Ted Binion's death and that Rick Tabish was believed to have been involved, he did not go to the police because he feared that Gratzer might retaliate against him. He also stated that the rumor about Binion's death and Rick Tabish's involvement had been circulated at the Testicle Festival.

Meanwhile, back in Las Vegas, the issue of the videotape made by Sandy Murphy's lawyer, William Knudson, depicting the inside of Binion's home the day after his death, had become a hot issue. The tape had been made to document items inside Binion's home because of the expected court wrangling between Murphy and Binion's lawyers over the massive estate. Lawyers for Binion's estate wanted the tape, but Murphy's criminal lawyer, David Chesnoff, argued that if it was turned over it might violate his client's right against self-incrimination. Although a copy of the tape had previously been promised to James Brown, Chesnoff argued that circumstances had changed since that promise had been made because of the homicide investigation and the "hostile position taken by the estate's lawyers."

The twenty-minute tape shows Sandy Murphy, her back to the camera, as she removes a wine glass from the kitchen counter and appears to place it into a handbag hanging over her right shoulder. However, when the tape is slowed down, it isn't clear what becomes of the glass. It also shows Murphy taking a computer disk from her bedroom's bathroom and an item, believed to be a package of cigarette papers, from the desk in Binion's bedroom.

The tape depicts a different Sandy Murphy. No longer is she hysterical, nor does she appear to be grieving over Binion's death. Instead she is heard using profanity, and, less than twenty-four hours after Binion's demise, is seen being materialistic over Binion's possessions as she moves through the house pointing out this and that and claiming her rights to certain items.

The detectives considered the taking of the wine glass as significant since it might have been used to force-feed Binion the potentially lethal cocktail of heroin and Xanax. Buczek and Thowsen would have loved to have gotten their hands on it so that they could submit it for testing to determine if there were any drug residues inside the glass. Now, they realized, it was gone forever and they might never know what role, if any, the glass had played in Binion's death.

At another point on the tape, as Sandy tours through the home, she is heard directing William Knudson to point the camera toward the grand piano. "I've got another pistol in there," Sandy says on the videotape, indicating the piano bench. "I bet they forgot about that one because they weren't smart enough to fucking look." After she opens the piano bench and the camera catches a shot of the gun inside, she says: "Here you go."

Tanya Cropp was present at Binion's home the day the videotape was made. According to Cropp, she once confronted Sandy regarding her role in Binion's death after reading a newspaper story in which it was revealed that investigators were theorizing that someone had forced the mixture of heroin and Xanax down Binion's throat and had finished him off by suffocating him. During that confrontation, Cropp said Murphy had mentioned the glass to her.

"She [Murphy] said it was all a lie," Cropp said. If Murphy had poisoned Binion, why hadn't the police taken the glass that was in the house? Cropp said that Murphy had asked her.

Cropp also told David Roger about a seven-page handwritten list of coins that Murphy had given to her and asked her to fax to Rick Tabish's MRT Transport offices in Missoula. Roger believed the list of coins referenced those missing from Binion's home. Cropp also said that she wanted to come clean, and admitted that Murphy had asked her to be less than truthful for her regarding two issues.

"I thought I was helping a friend," Cropp said. "She asked me to say I saw Ted give Rick Tabish some money . . . on the sixteenth of September." She also said that Murphy wanted her to testify that she had overheard Tabish say on September 18 that he "had something to take care of before Jim Brown gets his hands on it," the inference being that he was going to remove Binion's silver from the vault in Pahrump before the estate could gain possession of it. She admitted that she had misled the investigators as well as the grand jury regarding those two issues, but was now telling the truth.

Cropp also said that Binion had appeared jealous the day before his death and had asked her whether Murphy was cheating on him. She said that she had recalled how Murphy had once described Tabish as her new "significant other."

"I told him that I knew that the intentions were there," Cropp said. She added that she knew that Murphy had once truly loved Binion, and it was only after Binion began using heroin again, in March 1998, that Murphy began having an affair with Tabish.

She also described Binion as promiscuous and said that he had relationships on the side with women from Cheetah's while living with Murphy. Binion once had asked

Cropp if she "knew any redheads" that she could fix him up with.

The day before Binion's death, which was the day that Cropp had reported for her first day of work as Binion's personal secretary, she said that Binion was upbeat and in a good mood and had shown her a brand-new stack of $100 bills. He also spoke of making future investments and had offered to teach Cropp how to invest and make money and had stated how they "would make money together." Binion told Cropp how he "loved money and hated to part with it." However, she stated that Binion's upbeat mood quickly spiraled downward after she told him of Murphy's intentions of having an affair.

At one point the investigators learned of a Valentine's Day card that Cropp had sent to Murphy in February 1999. The card read: "I want you to know how much I love you. Thank you for being there when I needed you the most. I have a feeling this year is going to be rocky. I want you to know and feel that you can call me for anything. You are one of the four dearest people to me and I love you. Love you, Tanya . . . Our friendship is exactly the consistency of fudge. A beautiful thought, isn't it? Happy Valentine's Day."

The card clearly showed that Tanya held no animosity for Murphy and bore no grudges toward her, an indication that she was being truthful with investigators and was not just out to get Sandy Murphy by now coming clean with the information. However, Cropp had also stated that Binion's estate had allowed her to live rent-free in the Palomino Lane residence for eight months, and that private investigator Tom Dillard had offered her a job. The situation made it somewhat difficult to determine which side of the fence she was on, so to speak, or whether her actions had been somehow influenced by Binion's estate, but her statements were taken in the end as being truthful.

As the investigation continued, a statement was obtained from Jared Pace, one of Tabish's former truck drivers. Pace told the investigators that he had seen Tabish and Michael Milot, an MRT supervisor at the time, loading a pickup truck with silver dollars encased in plastic the day after Binion's death. Pace stated that the small plastic cases were similar to the cases that he had assisted Tabish and Milot with when Binion's silver was removed from the Horseshoe Casino. He had no idea where they were now.

On Tuesday, April 20, 1999, Tom Dillard was conducting an interview with Fred Schmidt and Michael Wells at RTI's offices when John Joseph called and asked to speak to Schmidt. At one point Dillard took the telephone and asked to meet with Joseph to conduct an interview, at which time Joseph assured Dillard that he would call back and arrange a meeting. However, Joseph never called back as promised.

The next day, investigators learned that Rick Tabish had called Michael Wells and left a message on Wells's voice mail. According to Wells, Tabish sounded "very angry and he seemed agitated." Tabish had "barked" that Wells was not authorized to provide Tom Dillard or the district attorney's office with any documents, and had warned Wells that if he did not heed his orders he would "take care of Wells and those around him." Only moments later, Rick Tabish had called Wells's cellular phone and had left an identical message, driving home the point that Wells was not to cooperate in the investigation in any way. Again, he threatened to retaliate against Wells and his loved ones if Wells cooperated with the authorities.

Tabish's actions made it seem like he was now in a panic, that as the police continued to move in and turn up the heat, his life was unraveling around him. And in reality it was, as was Sandra Murphy's, probably faster than either of them realized. Rumors were beginning to circulate around the courthouse that prosecutors were putting together a massive affidavit for a warrant for Tabish and Murphy, and that their arrests were looming in the background.

CHAPTER 18

Over the next two months, between April and June 1999, the Ted Binion death investigation continued to evolve. District Judge Michael Cherry delayed a hearing in which he was to decide whether to allow Sandy Murphy to move back into Ted Binion's home, citing that he needed additional time to review the court papers because Binion's sister, Becky, had filed papers seeking possession of personal and family items she believed to be in the Palomino Lane residence. He set the hearing date for Friday, June 11.

Rumors also continued to circulate that Prosecutor David Roger was getting closer to filing charges against Murphy and Tabish, but he had ceased commenting on the case. Speculation also ran high that Murphy and Tabish were thinking about leaving town. The telephone to their apartment in Henderson had recently been disconnected, as had Tabish's cellular phone.

It was amid all the rumors of impending arrests that Murphy's lawyers, David Chesnoff and Oscar Goodman, requested a hearing before Judge Cherry. At the hearing Chesnoff announced that he and Goodman were withdrawing as legal counsel for Sandra Murphy, and only said that it would be "inappropriate" if he outlined their reasons for leaving the case. By this time, Goodman had entered the race for mayor of Las Vegas.

Rick Tabish's attorney, Louis Palazzo, also bowed out without providing an explanation.

Murphy and Tabish quickly found new lawyers. She retained attorney Bill Terry on Monday, May 24, 1999, and Tabish retained attorney Steve Wolfson, a former prosecutor, that same day. Both attorneys were eager to represent Murphy and Tabish, particularly if it came to the point where charges were filed against their clients. Tabish, said

Wolfson, was looking forward to exonerating himself.

In the meantime, District Attorney Stewart Bell came out and publicly downplayed the rumors that arrests were forthcoming.

"There is nothing imminent, we're continuing our investigation," Bell said to a reporter for the Las Vegas *Sun*. "We may or may not be able to initiate charges in two weeks or two months or two years. It depends on whether the path leads to something or leads to a dead end . . . Murphy and Tabish are certainly among the people being looked at. That said, we look at people as much from the point of view of not being involved. We're looking at several people as to whether they should be eliminated or charged . . . It's certainly more complex than three shots to the head from a .44. But that's just a part of it. It's a very complex set of facts . . . you can buy a jigsaw puzzle for a child that has ten pieces and is very easy to put together. You can also buy a puzzle that has five thousand minute pieces and it's hard to know what it's going to look like, and how it goes together. This case is a lot like the latter."

At the June 11 hearing, Judge Cherry removed himself from the estate case because he had represented Becky Binion-Behnen on other matters and wanted to avoid the possibility of a conflict of interest. As a result, the long-awaited decision to see if Sandy Murphy could move back into Ted Binion's home was delayed again.

Murphy, obviously upset, made a scene in the hallway outside the courtroom afterward when she approached attorney Harry Claiborne and asked him why he had never offered to help a "very sick" Ted Binion prior to his death.

"You didn't care about him when he was sick," Murphy yelled. "I said, 'Harry, he's sick,' and you didn't come to help . . . where were you when he was alive? You called and told me you were going to help, and you never came."

As Claiborne tried to walk away from her, Murphy, crying and yelling, continued to criticize and rebuke Claiborne and called him a "liar" in front of reporters and television news cameras, according to the *Las Vegas Review-Journal*. One of her lawyers finally had to pull her away and send her to a restroom where she could calm down. Claiborne, however, indicated that he had not known that Binion was sick, and had also spent much time out of town in the weeks prior to his friend's death and wouldn't have known about any problems that Ted might have been having. Claiborne told reporters that he felt that Murphy's emotional outburst had been an act.

"This is a big act," Claiborne said. "She's trying to plant a seed that Ted was really sick and not murdered . . . She never called me, period."

Additional background on Sandy Murphy, dug up by KLAS-TV, revealed an abrupt change in her lifestyle and behavior from childhood to adult and two distinct sides to her personality. Before she was old enough to start kindergarten, her mother had enrolled her in tap dancing, ballet and gymnastics and, like many children, she also played tee-ball and softball. Always athletic-minded, by the time she was in middle school she was playing volleyball, basketball, softball, and was involved in track and field. In the eighth grade she was the captain of nearly every team she played on, and was given recognition as the athlete of the year. She also swam on Bellflower's city swim team, and every Wednesday night she taught handicapped children how to swim and became involved in Special Olympics. She also sat on the student councils of her elementary, middle, and high schools, and made good grades until her senior year when she met and moved in with a family friend ten years older than her.

"A few years after high school she came back to visit, and we went out," recalled a childhood friend. "She was doing well. I thought she seemed really successful. She was a finance manager, and she was very smart. My husband and I were buying a car at that time, and she was helping us understand the financing end of things . . . I just can't believe this has happened to her. Sandy was always the nicest girl. She is the kind of person who I would call if I was broken down on the freeway, because I knew she'd come to help . . . She was a really good-hearted girl."

"I don't know if Sandy worked for the clubs in Orange County," another acquaintance said. "I don't know what she did. But I can tell you that a lot of Southern California dancers go to Las Vegas a few days out of the month to dance. Girls make a lot more in Vegas, thousands in a weekend. Then they come back here and lead very normal lives."

When Sandy first hooked up with Ted Binion, their relationship had seemed relatively normal and they were known to do a lot of things together, such as fishing and horseback riding. There were times when they'd get up before dawn, take the dogs, and fish until it became too hot in the afternoon. But as she became more involved in Binion's lifestyle and business dealings, things began to change.

"At the very beginning she was happy," gardener Tom Loveday told reporters. "I mean, she was twenty-three or so, and Ted's a wealthy man who shows up at the club in a limo and spends a ton of money on her for lap dances. Then he takes her to this house, she sees this big house. That's what she was looking for, you know . . . She may have told herself that he loved her, and she may have told herself that she loved him. But it was about money."

She was soon drawn into the lives of the high rollers, and Binion began using her to network with them and even collect debts for him. On one occasion, in November 1995, he had sent Sandy and two Horseshoe employees to Taiwan to try to collect a gambling debt from a Taiwan businessman who was disputing what he owed the club. Since Binion was barred from running things at the Horseshoe by the Gaming Control Board, the action was viewed as unfavorable and she would end up taking the Fifth Amendment when called to answer the Board's questions about her activities.

After the Gaming Control Board's hearings, Sandy and Ted returned to their Palomino Lane home to unwind. Sandy was known to perform stripteases for Binion in the back yard at night by the pool, and they would make love by moonlight at the side of the pool. On the surface it seemed like their relationship was blossoming, but beneath it all, things were not what they had seemed.

"She took a lot of crap from him," Tom Loveday told reporters. "She would show me the bruises. She'd put makeup on to cover it, but you could see it. I would get Ted's side of the story and then her side. She got beaten a lot. Ted had a temper . . . She fought back, though. Ted used to show me where she scratched him. He'd say, 'I'd get rid of her if she wasn't so pretty.' Sometimes I'd come over and all her clothes would be packed, and she'd be saying she was going to leave, and then the next thing I know she's sitting in the living room next to the grand piano, staying . . . Partying was big with them, and sex was the thing with them, big time at first. But then after a while it petered out . . . when he went back on heroin, he couldn't perform sexually and that pissed her off."

Binion, however, seemed to genuinely care about Sandy, at least at first. In order to help keep her out of jail for her DUI offense in California, at a time when she was supposed to be on in-house arrest, Binion had purportedly persuaded a law enforcement official in Jordan, Montana, where the family's massive ranch was located, to write a letter on her behalf to the California authorities that indicated that she was adhering to her in-house arrest at the Montana ranch. He also paid $15,000 for her to attend an alcohol and substance abuse program, Sober Living by the Sea, in Newport Beach, California, to complete her DUI sentence, even though he had been allowing her to smoke marijuana inside his house. He also allowed her to go on trips to Europe.

Early in their relationship Sandy became pregnant.

When Binion learned of the pregnancy in 1996, he called his pal, Herbie Blitzstein, who had also become friends with Sandy. Not wanting any additional children at his age, Binion drove Sandy to Sunrise Hospital where Blitzstein met them. Between himself and Blitzstein, they convinced Sandy to agree to have an abortion even though it was against Binion's and Sandy's Catholic religious beliefs. They checked her into the hospital under a fictitious name, and the procedure to abort the embryo was performed. She was released a short time later, and the details of the abortion were, for the most part, kept quiet and out of the media.

In the spring of 1998, Binion's relationship with Sandy began to deteriorate. Upset with her when he had found out about her taping his telephone calls, Binion told Sandy that his mother had buried jars of cash beneath the flooring of the now-burned-out family home on Bonanza Road. Sandy took an ax and drove to the fire-damaged home. She purportedly tore up much of the flooring, but had found no money. Although Sandy may not have realized it at the time, the incident had allowed the materialistic side of her personality to show itself explicitly.

Besides the partying and purported physical abuse at Binion's hands, there were other problems that complicated Binion's and Sandy's lives. One of those problems was Binion's daughter, Bonnie.

Bonnie Leigh Binion adored her father despite his short-comings, and he had loved her just as dearly. When Bonnie was born, she had a minor birth defect in one of her legs, and Ted had blamed himself by thinking that he had passed on damaged chromosomes to his daughter because of his drug abuse. But he was crazy about Bonnie. He would sit around and watch *Sesame Street* with her, tell her stories and some of his biggest secrets, read to her, and he even let her sleep in the same bed with him until she was ten. But there was little love in Bonnie's heart for her dad's new girlfriend, whom she viewed as a poor replacement for her mother, and her relationship with Sandy was rocky at best.

"I actually told my dad that she would have to change her behavior and the way she dressed and acted," Bonnie once told Tom Dillard during the early part of the investigation into her father's death. "Because I wasn't going to have basically a whore living in our house."

Bonnie said that Sandy had threatened to shoot her and her father in 1997.

"And she threatened to hit me a couple of times," Bonnie said. "She would definitely get in my face. She would definitely scream at me . . . She just wasn't that mentally stable, and she had gotten kind of crazed . . . she was constantly jealous of my relationship with my dad."

Bonnie's relationship with Sandy continued to deteriorate with time. Bonnie on occasion would break into Sandy's room and take some of her designer clothes, which she would give away to friends. Afterward, following another bout with Sandy, Binion sent Bonnie off to an exclusive boarding school in Connecticut. While away at school, Bonnie encountered difficulties in being able to contact her father. Sandy would answer her calls, but would refuse to put Binion on the phone. Bonnie finally resorted to writing a letter to her father asking him to call her, and he had quickly responded. Bonnie announced to him at that time that she was coming home to visit, and wanted to spend much of the summer at the ranch in Pahrump.

When she had visited her father in June 1998, and was talking to him outside the Palomino Lane home, the last time that she had seen him alive, Sandy Murphy came running out of the house screaming at her and ordering her to leave.

"My father came out and got in the car, and Miss Murphy came outside and she was screaming and yelling at him and me . . . She didn't want me on her property, and said that she would call the police if I didn't leave," Bonnie said.

On other occasions, when Bonnie would become involved in a heated argument with her father, Sandy would come to her aid.

"She protected me a lot," Bonnie said.

At times it would seem like Binion had played Bonnie and Sandy against each other. According to Bonnie, Binion would sometimes say something bad about her to Sandy when Bonnie wasn't around, and would similarly say something unflattering about Sandy to Bonnie when Sandy wasn't around.

"That started some animosity," Bonnie said.

On another earlier occasion Bonnie, with Sandy's permission, had borrowed Sandy's new two-seater Mercedes convertible and had taken it out with her boyfriend on the condition that they return it within an hour. She had also borrowed a $9,000 Versace outfit of Sandy's, and left in the Mercedes.

"We had the top down and were going about one hundred twenty miles per hour out by Mount Charleston," Bonnie said. "Then we rolled the car seven times." It was a wonder that she and her boyfriend still had their heads, she said.

According to Bonnie's account of the incident, when Sandy arrived at the hospital emergency room she was very angry and literally began removing the $9,000 Versace outfit as Bonnie lay stunned in a hospital bed.

"She sent it to the dry cleaners, but it was ruined," Bonnie said.

According to Binion's sister, Becky, who lived only a few blocks from Binion's home, she and Ted customarily had breakfast together nearly every morning while Sandy slept in late, until the last year of his life. During that year Becky was never at his house. "Sandy saw to that," Becky said. "She systematically eliminated everyone from his life who threatened her control. She taped all of his calls . . . Ted usually went along with her just to appease her . . . He used to tell me, 'Whatever I say on the phone, just go along with it.' "

The last ten days of his life, Becky related that she had called her brother every day. According to Becky, Ted suspected that Sandy was seeing somebody and cheating on him, but he never suspected that the man she was seeing was Rick Tabish. Becky said that she had urged Ted to break off the relationship.

"My husband and I both told Ted to get rid of Sandy," Becky said. "I told him, 'She'll kill you in your sleep,' but . . . he didn't listen."

Finally, by Monday, June 21, 1999, Prosecutor David Roger was ready to bring to fruition all of the rumors that had been circulating for nearly two months. He and detectives James Buczek and Tom Thowsen had put together an extensive 109-page affidavit in support of arrest warrants for Rick Tabish and Sandy Murphy, as well as for David Mattsen, Michael Milot, Steven Wadkins, and John Joseph, which he and Buczek signed and Thowsen witnessed. Roger presented the affidavit to Clark County Justice of the Peace Jennifer Togliatti, and the arrest warrants were signed.

Three days later, on Thursday afternoon, June 24, 1999, Buczek and Thowsen had asked members of Metro's Repeat Offender Program (ROP) to conduct surveillance at Murphy and Tabish's apartment in Henderson. They wanted to arrest Murphy and Tabish at the same time to enable their cases to be tied together, and didn't want to take a chance on, for example, Tabish being in Montana while Murphy was in Las Vegas. Finally, at approximately 5:00 p.m., the ROP officers observed Murphy and Tabish exit the apartment, get into their car, and leave together. The officers followed them to a Smith's supermarket in Henderson, and reported their findings to Buczek and Thowsen, who were on their way home from work at the time. The ROP officers asked Buczek whether they should make the arrests or wait for Buczek and Thowsen to arrive, but Buczek told them to go ahead and take the two suspects into custody.

It was at approximately 5:30 p.m. when the ROP officers entered the grocery store and presented the arrest warrants to Murphy and Tabish. The officers read them their Miranda rights, and took them into custody without incident. They were leading Murphy and Tabish out of the store just as Buczek and Thowsen arrived. By the time the detectives drove the two suspects into the garage of the Clark County Detention Center in downtown Las Vegas, the news media had heard of the arrests and were waiting with cameras rolling as the two suspects were driven past them. Murphy and Tabish were booked into the jail and charged with Ted Binion's murder, as well as conspiracy, robbery, grand larceny, and burglary. Tabish was also charged with extortion and assault with a deadly weapon with regard to the Leo Casey incident. Both were initially held without bond.

"No one incident brought us to this point today," Lieutenant Wayne Petersen said after the arrests. "It was a culmination of months of work on a complex case. The file for this case is the largest in the office, and the biggest I've ever seen in the more than two years since I joined homicide." Petersen added that the file was approximately four feet tall.

"Detectives Jim Buczek, Tom Thowsen, and Sergeant Ken Hefner have been working on this since the beginning," Petersen told the Las Vegas *Sun*. "It means something for the officers to be able to go down, put the handcuffs on and make an arrest after so much work."

The following afternoon, Steven Wadkins turned himself in at the Clark County Detention Center. Similarly, John Joseph was arrested by police in Orange, California, and booked into the county jail to await extradition proceedings. He was held on $100,000 bail. Both Joseph and Wadkins were charged with conspiracy to commit extortion, conspiracy to commit kidnapping, first-degree kidnapping with the use of a deadly weapon, assault with a deadly weapon, and extortion with the use of a deadly weapon, all in connection with the Leo Casey incident. Wadkins made bail later that evening and was released, but Joseph remained in jail for the time being.

The following Monday, June 28, 1999, Michael Milot turned himself in at the Clark County Detention Center, and the following day David Mattsen surrendered in court with his attorney, Bucky Buchanan. Milot and Mattsen, along with Tabish, were each charged with conspiracy to commit burglary and/or grand larceny, burglary, and grand larceny, in connection with the attempted theft of Binion's silver from the vault in Pahrump. Milot, Mattsen, and Joseph each posted bail over the next few days and were released pending trial.

The bail hearing for Murphy and Tabish was held on Wednesday, July 7, 1999, before Justice of the Peace Jennifer Togliatti. Now shackled in chains and wearing drab blue jail clothing, Tabish and Murphy listened intently as Prosecutor David Roger argued against bail by citing that the two murder suspects were not only flight risks but were also a danger to the community.

"The defendants are now privy to the vast amount of evidence establishing their guilt," Roger said. "The defendants may face the death penalty. The stakes are high, and the risk of flight is great." Roger indicated that his office believed Murphy and Tabish had access to vast amounts of money—much of which was believed to have been Binion's—with which to flee the state or even the country.

In addition to Murphy contacting and badgering witnesses, Roger told the judge, she also had a tendency toward violence. Roger cited a reported incident in which Murphy had told Binion's brother-in-law, Nick Behnen, through an intermediary, to keep his mouth shut or end up "dead on the street." Murphy purportedly wanted Behnen to "watch the pigeon" scene toward the end of the 1967 movie, *Bonnie and Clyde*. The implication one might read into her threat was that Behnen might be ambushed but, unlike the movie, not by the police.

In another incident, said Roger, Murphy had been eaves-dropping on a telephone call that Ted Binion had made to one of his old girlfriends and had heard the former girl-friend advise Binion not to include Murphy in his will. When she had heard the comment, Murphy got on the line. "Listen, you cottage cheese–ass, red-headed has-been from hell, ugly old bitch," Roger quoted Murphy as having said. "Who do you think you are? I'm going to kill you."

According to Roger, Murphy had gone on to tell Bin-ion's former girlfriend that she was going to her home and would shoot her in the head with a shotgun as she slept. Roger, in his attempt to show that Tabish was also a danger to the community, cited the Leo Casey incident at length, and quoted the threats that Tabish had made to Casey about harming him and his loved ones.

"Someone forced that heroin down Ted Binion's stom-ach," Roger said. "This was not suicide. This was not an accidental overdose. This was murder."

In their attempts to obtain bail for their clients, attorneys Bill Terry and Steve Wolfson argued that Murphy and Ta-bish were not a flight risk because they had remained in the community for the nine months since Binion's death even though they had known that they were being looked at as the prime suspects in the investigation. The attorneys argued that Murphy and Tabish could be placed on house arrest and that it be mandated that they check in with the authorities on a daily basis, either by phone or in person.

Roger countered that Tabish and Murphy had remained in the area because they had convinced themselves that they would not be held accountable for Ted Binion's death and the crimes surrounding it. Now that they knew what they were facing, the chances of them fleeing were far greater.

The following day, Togliatti granted bail for Sandra Murphy. She set her bail at $3 million, but Murphy could be released from jail if she posted ten percent of that amount. She would also have to surrender her passport, which had previously been found by security guards in the back yard of the Palomino Lane home. Togliatti ordered that Rick Tabish be held without bail, citing that she considered him a flight risk and a danger to the community.

That afternoon Murphy's Irish friend, William Fuller, brought in a cashier's check for $300,000 and posted her bail after having the money transferred from one of his overseas accounts.

"I think she's a nice person, and I think she is innocent," Fuller said. "That is the main reason. I think I'm a good judge of people."

Prior to Murphy being released, however, the court required that Fuller provide evidence of his credibility and show where he had obtained the $300,000 that he was so willing to put up for Murphy's release. Although it took a few days, Fuller convinced the judge through documentation that the source of his money was legitimate and that he had obtained it from the sale of property he owned in Dublin.

Murphy ended up spending a few more days in jail, but was finally released from custody the following Thursday, July 15, 1999, and transported to her apartment in Henderson where she would remain under house arrest. She was required to submit to electronic monitoring, accomplished by wearing an electronic ankle bracelet that would alert authorities if she left the apartment without first obtaining permission. She was also ordered to have no contact with any of the other defendants in the case, and she was not to contact any of the witnesses unless she was in the presence of her attorney.

CHAPTER 19

As time raced toward August 1999 and the start of a pre-liminary hearing to determine whether Sandy Murphy and Rick Tabish would stand trial for the murder of Ted Binion, a number of developments occurred. Among them was a decision by District Court Judge Michael Cherry, in which he denied Murphy's request to gain possession of Binion's house. Cherry said that he would not consider the matter further until Murphy's guilt or innocence in the case was determined, or until the Nevada Supreme Court issued a ruling on the estate's appeal of a prior decision in which Murphy was granted ownership of the house. Under Nevada law, someone convicted of murdering the person from whom an inheritance is received is not entitled to the inheritance. Similarly, the $300,000 Murphy was awarded would remain in an interest-bearing account.

Another development involved information from Tanya Cropp, who told Buczek that Murphy had confided in her that even though she was engaged in a sexual relationship with Rick Tabish, she feared Tabish because of purported beatings that she had sustained at his hands.

"She would call me and say that she got her punishment last night," Cropp said. "I'd ask her what she meant by 'punishment,' and she'd say that Rick would beat her up, you know, hit her, whatever, throw her around . . . so yeah, she was afraid of him physically . . . She always, for some reason, referred to her being beaten up as 'punishment' . . . "I told her I thought she was stupid, and I thought that she should just leave Rick if Rick was beating her up."

Murphy, however, told Cropp that she couldn't leave Tabish because she "loved him so much." She also said that Murphy received money from Tabish anytime she needed it after Binion's death.

Cropp also told Buczek that Murphy was concerned that her friend, Linda Carroll, "was going to open her mouth and she would have to take care of her."

Buczek and his partner had also learned that the computer disk seized during the search of Murphy and Tabish's apartment several months earlier was likely not the same disk that Murphy was seen pocketing during the videotaping of Binion's home on September 18. As a result, the contents of the hard drive of Binion's computer were being analyzed for any information that might be significant in the investigation into his death, though it seemed doubtful that anything useful would be found on it.

It was also revealed that Murphy had filed a palimony suit against Binion's estate a few weeks prior to her arrest, seeking $2 million for "unique and extraordinary" services, including maintaining the home, cooking for Binion and helping him entertain visitors, and so forth, all the while sacrificing her own interests, both personal and financial.

"She just is incapable of suppressing her true motives," Richard Wright, attorney for Binion's estate, said. "This lawsuit speaks eloquently to her character."

It was generally opined that because of her cohabitation agreement with Binion, her palimony suit would eventually become a moot issue.

In another development, Nick Behnen, Binion's brother-in-law, told a reporter for the Las Vegas *Sun* that Ted had told him, about a week before his death, that he was concerned that Murphy had been secretly tape-recording his conversations with a number of prominent people and may have been planning to use the tapes against him. According to what Behnen told the reporter, Binion had appeared almost panic-stricken while searching for the tapes that he said contained information that could send him to prison.

"He said she was crazy and he wanted to get these tapes away from her," Behnen told the reporter. "It was of great concern to him. He said, 'She could put me in the penitentiary.' " Behnen said that Binion had told him that Murphy admitted that she had recorded some of his conversations and that she had placed the tapes in a safe deposit box so that she could use them to obtain money if they separated. Binion told Behnen that, to make the recordings, he believed Murphy was using a parabolic microphone he had purchased which was capable of picking up conversations from one hundred yards away. Behnen said that he did not know whether Binion had been able to obtain the tapes from Murphy.

According to Behnen, Binion also related to him an incident in which Sandy had pointed a gun to his head and said that she was going to "blow his brains out." Binion said he had been able to talk her out of shooting him, but purportedly told Behnen the day before his death that "the bitch is trying to kill me."

"He said she was a dangerous person," Behnen said. According to Behnen, Binion also told him that he believed that Murphy was cheating on him, possibly with three different men.

As the preliminary hearing got underway on Tuesday, August 17, 1999, Sandy Murphy showed up in court with her electronic ankle bracelet. Instead of its normal black color, Murphy had spray-painted it beige to match her outfit and shoes. When asked about it, she commented that she was considering painting it daily so that it would match her outfits. On the surface it seemed like she was more concerned over her appearance than she was about the gravity of the charges she was facing, and her attitude about her overall predicament reeked of arrogance toward authority.

One by one the witnesses were called to the stand to recount what they had already told the investigators: Binion's maid, Mary Montoya-Gascoigne; gardener Tom Loveday; manicurist Deanna Perry; employees from the Peninsula Hotel in Beverly Hills; real estate agent Barbara Brown; Tanya Cropp; Leo Casey; and so forth. It wasn't until the prosecution called Dr. Michael Baden, a renowned pathologist from New York hired by Binion's estate, that anything new surfaced. Although the defense had been apprised of Baden's impending testimony, his appearance came as somewhat of a surprise to the general public who had been closely following the developments related to this unusual case.

Baden, who has performed more than 20,000 autopsies and works as the director of the Medicolegal Investigations Unit of the New York State Police, testified that at first he was inclined to agree with Dr. Lary Simms's findings that Binion had died as a result of a drug overdose. However, after further examination of the autopsy reports, tissue slides, and photographs, he had changed his mind and now held the opinion that someone had obstructed Binion's ability to breathe, possibly by using a hand or a pillow.

"The mouth and nose area were obstructed," Baden testified.

Baden said it was possible that the amount of drugs that Binion had ingested would be capable of killing some people, but he believed that most people would have survived the dosage.

"One hundred thousand heroin addicts walk around New York City with higher levels than [that found in Binion's body], shooting up four times a day," Baden said. "Maybe one will die . . . it's the most amazing thing how the body is resistant to dying from these infectious agents . . . my opinion is that he died from some obstruction to his nose and mouth . . . and pressure on his chest."

Baden testified that Binion, as an experienced heroin user, would likely have a higher tolerance for the drug and the level required for an overdose would have to have been greater than that found in Binion's body. His testimony sharply conflicted with that of Dr. Simms, Clark County's chief medical examiner, who had indicated that a lethal level of heroin would not be affected by the user's experience or amount of use. Baden also indicated that he did not believe that the combination of drugs found in Binion's body had greatly increased the risk that death would occur from the drugs alone.

"Theoretically," Baden said, "the answer should be yes, but practically, in the case of Mr. Binion, the answer would be no." He indicated that, based upon the amounts of the drugs found during the autopsy, none of them either by themselves in the quantities discovered or by mixing them together, would be sufficient to cause death. "It's zero plus zero . . . what's unique about heroin is that . . . in half of heroin addicts who die of overdoses, we find froth coming up the windpipe, coming out of the nose and mouth. It's internal drowning almost . . . that was not described and did not happen here."

Baden testified that he considered the bruises and abrasions on Binion's body to be "fresh," and said that they could have occurred a short time prior to death or even shortly after death. He indicated that one of the wrist abrasions was consistent with the pattern caused by the use of handcuffs as a restraint. He also noted the injuries in the area of Binion's face, the "rubbing off of skin and dried superficial abrasions" in the areas of the nose and mouth, which "look like pressure marks to me. There was pressure against Mr. Binion's mouth . . . this appears to have occurred about the time of death." The abrasions and bruising on his chest may have been caused by buttons on Binion's shirt, and hemorrhaging beneath the skin on the left side of his chest, he opined, could have been caused by pressure being applied. He also noted the bruising on Binion's back, which could also be indicative of pressure marks. Baden also talked about the hemorrhaging in Binion's eyes, capillaries that had burst.

"[That] occurs when there's an increase in blood pressure in the face area," Baden said, bolstering the possibility that the hemorrhaging of the eyes could have been caused by someone suffocating Binion. Baden noted that capillaries sometimes burst in the eyelid following a bout of coughing, but because there were multiple broken capillaries he opined that coughing was not what had caused them to rupture in this case. He added that suffocation is one of the most difficult causes of death to determine.

Baden also noted that Binion's preferred method of using heroin, "chasing the dragon," was the safest possible manner in which to use the drug. He said it was highly unlikely that Binion had overdosed on the drug using this method. If Binion's death was a case of overdose from inhalation of heroin smoke Baden said, "I think it would be the first one in the United States."

Following Dr. Baden's testimony, Prosecutor David Roger amended the criminal complaint against Murphy and Tabish to include the theory that Binion was killed "by means of asphyxia due to manual suffocation."

"We are offering two alternative theories," Roger argued. "The jury [when the case goes to District Court] may accept one or both or reject both of them." Roger added that the state of Nevada has the right to amend a criminal complaint to properly reflect the appearance of new evidence.

"These are not alternative theories," attorney Steve Wolfson objected. "They are inconsistent theories."

Justice of the Peace Jennifer Togliatti allowed the prosecution's amendment to the criminal complaint.

As the preliminary hearing continued, Kurt Gratzer took the stand. Often, his testimony was somewhat inconsistent with the information that he had provided to the investigators earlier, and at times he even recanted some of those previous statements. Instead of simply answering yes or no to a number of questions, he often rambled on and offered statements without being asked despite being admonished by Togliatti to provide direct responses. "All I'd like you to do is answer a simple question," Togliatti told Gratzer. "It's not that tough."

When asked about telling the police that Rick Tabish had told him about wanting a wealthy casino owner in Las Vegas killed, Gratzer responded: "I can't remember Rick telling me *per se* that the man is a wealthy casino owner in Las Vegas and he wants him killed. I don't remember him saying that." When Prosecutor Roger confronted him about the statements that he had given to the investigators regarding Tabish, Gratzer repeated most of the allegations that he had previously related to the police. Gratzer was being difficult, and it was difficult to determine why. Some thought that it was because he found it awkward to have to relate what he'd said to the investigators now that he was facing his former friend in court.

At another point in the proceeding, the prosecution showed the videotape that Murphy's lawyer at that time, William Knudson, had made, and Roger pointed out that the tape showed Murphy's "true colors."

"Make sure you get a complete inventory of everything," Murphy is heard telling the camera operator. "I want everything shown. I don't want anything missing."

Murphy is seen moving through the house, opening and closing drawers and cupboards for the benefit of the photographer, and at one point claims that the best china is missing. She also makes angry comments to attorney James Brown.

"I thought you were my friend," Murphy says to Brown in the tape. "You're in here loading up my fucking shit to take to give to Doris," she tells him, referring to Binion's ex-wife. At another point on the tape she says: "There was $20,000 in the house and it's not here now."

Prosecutor David Roger told Togliatti that Murphy's statement about the missing money was an attempt to "point the finger at someone else."

There were many instances in the proceeding when Sandy Murphy would sigh loudly or blow out her breath audibly after Roger made a statement that she didn't agree with, and it caught the attention of many in the courtroom. At one point Roger became agitated at Murphy's behavior when he was attempting to describe the "cruelty" involved in Binion's murder, and he asked the judge to direct Murphy to cease her "huffing and puffing." Afterward, Murphy apologized and sat quietly.

Although Sandy Murphy had fought authorities in their attempts to obtain handwriting samples that could be compared to the handwritten list of rare coins that had been faxed to Tabish's offices in Montana, she ultimately lost and was required to provide specimens of her writing. It was brought out in the preliminary hearing that a police handwriting expert believed that it was "highly probable" that Murphy had written the document.

The prosecution also attempted to establish the romantic relationship between Murphy and Tabish, and called Tanya Cropp to the stand. Cropp testified that Murphy, usually physically fit, had appeared to be gaining weight when she saw her in March 1999, and had related to Cropp that she was planning to have a "personal procedure" performed in the near future and had planned to take Tabish with her.

"I assumed that she was pregnant," Cropp said. Cropp added that she told Murphy that it wouldn't be wise to bring Tabish along if she was planning to have an abortion performed in Las Vegas. She said that she had seen Murphy again several weeks later, and it "looked like she had started losing weight."

Cropp also testified that she had provided false information to investigator Tom Dillard at Sandy Murphy's request. She said that there were two false statements that Murphy had asked her to provide to Dillard. In one of the statements she had told Dillard that she had witnessed Binion give money to Rick Tabish on September 16, the day prior to Binion's death, that could have explained why Tabish had in his possession the one-hundred-dollar bills, consecutively numbered, that had been ultimately traced back to Binion. The other statement involved her telling Dillard that Tabish was angry after providing a video camera for attorney William Knudson to use to record an inventory of the home's contents. She had told Dillard that Tabish had said to Murphy: "Sandy, I'll talk to you later. I've got to go take something before Jim Brown gets his hands on that, too." Although she had previously indicated to the police that Tabish had asked her to lie to the investigators, Cropp now told the judge that it was not Tabish who had asked her to make false statements. It had been Murphy.

"I didn't know what the outcome would be if I didn't [provide the false statements]," Cropp reasoned. "I thought I was helping a friend."

Leo Casey was called to testify, and for several hours he recounted his torturous ordeal in the desert with Tabish and Steve Wadkins, and related how Tabish, Wadkins, and later, John Joseph, had coerced him into signing over his shares of the Jean sand pit and how Tabish then ordered him out of town, or else. The defense lawyers countered his testimony in part by calling him a liar and a thief, accusing him of stealing more than $500,000 from the company in which he had shares. But Casey explained that he had diverted money and assets from the company as part of an unwritten agreement he had made with John Joseph so that his actions would escape the attention of other investors.

"This case is fraught with immunity, paid testimony, perjury, and heavy involvement of interested parties," Murphy's attorney, Bill Terry, argued.

"There is no evidence whatsoever that Mr. Tabish was at the house [the day of the murder]," Steve Wolfson declared. "So I submit to you there is no evidence that he committed this murder."

During his closing arguments, Prosecutor David Roger painted a dark, grim picture of cruelty and calculated cold-bloodedness with regard to Ted Binion's murder. Roger said that detectives believed Murphy and Tabish killed Binion sometime between the hours of 9:00 a.m. and 12:30 p.m., while gardener Tom Loveday was mowing Binion's lawn. Roger said that evidence would show that Binion had kicked Murphy out of his home earlier on the morning of his death, and that she might have gained access to get back inside the house by going through an open bathroom window adjacent to her bedroom.

"Something unexpected happened that day, and it was Tom Loveday," Roger said. Roger told the judge that investigators believed Murphy or Tabish had softened or dissolved the tar heroin that Binion had purchased on the previous evening and mixed it in a wine glass, restrained Binion with his own handcuffs, and forced him to drink the potentially lethal mixture of drugs. After he became incapacitated, and after they saw Loveday attempting to peer into the doors and windows of the house, they decided that they couldn't wait to see if the drugs they had forced down Binion's throat would accomplish the desired effect of death and decided to finish him off by suffocating him.

"She had a new flame in her life, and she wanted to move on based on Ted Binion's money," Roger argued. Roger verbally painted a picture that showed that the motive for Binion's murder was for financial gain. He explained how Tabish was more than a million dollars in debt, and how he also needed an additional half million dollars to keep his stake in the Jean sand pit afloat. Roger charged that Murphy and Tabish stole most of Binion's valuable collection of rare coins and currency from his house before reporting that they had discovered his body on the afternoon of September 17, and outlined the attempted silver theft from Binion's vault in Pahrump less than two days after Binion's death. He called the theft from Binion's home and the attempted theft of the Pahrump silver "signature crimes" by citing that only a single silver dollar was left behind in the vault and a single dime was left inside the safe in Binion's home. After all that, he said, they then staged the death scene.

"The killers had to stage a suicide or accidental overdose to get away with the crime, and that's exactly what they did," Roger said.

To top it all off, Roger said, someone, presumably the killers, had affixed a Halloween decoration to a light fixture at the entrance to Binion's home that read, "R.I.P."

"What a cruel, cruel thing to do to a dead person," Roger said.

With over thirty witnesses testifying, the preliminary hearing turned out to be one of the longest in Clark County history, and ran into the evening hours and on Saturdays. Because the burden of proof to bind the case over to District Court for trial is much less than that required of an actual trial, the defense strategy was to not tip their hands by presenting their cases fully at that time.

On Monday, September 13, 1999, nearly a year after Ted Binion's death, Justice of the Peace Jennifer Togliatti ruled that there was sufficient evidence to bind all of the defendants over for trial. She set their arraignment for September 27, before District Court Judge Joseph Bonaventure.

Afterward, Togliatti said that she had not unequivocally evaluated Leo Casey's credibility as a witness, even though prosecutors had contended that other witnesses corroborated Casey's testimony. Because of the uncertainty over the legality of some of his business dealings, Togliatti indicated that Casey had made a good victim in that he was reluctant to inform the police of what had purportedly happened to him.

"Stories written in hell don't have angels for characters," Togliatti said.

By the time of the arraignment for the six defendants, it seemed like a game of musical attorneys was being played. Steve Wolfson was now out of the case, and attorney Louis Palazzo re-entered the picture as Tabish's attorney and was paired with attorney Rob Murdock. Tabish, when he appeared before Judge Bonaventure, was wearing a blue blazer instead of the traditional blue jail clothing that he had been required to wear at prior court appearances. Due to the extensive media coverage that the case had generated, including live television broadcasts of the courtroom proceedings, Palazzo asked the judge if Tabish could continue wearing civilian clothing during future court appearances and appear without wearing shackles. The judge granted the request with the stipulation that there not be any security issues regarding Tabish. In other words, if Tabish remained on good behavior he could continue to wear civilian clothes to court and would not be shackled.

All six defendants pleaded innocent to the multiple charges facing them. A request was made that Michael Milot and David Mattsen be tried separately from Murphy and Tabish, citing guilt by association and the manner in which a jury might view such a connection. Lawyers for John Joseph and Steve Wadkins asked that their clients be tried separately from all of the others as well. Bonaventure agreed to three separate trials, and set a date of March 13, 2000, for Murphy and Tabish. He said that Milot and Mattsen could be tried either before or after Murphy and Tabish's trial, and that Joseph and Wadkins would be tried after the other four defendants.

However, on Monday, October 4, 1999, Sandra Murphy filed court papers through her attorney, Bill Terry, requesting that she be tried separately from Rick Tabish in three separate trials, one trial for each of her charges. She also asked in her motion that she no longer be confined to house arrest, and that her cash bail be reduced from $300,000 to $100,000 because she had shown that she would not flee the area.

"She is totally committed to the defense of her case," Terry wrote in his motion.

Similarly, Tabish's attorneys asked Bonaventure to set bail for their client at $100,000, because "there must be a substantial amount of proof in order to hold someone without bail. There is absolutely no competent evidence which has been presented which would rise to such a level," his attorneys wrote.

Tabish's wife, Mary Jo, in the meantime had written an impassioned letter to the court pleading that her husband be released on bail. She said that she had run out of money and out of things to sell, and that she would be in financial ruin, along with her two small children, if Tabish were not released and allowed to return to work.

"I know him better than anyone," Mary Jo Tabish wrote, "and at this time his main concerns are to clear his name, repay his debts and take care of his family . . . [The children] need Rick and Rick needs them, and with every day that passes a bigger hole is created in their lives . . . the vultures are circling, and with every day he spends incarcerated they loom even closer."

Before Judge Bonaventure ruled on Murphy's motions, Chief Deputy District Attorney David Roger sought to have bail revoked for Murphy. In his request, Roger cited the letter that Binion had persuaded a sheriff in Montana to write to California authorities on Murphy's behalf. In that letter, the sheriff had indicated that Murphy had completed house arrest at Binion's ranch in Montana for her DUI offense in California. However, Roger had received information from a California investigator that showed that Murphy had not completed the terms of her house arrest and in fact had only spent two to three weeks in Montana. The California court had ruled that she spend seventy-five days under house arrest. Roger also stated that an agent from the Gaming Control Board had provided records showing that during the time Murphy was supposed to be serving house arrest in Montana, she was living in Las Vegas and using Horseshoe casino limousines.

Roger also asked Bonaventure not to grant separate trials for Murphy and Tabish, citing Murphy's "cavalier attitude toward authority" and stating that the events surrounding Binion's death between her and Tabish are inextricably linked together.

On Friday, October 15, 1999, Bonaventure agreed that the charges against Murphy and Tabish are "inextricably intertwined" and ordered that the two defendants be tried together. Bonaventure denied Murphy's request that she no longer be under house arrest, and Roger's request that Murphy's bail be revoked. He also denied her request that her bail be lowered from $300,000 to $100,000. He did, however, grant approval for Murphy to speak to the witnesses and the other defendants, citing that otherwise her ability to participate in her own defense could be unfairly hampered.

Regarding Tabish, Bonaventure denied Louis Palazzo's motion to ban television cameras from the courtroom during the trial, and denied his request that Tabish's bail be set at $100,000. Despite the impassioned plea from Tabish's wife that her husband be freed on bail, Bonaventure ruled that Tabish would remain jailed until the outcome of the trial.

"Rick Tabish is a flight risk and a threat to the safety of the community," Bonaventure said. He based his decision in part on Tabish's prior criminal record of felony convictions, the alleged threat made to the attorney for RTI, and the brutal and cruel nature of the allegations against him associated with Ted Binion's murder.

A little more than a week later, Sandy Murphy found herself back in jail. She had violated the conditions of her house arrest by refusing to tell Sergeant Barry Payne, who supervises Clark County's house arrest program, where she had spent eight hours on Wednesday, October 20. According to information that the house arrest program provided to Judge Bonaventure, Murphy had called at 9:30 a.m. on Wednesday to say that she had an appointment with her attorney, and called again at 5:30 p.m. to report that she had returned home. Later that evening, at about 9 p.m., a corrections officer called Murphy to verify where she had spent eight hours that day. Murphy replied that she had been at her attorney's office, but refused to specify which attorney she had seen.

"Murphy became agitated and told me she would not have any further conversation with me without her attorney present and hung up the telephone," the corrections officer wrote in the letter to Bonaventure. "After she hung up the phone, I made three attempts to call her residence and there was no answer."

"If she had cooperated, she probably would not be in jail," Payne said. "She would not account for her whereabouts . . . ninety-nine percent of the people [on house arrest] comply, because they know that if they don't comply they go back to jail."

It was later learned that Murphy had been hiring a new attorney, John Momot, that day, to represent her in future court proceedings regarding the criminal charges, while Bill Terry exited through the case's revolving door of attorneys. Momot confirmed that she was with him in his office for nearly eight hours going over her case with him. Murphy spent a week in jail while all of the details surrounding the issue were worked out, and was released and returned to house arrest the following Thursday, October 29. Momot indicated that he would be submitting subsequent requests for visits from Murphy in writing to avoid such a misunderstanding in the future.

Meanwhile, in issues related to defendant David Mattsen, a federal grand jury indicted him on seven counts of being an ex-felon in possession of a firearm and on four counts of being an ex-felon in possession of ammunition. U.S. Magistrate Judge Lawrence Leavitt also ordered Mattsen to register with the State of Nevada as a sex offender for his 1972 conviction in Wisconsin for having sexual intercourse with a minor. Mattsen posted $10,000 bail, and remained free pending the outcome of his trial.

CHAPTER 20

Shortly after Murphy was released from jail and placed back on house arrest, she accused Clark County jail officials or the police, she didn't know which, of stealing her black panties after she had been booked into the jail. Murphy, through her attorney, John Momot, said that her clothes had been confiscated and inventoried at her booking. She claimed that she had shoved the panties into a pocket of her jeans, after which her items were placed inside a plastic bag and sealed. However, when her belongings were returned to her upon her release, the panties were missing.

Momot, in a motion he filed to obtain the return of Murphy's panties, implied that authorities had taken the panties so that they could be subjected to testing of her bodily secretions. He demanded their return, and asked that any evidence obtained from the panties be ruled inadmissible in court.

"The court is further requested to conduct an evidentiary hearing to determine how Ms. Murphy's panties managed to mysteriously disappear while in the custody of the detention center to get to the bottom of this matter," Momot wrote in his motion.

Chief Deputy District Attorney David Roger took umbrage at the accusations, and said that neither his office nor the police investigators were attempting to gather evidence against Murphy from the panties.

"There is absolutely no truth to her allegations," Roger said. Roger also stated that if the investigators had wanted to obtain that type of evidence, they would have sought a court order. "What a terrible waste of court time. We have murder cases that are waiting to go to trial, and we are going to take hours of precious court time to find the missing panties?"

As jail officials were making every effort to locate Murphy's panties, a local radio station had a heyday over the controversy. A couple of morning DJs put out a request over the air that women come down to the station and strip nude, donating their panties to the "Sandy Murphy panty fund." Several women actually showed up at the station and did what was asked of them, and soon after, Murphy was being referred to on that particular station's news broadcasts as "Slutty Murphy."

At one point, jail employees notified Murphy that they had found four pairs of black panties and requested that she come down and identify which pair belonged to her. When Murphy showed up at the jail, she said that none of them belonged to her.

"The State of Nevada has meticulously followed the letter of the law in its search for the truth," Roger wrote in a document filed with the court. "It is absurd to suggest that law enforcement secretively seized defendant's undergarments. In sum, there is no evidence to suggest that the State of Nevada has seized defendant's panties for any purpose . . . if the defendant's panties are ever recovered, the state will notify the defendant and the court."

District Judge Joseph Bonaventure ruled in a proceeding that was broadcast on live television that Murphy had failed to establish that officials stole her panties for the purpose of evidence-gathering and testing.

"If the underpants are ever recovered," Bonaventure ordered, "the state is directed to notify the court and the defendant immediately."

As Detective James Buczek pushed on with his investigation of Ted Binion's murder, he soon found himself in the middle of an alleged bribery plot involving Rick Tabish. Buczek was contacted by investigators in Missoula who told him that they had obtained handwritten notes that had been given to them by the wife of Jason Lee Frazier, 28, who had found them inside her husband's briefcase. Frazier's wife, Bobbi, turned over 52 pages of handwritten notes to Missoula authorities, many of which had been written on Rio Hotel and Casino stationary.

"It was readily apparent . . . that these notes are notes outlining a false alibi for Richard Tabish," Buczek wrote in an affidavit to secure a material witness arrest warrant for Frazier. "Also, the notes reflect that the alibi witnesses were to be paid for their testimony." Buczek described Frazier as being a critical witness for the prosecution, with the knowledge that several people had been "promised money in exchange for their testimony."

Tabish's attorney, Louis Palazzo, had previously filed notice that Tabish intended to put on an alibi defense at his and Murphy's upcoming trial.

Buczek learned that Frazier was a friend and business associate of Tabish's who ran a trucking business, and that he was making preparations to flee the country before being arrested and exposed as a participant in the bribery plot. Frazier was arrested as a material witness by Missoula police and was held on $1,000,000 bail at the request of Prosecutor David Roger. Frazier subsequently struck a deal with Roger and said that he would cooperate fully with the Binion investigation in return for an agreement that he would not be charged in the case. Roger agreed.

As he examined one of the notes that had been passed to Frazier from Tabish in jail, Buczek read: "Three guys, $2,000 up front. The rest the day after they take the stand—$4,000 later."

Another note, dated August 12, 1999, read: "Roger and Marty will be here tomorrow night. Final prep and it is done." After some investigation, Buczek had reason to believe that "Roger" and "Marty" referred to Roger M. Davis, and Martin A. Frye who had been listed as possible defense witnesses at the trial.

In another note Tabish wrote: "I need Roger to get hold of Jim Mitchell concerning September 17, 1998, at All Star. We really need an affidavit from him saying we were working on the sand screw from 7–11:30 a.m. My life is on the line, and we need to fight fire with fire and I will pay for an attorney for him . . . be careful about what you do. Everything will be fine. Let's get some stuff handled and pay attention to business."

Buczek learned that Tabish was referring to paying an attorney for legal problems that Mitchell was having at that time. Mitchell, he also learned, was listed as a potential witness in court records for the defense.

Another note from Tabish read: "Tell Mitchell we will take care of any legal concerns he has, but his testimony is crucial to me being set free . . . this is a slam dunk if everyone sticks in . . . tell everyone when I owe someone something, the rewards are huge, and I think they know."

Another alleged alibi witness, Michael P. Geary, an All Star Transit Mix employee, was to receive a payoff from Tabish, according to Tabish's notes. Buczek recalled that Steve Wadkins was one of the owners of All Star Transit Mix at that time, and he, too, was listed on court documents as a potential defense witness. Armed with the new information, Buczek applied for and received court authorization to conduct wiretap surveillance on Wadkins's and Geary's phones.

In one of the conversations that Buczek had monitored, he heard Wadkins tell Geary that Michael Milot had visited him: ". . . there's two guys that are going to testify that Rick was there that early morning."

"They're pretty hard-core guys, very good witnesses," Buczek quoted Wadkins as having said during the conversation. "That's why we want you to testify as well that we were having problems. . . ."

"Yeah, no problem," Buczek quoted as Geary's response.

Buczek learned that Jason Frazier had begun visiting Tabish in jail on June 25, 1999, and had visited him several times afterward in July and August. According to what

Buczek learned, many of the notes had been passed to Frazier during the jail visits.

Frazier, told Buczek, in an interview, that he had paid a man who he only knew by the name of Ishma $3,000 to locate three additional alibi witnesses for Tabish. He said he had paid the money to a woman who said she was Ishma's girlfriend, not to Ishma directly. Frazier told Buczek that he was never informed of the identities of the witnesses, but they were to be paid $1,000 each for their testimony. He said that he never learned whether the witnesses were actually paid or not, but at one point, he said, Ishma had told him that they wanted cocaine as payment for their statements. Frazier described Ishma as a slender, dark-skinned man of Hispanic descent, and said that he believed he might be a drug dealer. Frazier also told Buczek that he believed that Sandra Murphy was aware of the alibi plot and that he believed that she knew Ishma as well.

"She was aware of most everything that was going on," Frazier told Buczek. He said that he had stayed with Murphy at her apartment in Henderson. "I believe that she knew about the money situation and that I was going to take care of it after Rick's approval."

Frazier also stated that Tabish was hoping to recruit witnesses who could help clear him of the charges involving the kidnapping and torture of Leo Casey.

In another note that Tabish had written from jail and had passed on to Frazier, Tabish wrote disparaging remarks about investigator Tom Dillard: "Half of the 109-page [affidavit for an arrest warrant for Murphy and Tabish] comes from this uneducated moron. This man has no business savvy. Thank God for us he has no ethics either."

"He thinks he's the puppet master, but his strings have been severed," Dillard told the Las Vegas *Sun* later, after details of Tabish's notes had been made public by the newspaper.

"Frazier has provided crucial information that will eliminate Rick Tabish's alibi for the day of Ted Binion's murder," Prosecutor David Roger stated in court documents.

As for Ishma, Roger said that investigators were looking for him and trying to fully identify him. Roger indicated that it was possible that charges would be filed against him.

Louis Palazzo suggested that the prosecution was only attempting to intimidate potential witnesses, but despite the objections, Judge Bonaventure ruled that Tabish's jailhouse notes to Frazier could be used by prosecutors at the trial.

While interviewing Frazier, the name Salvatore Galioto had come up, as had Joseph "Joey" Cusumano's, with regard to Rick Tabish. According to Frazier, Tabish had boasted that he had sold the rights to his story for $200,000 to $300,000 as part of a movie deal. Frazier said that Tabish had promised to pay him $50,000 from the proceeds of his rights sale to help him run his trucking business. Frazier said that he couldn't be certain that the deal had been made because he had not seen a contract or agreement.

Frazier said that he, Tabish, Galioto, and another man identified only as "Joey" had dinner together in 1995. At that time Tabish had informed him that Galioto could be accommodating with regard to Frazier's trucking company because of his union connections. Frazier later identified "Joey" as Joseph Cusumano.

When Buczek checked the jail log records for visitors, he learned that Tabish had been visited in jail a few months earlier by Galioto, a reputed mob associate from Chicago with former ties to the movie industry. Galioto, according to the jail's visitor register, had shown up on August 16, 1999, one day prior to the beginning of the preliminary hearing. Buczek subsequently learned that Galioto was known by the Chicago Crime Commission with ties to "The Outfit" in Chicago, and known by association to have ties with Cusumano.

Tom Dillard ended up flying to Chicago at the request of Ted Binion's estate to try to uncover any firmly established ties between Salvatore "Sammy" Galioto and Tabish.

Dillard had learned from Tabish's cellular records that Tabish had placed a number of calls to a beeper number in the Chicago area, both prior to and after Ted Binion's death. Dillard subsequently learned that the beeper number belonged to Galioto, and that Tabish had called that number after Binion's death prior to going to Pahrump to remove Binion's silver.

"There has been speculation that the silver may have had a Chicago connection," Dillard said. "That's one of the things we're looking into."

However, Dillard's attempts to interview Galioto were in vain. Galioto would not speak to him, leaving many of those working on the case wondering whether a more solid tie between Tabish and Galioto would ever be established. At this point they had Frazier's sworn testimony, the jail's visitor log, evidence of Tabish's phone calls to Galioto's beeper that tied them together, and little else. Investigators couldn't be certain that the man who had signed in at the jail to visit Tabish as Salvatore Galioto was the same Salvatore Galioto from Chicago with reputed mob connections.

Buczek, meanwhile, received an anonymous telephone call from a man who claimed to own an airline service in Southern California. The tipster claimed that someone had offered to pay him a fee of $200,000 to fly Sandy Murphy to the Philippines. The amount that the man was offered seemed significant because it was the same amount by which Murphy had unsuccessfully tried to get her cash bail reduced.

A short time later Buczek received another anonymous tip, this time from a man who claimed to be a locksmith. The man said that he had been offered money by someone to remove Murphy's electronic ankle bracelet.

As a result of the tips and amid fear that she was planning to flee the country, the investigators placed Murphy under twenty-four-hour surveillance. They also sought and obtained a sealed court order to install a pin register on Murphy's telephone that would trace all of her incoming and outgoing calls. However, Murphy stayed put and seemed to comply with the conditions of her house arrest, for the time being.

As the case moved closer to the trial date, District Attorney Stewart Bell announced that his office would not be seeking the death penalty against Murphy and Tabish. He said that the death penalty was not appropriate in this case, but otherwise would not comment on why that decision had been made.

Many in the legal field speculated that it was in the state's best interest not to seek the death penalty. A jury might be more willing to convict if the threat of death wasn't looming over a case that was based almost solely on circumstantial evidence.

CHAPTER 21

Yet another twist was added to the case when Buczek learned that two freshly dug holes were discovered in late August 1999 at Ted Binion's ranch in Pahrump. The holes were dug in front of Binion's home, manually, in the middle of the night without the use of any heavy equipment, and they measured approximately two feet in width by three feet in length. Ranch manager Ed Raap, who had taken over David Mattsen's former position, had discovered the holes and reported them at that time to the Nye County Sheriff's Department. Buczek speculated that whoever had dug the holes had been looking for something of value that they believed Binion had buried there.

Recalling the map of Binion's ranch that had been seized during the raid on Murphy and Tabish's apartment, and the fact that Murphy had previously attempted to persuade Jack Binion to split anything that was found on the property with her, Buczek knew that the holes were not a matter of mere coincidence and that the incident required further investigation.

According to Nye County Sheriff Wade Lieske, Ted Binion had told him approximately two weeks before his death that he had buried items beneath trees growing near the irrigation system. The holes, Buczek was told, had been dug near a number of fruit trees. According to the information that he received, the dirt that had been removed from digging the holes wasn't sufficient to fill them back in, a strong indication that Binion might have buried something there. Although there was no way of knowing for certain whether anything was taken or what had been buried there, the smell of buried cash came quickly to mind. Unfortunately there were no witnesses to the digging, and

Buczek was certain that the digger or diggers would not be coming forward on their own.

Meanwhile, attorney Harry Claiborne filed a wrongful death lawsuit against Sandra Murphy and Rick Tabish in District Court, on behalf of Ted Binion's daughter, Bonnie. The lawsuit charged that Murphy and Tabish were involved "in a secret sexual relationship" in which Murphy "intentionally misrepresented" herself to Binion, and together Murphy and Tabish "planned, confederated and conspired together" in a plot to murder Ted Binion. They "inflicted great physical pain and suffering" on him and deprived Bonnie of her father's "companionship and comfort."

In a motion filed later by Claiborne, Bonnie also sought any compensation that Murphy or Tabish might receive from their purported movie deal should she win the wrongful death lawsuit. Her actions and the motion were based on a 1993 Nevada law that prevents criminals from profiting from their crimes and ensures that any proceeds received or promised from the sale of any of their rights go to the family of the victim.

"If in fact Tabish and/or Murphy are receiving now, or are entitled to receive in the future something of value for contributing anything," Claiborne wrote in his motion, "including the right to use their name to a movie, then if Bonnie obtains a judgment against them for the murder of her father, Bonnie is entitled to the proceeds."

In pre-trial legal maneuvers, Judge Bonaventure ruled that both Tabish and Murphy were indigent and were entitled to receive up to $20,000 each in taxpayer money to help pay for their defense, despite the fact that they had retained private attorneys. Bonaventure also declined a defense motion for a change of venue, even though Prosecutor David Roger hadn't opposed it. In fact, Roger indicated that he wouldn't have minded having the trial occur in another county, such as White Pine County, which is known as cowboy country. Ted Binion was a cowboy, and it was Roger's opinion that the defendants wouldn't "play well" to a jury made up of fellow cowboys and cowgirls.

In yet another unexpected development, allegations were made by Tabish's lawyer, Louis Palazzo, and Murphy's lawyer, John Momot, that the prosecution had placed an informant in Tabish's jail cell. Palazzo charged that David Gomez, a career criminal who had been charged with robbery and sexual assault, among other things, and reputedly was a member of the Mexican Mafia out of Southern California, had been placed inside Tabish's cell to funnel information to the prosecutors. Gomez, it turned out, had stated that he had information that Tabish was involved in a plot to kill Binion's gardener, Tom Loveday, before he could testify at the trial. Gomez claimed to have a handwritten note from Tabish in which Tabish had said that he was willing to pay someone $200,000 to have Loveday killed.

"The misconduct at issue is so flagrant that nothing short of dismissal will serve to deter such unlawful and egregious tactics in the future," Palazzo and Momot wrote in their motion to Judge Bonaventure to dismiss the charges. "Further, it is believed that this informant has purloined personal notes and work product documentation relating to the defense of Mr. Tabish in the upcoming trial from Mr. Tabish's cell on behalf of the district attorney's office . . . The documents at issue include matters impacting upon trial strategy, as well as matters concerning impeachment material of various state witnesses."

"There is absolutely no truth to the allegation that the prosecution planted an informant in Tabish's cell," Prosecutor Roger told a reporter for the Las Vegas *Sun*. "We are confident with our case, and we would not jeopardize the prosecution by using jailhouse informants." Roger characterized Palazzo's allegation as "another example of the young lawyer going off half-cocked."

In a follow-up investigation, detectives determined that Gomez's information was not accurate and that the note in his possession had not been written by Tabish. Investigators believed that Gomez may have concocted a scheme in which to obtain money from Tabish. The possibility that Tabish had made up the story and enlisted Gomez's aid to embarrass the prosecution prior to trial was also considered. When Gomez was called to answer questions before Judge Bonaventure, he took the Fifth Amendment.

At the conclusion of a hearing in which several corrections officers were called to testify regarding Tabish's allegations, Judge Bonaventure found no evidence that prosecutors had planted Gomez in Tabish's cell and denied the defense motion to dismiss the charges.

"The defense has not met its burden," Bonaventure said. "The defense has shown this court supposition upon supposition and inference upon inference."

In February 2000, despite the fact that Judge Bonaventure had declared Sandy Murphy indigent, she moved into an expensive apartment at the exclusive Regency Towers at the Las Vegas Country Club. It was generally believed that Sandy's benefactor, William Fuller, was paying the bill, but there was also speculation that she was living off money that she had taken from Binion after his death.

Further investigation revealed that Murphy was once again in flagrant violation of the terms of her house arrest conditions and that she had lied to the authorities regarding her whereabouts. On February 17, 2000, she was observed at Walker Furniture Store picking out her new home's furnishings after she had told authorities that she was going to see her attorney. Employees placed her at the store on two occasions that day. She was also seen at a car dealership looking at a new Mercedes with Fuller.

Murphy had been seen at a number of locations around town while she was supposed to be under house arrest, but investigators with the house arrest program had not been able to confirm any of the sightings until they talked with the employees at the furniture store. Law enforcement officials viewed Murphy as having total disregard for the judicial system. "She lied to us," Sergeant Barry Payne, the officer in charge of the house arrest program, said. "We don't want to put her back in house arrest. She's really a challenge." It seemed like she thought she was entitled to do whatever she pleased, and that she was living in some kind of a dream state in not taking her predicament seriously.

Murphy was again placed in custody on March 16, 2000. This time Prosecutor David Roger was determined to keep her in jail pending the outcome of her trial. Judge Bonaventure had moved its beginning two weeks, to early March, after the defense attorneys insisted they needed time to address new charges involving Tabish's alleged plot to bribe alibi witnesses and to pay certain individuals to provide false testimony.

"If she violated house arrest, then she should remain in custody," Roger told a reporter for the Las Vegas *Sun*. "She's been given way too many chances."

"It is as though she does not comprehend the multiple life sentences that she's facing and that everyone else facing multiple life sentences are sitting in jail," Deputy District Attorney David Wall, who had been brought into the case as co-prosecutor with David Roger, told the judge.

Judge Bonaventure agreed, and ordered her held without bail until the outcome of the trial was determined. "The situation you now find yourself in is a result of your own doing, your own contemptuous actions," Bonaventure told Murphy.

Her attorney, John Momot, however, said that she was being discriminated against and picked on by authorities.

"To claim now on the eve of trial that you will somehow be prejudiced if you are in custody is without merit," Bonaventure said. Bonaventure, in his admonishment of Murphy, told her that she had repeatedly shown "disregard for the instructions of the judicial system."

"Now, the defendant must suffer the consequences during the remaining months of this litigation," David Roger said.

Two weeks before Southern Nevada's "Trial of the Century" was set to begin, authorities in Missoula, Montana, contacted Detective Buczek. Acting on a tip regarding silver coins, Montana lawmen were led to Dennis Rehbein, Tabish's brother-in-law. Confronted with information that they had received indicating he might be in possession of stolen property, Rehbein turned over more than one hundred pounds of silver coins, as well as Horseshoe gaming chips, to the Montana investigators. Through his lawyer, John E. Smith, Rehbein indicated that he wanted to cooperate with the Nevada investigators in return for immunity from prosecution.

Rehbein, 37, employed in his family's construction business, was described by his lawyer as a "law-abiding citizen" who wanted to tell the truth regarding his knowledge about the coins.

"He's stuck in the middle of this only because he accepted these coins from Rick Tabish," Smith said. Smith said that his client felt like he was a victim of circumstances. "This is very difficult for the family . . . there has never been any insinuation or belief expressed to me by anyone in law enforcement that Dennis Rehbein has done anything wrong."

Judge Bonaventure, after hearing the details about the coins, granted Rehbein immunity from prosecution and listed him as a material witness for the state's case against Tabish and Murphy. Buczek and Thowsen, joined later by co-prosecutor David Wall, flew to Montana to retrieve the coins and to interview Rehbein.

Rehbein told the detectives and Wall that he had a meeting with Tabish at MRT's Montana offices on November

1, 1998, at which time Tabish had asked him if he wanted to buy the coins. When Rehbein declined, Tabish then asked him for a $25,000 loan to help him pay for his legal defense. He said that Tabish, at one point, had shown him a list of coins. The list, the detectives learned, was the same seven-page list that Tanya Cropp had faxed to Montana, and which Metro's fingerprint expert Ed Guenther had found Murphy's and Tabish's fingerprints all over the original copy.

"With the trouble that Rick was in, I didn't really want these coins," Rehbein said. He said that some of the boxes containing the coins had sand in them. When he had asked Tabish about it, Tabish told him that it became necessary for him to bury the coins at a location near the Jean sand pit after his arrest for attempting to steal Binion's silver. Tabish, he said, had not wanted the coins in his possession after the trouble in Pahrump.

Rehbein said that he had loaned the $25,000 to Tabish, but when Tabish failed to repay the loan he accepted the coins as collateral. Rehbein told the investigators that Tabish had told him the coins were a payment from Binion for work that he had done for him.

Buczek, Thowsen, and Wall believed otherwise. They were convinced that the coins were the same ones that had been stolen from Ted Binion's safe, and were what one of Tabish's former employees had seen him loading into the back of a pickup truck the day after Binion's death. Although that employee had reported seeing plastic coin *cases*, the investigators now felt confident that the employee had witnessed the loading of the actual coins. The investigators packed up the silver coins and brought them back to Las Vegas to use as additional evidence against Tabish at trial. The question of what had happened to Binion's rare silver coins minted in Carson City, estimated at being worth $10 million to $15 million, remained a mystery.

On Tuesday, March 7, 2000, David Mattsen stood trial

in federal court on multiple charges of being an ex-felon in possession of firearms. It was a jury trial, held before U.S. District Judge Philip Pro.

During opening statements Mattsen's attorney, James "Bucky" Buchanan, said that his client never denied that the guns in question were in his home when police investigating the Binion case found them. He did, however, deny that he had ever used them or had any control over them.

"He didn't want them," Buchanan said. "He didn't care about them. They belonged to his boss." Buchanan stated that the only reason Mattsen was on trial for the weapons was because the prosecutors in the Binion case were trying to force him to testify against Rick Tabish and Sandra Murphy. A few weeks earlier he had offered to cooperate with prosecutors in that case in return for immunity from prosecution and for probation on the weapons charges, but the proposed deal had fallen apart during negotiations.

Buchanan said that when Mattsen had worked as Binion's ranch manager and was allowed to live on the ranch, Binion had owned numerous guns, anywhere from one hundred to two hundred, and kept them every place imaginable.

"None of them are my guns," Mattsen testified. "I never had possession of those guns."

Mattsen's wife, Thressa, testified that Binion frequently gave guns to her to take to the ranch house, and sometimes she stored them inside the mobile home where she and Mattsen lived on the ranch property. When Mattsen was arrested for the attempted silver theft in Pahrump, she said, she was given orders to move off the property. She said that friends had helped her hastily move out of the mobile home, and some of Binion's guns had been packed up and moved to their new home by mistake. When she learned of the mistake, she said that she took the guns and hid them in various locations in their bedroom. Terrified of guns after having once been shot in the head, she said that she wanted them kept out of sight.

The jury of seven men and five women acquitted Mattsen of all of the weapons charges after deliberating for ninety minutes. "I respect the jury's verdict," Assistant U.S. Attorney Thomas O'Connell said afterward. "Obviously, I'm a little surprised."

Mattsen's acquittal on the weapons charges ended one chapter of his ordeal, but he still faced trial in state court, along with Michael Milot, on charges stemming from the attempted theft of Binion's silver in Pahrump.

CHAPTER 22

On Monday, March 27, 2000, a long line of people filed through the metal detectors on the first floor of the Clark County Courthouse at Third Avenue and Carson Street in downtown Las Vegas to try claiming a seat in the Honorable Judge Joseph T. Bonaventure's courtroom. Sandra Murphy's and Rick Tabish's parents were there, as were several other relatives and friends of the two defendants. Several members of Ted Binion's family were also present. But mostly there were the curious trial watchers, people who knew neither the defendants nor the victim but who had been waiting for nearly a year and a half for Southern Nevada's "Trial of the Century" to begin. Court TV had its cameras set up in the courtroom, as did a local television station, so that the world could experience a courtroom drama that would ultimately play out better than a *Perry Mason* episode.

A native New Yorker, Judge Joseph T. Bonaventure was born in Queens. The son of a cab driver and a Garment District seamstress, Bonaventure was the youngest of eight children. Although noted for judicial fairness and a sense of humor, Bonaventure can exhibit a "wrath of God" manner at times inside his courtroom. The silver-haired jurist received both his undergraduate degree and his jurisprudence degree from the University of Arizona, and after graduation in 1967 moved to Los Angeles where he obtained his first job as a deputy probation officer. He moved to Las Vegas in 1970, and worked as an investigator for the Clark County District Attorney's office, after which he worked as a law clerk in the Eighth Judicial District Court. Before being elected a judge, he held the position of Chief Public Defender and worked in private practice in the areas of civil as well as criminal law. In 1978 he began a stint as a justice of the peace, and was elected a District Court Judge in 1989. Married and the father of two sons, Bonaventure is generally regarded as a no-nonsense judge who has presided over a number of high-profile murder cases. The Binion case became the biggest and most complex case of his career.

A hushed silence fell over the courtroom as corrections officers led Sandra Murphy and Rick Tabish in through a rear door. Allowed to wear civilian clothing without being handcuffed or shackled, Murphy somewhat pale, was dressed in a beige designer pantsuit and Tabish was wearing a navy coat and tie. They were seated on the left side of the courtroom with their attorneys, facing Judge Bonaventure. Murphy, though at first nervous, later began smiling frequently and appeared carefree, and at times jovial, as the day wore on. As with most of her prior court appearances, she appeared to possess a certain disregard for the proceedings, and just didn't quite seem to get it. Judging by her demeanor, Murphy might just as well have been attending a fashion show instead of fighting for her freedom and credibility in a court of law.

The jury selection process took barely two days. By late Wednesday afternoon, March 29, a jury of nine women and three men had been seated, with six alternates, out of a one hundred-person jury pool. The panel consisted of a retired aerospace company supervisor, a computer programmer, a lab technician, an administrative assistant, a pharmacist, a small business owner, an assistant in a finance firm, a software engineer, a housewife, a plumber, a wildlife biologist, and a retired medical assistant. It was as diverse and intelligent a jury as Clark County had seen in recent history, and both the prosecution and the defense teams were satisfied that they could be fair and open-minded in hearing the testimony, analyzing the evidence, and rendering a verdict in the biggest, most sensational murder trial that Las Vegas had ever seen.

Chief Deputy District Attorney David Roger, the lead

prosecutor, looked surprisingly refreshed and confident as he prepared to give his opening statement. With a large photograph of Ted Binion's corpse in the background, the slightly-built prosecutor faced the jury and told them in a soft, calm but authoritative voice that Ted Binion was a troubled man, a heroin addict who frequented topless bars, associated with reputed mobsters, and lost his gaming license due to his less-than-savory lifestyle. Roger also described how Binion's marriage ended in divorce, how he met Tabish and Murphy, and how Binion had even boasted to friends about beating Sandy.

"We're not about to paint a picture of a saint," Roger said. "However, he was a human being . . . [It wasn't] always a day at the beach living with a drug addict . . . but Sandra Murphy led a pretty good life when she lived with Ted Binion."

Roger described how Binion had purchased a Mercedes for Murphy, had provided her with thousands of dollars in cash, and had given her a MasterCard with a $10,000 limit for her day-to-day expenses. She also had a secretary who paid the bills for her. She lived a pampered life of luxury with Binion, Roger told the jury. He also countered defense claims that Binion had died from a self-induced drug overdose, either by accident or by suicide. He described Binion as an experienced drug user who smoked heroin because he knew that he wouldn't overdose by using that method, and cited a number of witnesses who would testify that he was not suicidal.

"Although Ted Binion was down, he was not out," Roger said. The prosecutor said that Binion was looking toward the future and had told others of the plans he was making to regain his gaming license. Instead, Roger said, the medical evidence suggested that Binion was drugged, restrained with handcuffs, and then suffocated with a hand or pillow in a method that Dr. Michael Baden would describe as "burking."

"Burking," it was pointed out, dated back to nineteenth

century Edinburgh, when a man named Burke, along with another man named Hare, would rob graves so they could sell the bodies for anatomical dissection. Desiring to make their work easier, the two eventually resorted to getting an individual drunk, after which Burke would sit on the victim's chest to inhibit his ability to breathe while at the same time covering the victim's mouth and nose, ending with the death by suffocation. Hence the term "burking."

In his portrayal of Tabish and Murphy, Roger said that they, too, were looking toward the future, but it was a future without Ted Binion. Although Sandra Murphy had everything that a person could want, it still wasn't enough for her and she engaged in a romantic affair with Tabish. Roger described Tabish as a businessman with financial problems who chose to ignore the wife and children he'd left behind in Montana to carry on the affair with Murphy. On a weekend that he'd promised to visit his family, Roger said, Tabish instead chose to run off to Beverly Hills with Murphy for a romantic tryst at a posh hotel.

"I want you to remember two words," Roger said. "Witness manipulation." It was an obvious reference to Tabish's attempts to bribe witnesses to provide false testimony on his behalf.

"Ted Binion was murdered for lust, murdered for greed, by someone he trusted and her new companion," Roger said.

Murphy's attorney, John Momet, countered Roger's remarks during his opening statement by telling the jurors that Sandy Murphy and Rick Tabish were on trial not because they had murdered Ted Binion but because the powerful Binion family had hired a private investigator who took a simple case of drug overdose and twisted the facts to make it look like a homicide.

"Why?" Momet asked. "Because Sandy was not a Binion, that's why."

For the first time, Momet acknowledged that Murphy

and Tabish were having an affair, but he insisted that that had no basis in determining their guilt.

"It existed. So what? Is that against the law?" Momet asked. "If you don't take care of your woman, someone else will. That's what happens when you love drugs more than your woman."

Momet argued that Binion's death was not a result of murder, but of his long-term addiction to heroin. Referring several times to the "Binion money machine," Momet told the jury that Binion's family would point the finger of blame on Murphy and Tabish, "But where were they [his family], with all that drug addiction?" he asked.

Momet portrayed Murphy as a "nice young woman" who had become dazzled and overwhelmed with Binion's wealth, who fell in love with the casino scion who also happened to be an abusive drug addict. While the Binion family bickered among themselves over money, Momet said, Murphy was there, taking care of Ted, cleaning his vomit off the floor, caring for his daughter, Bonnie. Pointing toward the prosecution's photo of a dead, partially clad Ted Binion, Momet told the jury that that was how Ted Binion looked as a result of his addiction.

"That's how he walked around [in his underwear]," Momet said. "That's how he lived . . . this case is not about homicide. It's about heroin . . . Sandy Murphy didn't get the heroin. Sandy Murphy didn't get the Xanax prescription."

Tabish's attorney, Louis Palazzo, told the jury that his client was simply following Ted Binion's orders when he dug up the silver from the vault in Pahrump. He described the single silver dollar that had been left in the vault, and said that it supported Tabish's statements to police in which he had compared the single silver dollar to putting a small amount of money inside a new wallet for luck, which is what he claimed that Ted had instructed him to do. While it didn't make much sense to those hearing the account of why the lone silver dollar had been left behind, Palazzo

was insistent that those were Ted's instructions. He said
that one of Binion's lawyers, Tom Standish, corroborated
that arrangement in an interview conducted by Tom Dillard.

"It's like a superstition," Palazzo said. "Ted told him to
do it." He said the only thing Tabish was guilty of was
being "felony stupid" for going to Pahrump to unearth the
silver, and nothing more.

One by one over the next several weeks, the witnesses
were called to the stand and they told the jurors the same
things that they had told the detectives and private investigators during the course of the investigation. Doris Binion, James Brown, Deanna Perry, Kurt Gratzer, crime scene
analyst Mike Perkins, Tanya Cropp, Jason Frazier, Dr. Michael Baden, Dennis Rehbein, Nye County sheriff's deputies, and so forth, each took the stand and provided
damning testimony to the jury. At one point Sandy Murphy's interview at the hospital with Detective Mitchell was
played, and because of all of her sobbing it quickly became
known as her "boo-hoo" interview. Her emotional displays
were considered by many, including medical personnel, to
have been an act.

At varying points throughout the trial, the defense presented expert medical witnesses whose testimony made a
strong case that often countered the testimony of Dr. Baden,
who had maintained that Binion was suffocated. One of
those witnesses was Dr. Cyril Wecht, a forensic pathologist
who had worked on a number of high-profile cases including JFK's assassination, Elvis Presley's death, and the
JonBenét Ramsey case, among others. Wecht testified that
it was his opinion that Ted Binion had died of a drug overdose, and that he had not seen any evidence of homicidal
suffocation. In fact, he testified that he thought Binion's
death was a suicide but might reconsider that opinion if
additional information were to be supplied to him.

"I do not find any evidence to support the contention
that he was suffocated," Wecht wrote for the defense in a
pathological report that was admitted into evidence. "I be-

lieve that Mr. Binion initially inhaled heroin smoke, as he had in the past, and this led to thoughts of suicide."

The defense also presented testimony from another forensic pathologist, Dr. Robert Bucklin, who opined that the marks and abrasions around Binion's mouth were not caused by trauma, as the prosecution contended, but by new beard growth. Bucklin also said that he didn't find any petechial hemorrhaging in Binion's eyes to suggest death by suffocation, and that the abrasions on Binion's wrists were not consistent with the use of handcuffs. It was his opinion that the drugs found in Binion's body were sufficient to kill him, and he subscribed to Dr. Lary Simms's original finding of an "undetermined" death, citing that there was insufficient evidence to show whether Binion's death was a result of accidental drug overdose or suicide.

Yet another forensic pathologist, Dr. Jack Snyder, testified that Binion died of a "triple whammy" of Xanax, Valium, and heroin. He said that he could not find the petechiae in Binion's eyes that Dr. Baden had found, and instead opined that what was being looked at as petechial hemorrhaging was in fact vascular congestion indicative of death by an overdose of drugs. Snyder claimed that Dr. Baden was "behind the times" in his findings, and said that he found no indications of foul play. Snyder believed the marks on Binion's body were caused after death, most likely by the paramedics who had moved Binion's body while transporting it to the morgue.

When Leo Casey was called to testify, the prosecutors painted a picture of how Rick Tabish had kidnapped and tortured him to coerce him to sign over his rights to the Jean sand pit. The defense, on the other hand, called Casey a liar, an embezzler, and a man who cheated on his taxes, and ridiculed the allegations that he had previously made to the police about Tabish.

"Did you at any time shout to the lawyer, 'I was beaten, this is all under duress, I didn't take anything from the company, it's all a big mistake'?" Palazzo asked.

"Like I've told you several times, I wasn't shouting to nobody," Casey replied. "My life was threatened."

When questioned further, Casey admitted that his financial dealings with John Joseph's company appeared shady on the surface, but insisted that they were carried out at Joseph's direction as part of a secret agreement. Casey also admitted that he had not paid taxes for several years.

"Do you have a secret agreement with the IRS?" Palazzo asked.

At one point Palazzo told the judge that he wanted to attempt to re-create the telephone book beating allegedly committed against Casey. He asked Judge Bonaventure for permission to beat Tabish over the head with a phone book.

"You want to beat the hell out of your client now?" Bonaventure asked, somewhat stunned by Palazzo's unusual request.

"As hard as I can," Palazzo replied.

"I heard you were a hard-charging attorney, but not a hard-hitting attorney, Mr. Palazzo," Bonaventure said, laughing.

Palazzo's argument was that if Casey had been beaten as hard as he had told the police he was, there would be telltale signs of the beating such as bruising and bleeding.

"There was nothing to indicate that there was evidence of a beating whatsoever," Palazzo said.

"What is happening to this case, Judge," interjected Roger, "is that it is turning into a circus, a Hollywood drama."

Bonaventure apparently agreed, and denied Palazzo's request to beat Tabish in court.

"I can't allow it," Bonaventure said. "We've had nice control over this case, and we're not about to lose it now."

And on it went. Each day brought forth shocking testimony from the prosecution witnesses who told the jury what they had told the investigators months earlier, and each day the defense lawyers did their best to counter the prosecution's theory that Binion was murdered. Following seven weeks of testimony from nearly 150 witnesses, 89 of whom were called for the prosecution, and voluminous circumstantial evidence, both sides were ready to present their closing arguments.

"I suppose the inference that the defense wants you to draw was that Ted Binion wasn't worth your time as a jury and you shouldn't find the defendants guilty of murder," David Roger said. "Ladies and gentlemen, Ted Binion, for whatever he was, was entitled to the same rights as these defendants here in court."

"It is the state of Nevada's theory," Roger continued, "that Ted Binion was given a cocktail by his killers." He suggested that at least a portion of the drugs found in Binion's body were placed into one of his drinks covertly, after which Murphy and Tabish waited for the drugs to take effect. But, he said, they made "a major 'oops.' They called off the maid but forgot the gardener." Roger said that because of Tom Loveday's unexpected arrival, Murphy and Tabish had been forced to accelerate Binion's death by sitting on his chest to keep his lungs deflated and by holding a hand or a pillow over his face.

Roger played portions of the twenty-minute video that Murphy had directed attorney William Knudson to make the day after Binion's death, which showed her pick up a wine glass and appear to place it in her purse or shoulder bag. He also described how he believed that Murphy and Tabish had staged Binion's death scene by leaving an empty bottle of Xanax by his body and placing Binion on the floor in a mortuary pose. He described how he believed the killers had ransacked Binion's house and had emptied his safe of everything except for a single dime after his death, and how Rick Tabish was arrested in Pahrump less than two days later after cleaning out his underground vault of everything except a single silver dollar.

"It's arrogance when you kill someone and you then leave behind clues to that crime," Roger said.

Roger also attempted to diminish the defense position

that Binion had been suicidal by saying that all of the people who testified to knowing Ted Binion knew him better than any of the defense's expert medical witnesses. In one instance, said Roger, Binion had threatened suicide in order to get his wife, Doris, to come back to him.

"The only time he spoke of suicide was when he was manipulating his wife to come home," Roger said. He further stated that the defense team likely would not have been so quick to attack Binion's character if he had truly died of suicide.

"If he committed suicide," Roger continued, "then why talk about what a rotten person Ted Binion was? If he committed an accidental overdose, then why commit this character assassination and ask his former wife about how rotten he was, asking the maid if she has seen domestic violence? Ted Binion was a human being, he was a father and a brother, and that's all that matters . . . It is the state's position that the motive for the murder of Ted Binion was to obtain money for the Jean sand pit . . . [The defendants] did it for greed, they did it for lust, they did it for money . . . The evidence proved beyond a reasonable doubt that the killers in this case are the two people he trusted, the two people who had a secret affair behind Ted Binion's back, the two people who talked about killing Ted Binion [to others], the two people who betrayed Ted Binion, who stole everything Ted Binion had, including his life."

"Money, love, greed, lust. All classic motives for murder," co-prosecutor David Wall said in his closing argument. Wall described the deteriorating relationship between Murphy and Binion when Rick Tabish walked into Murphy's life. He charged that Murphy couldn't just leave Binion and make public her affair with Tabish, or she would risk losing everything. "If Ted Binion was going to find out," Wall continued, "he was going to kick her out. She wouldn't have the money, and I suspect that Rick Tabish wouldn't want her either."

It was under that premise, said Wall, that Murphy and

Tabish hatched the plot together to kill Binion and make it seem like a drug overdose or suicide.

"It doesn't matter who suffocated him," Wall said. "It doesn't matter who poured the drugs down him. They are both responsible."

Wall said that it was preposterous to believe that Tabish had taken Binion's silver in Pahrump for Bonnie, as his attorney had portrayed. "Think about the absurdity of that," Wall said. "Rick Tabish hardly knew Bonnie Binion. He's having an affair with Sandy Murphy, who hates Bonnie Binion."

Wall placed a large chart in front of the jury that listed all of the prosecution's witnesses. At the top of the chart it read: MUST ALL BE LYING OR MISTAKEN? He told the jury that the defense would have them believe that the state's case against Murphy and Tabish was a big plot perpetrated by the "Binion money machine."

"I guess all those people," Wall said, pointing to the chart, "were influenced by the 'Binion money machine' and are lying. They don't know each other. Leo Casey doesn't know Deanna Perry, who doesn't know Michael Wells . . . The 'Binion money machine' working to frame Rick Tabish and Sandra Murphy . . . if this case didn't involve a murder, the irony would be laughable, because it's the Binion money that these two wanted more than anything else. It's the whole purpose for all of these crimes . . . it was the money that drove Sandy Murphy . . , it drove both of them . . . Now look the defendant Sandy Murphy and the defendant Rick Tabish in the eye and say they are guilty of the offenses."

"The true fact is Sandy Murphy did not kill Ted Binion," John Momet countered during his closing argument. "But the sad fact is that Ted Binion did die of a conspiracy, and it was a conspiracy between himself and heroin . . . you have to have the strength of Hercules to deal with this [heroin addiction] on a day-to-day basis. She loves him, and he loves heroin."

Momet charged that the "Binion money machine" tried to "grind this woman up" in pointing the finger at her in Binion's death.

"They humiliated her, they mocked her, and they pushed her around, up to and including today," Momet charged. They even kicked her out of her house where she had lived for three years, said Momet, with only the clothes on her back.

But, Momet insisted, it was Binion's own addiction to heroin, a "curse," that had brought about his demise.

"He had a gaming license, he came from a famous and wealthy family . . . But Ted Binion couldn't stop using heroin . . . everybody here, including the state, is in denial about that," Momet said. "I don't want to let Ted Binion's addiction destroy Sandy Murphy."

Palazzo, in his closing argument, blamed the "Binion money machine" for bringing private investigator Tom Dillard into what he portrayed as a deceitful investigation in which Dillard was not restrained by having to obtain search warrants or the use of other legal standards.

"He was just on his own with no oversight," Palazzo charged. "It's like being in Nazi Germany."

Palazzo also pointed toward Peter Sheridan, who had supplied Ted Binion with heroin, and how Sheridan was never charged with a crime despite the fact that he had not been provided immunity from prosecution.

"How about having the benefit of a confession from Peter Sheridan?" Palazzo stated. "Doesn't that stink?

"Heroin junkies overdose all the time," Palazzo said. "This is probably just drawing more attention because it is Ted Binion . . . There is no evidence at all that Rick Tabish was present at the scene on September 17, 1998 . . . I would just urge you to spend time examining the evidence. We are entitled to the benefit of the doubt . . . you promised me at the early part of the case that you would be able to look the state in the eye and tell them that they didn't prove the case."

During his rebuttal, co-prosecutor David Wall outlined the circumstantial evidence that placed Rick Tabish at the scene of Binion's murder. Wall said that Sandy Murphy's telephone calls to Rick Tabish suddenly ceased on September 17, 1998. He said that on nearly every other day of that month, Murphy had called Tabish, sometimes up to thirty-one times a day, even when he was in Montana visiting his family.

"Even a schoolgirl doesn't do that," Wall said sarcastically. "The only time she doesn't call him is when she's with him."

Wall also pointed out for the jury's benefit the statements that Tabish was said to have made to Nye County authorities that he had been at Binion's home the day that he died. In his official statement Tabish had said that he was at Binion's home the day prior to his death. However, Nye County deputies had indicated that Tabish had also stated that he was at Binion's home on September 17, 1998. He also pointed out how Tabish had given over a hundred pounds of Binion's silver coins to his brother-in-law, Dennis Rehbein, as collateral for a $25,000 loan, and how Tabish had made plans to purchase an alibi. He also pointed to the fact that Sandy Murphy had claimed that she had left her purse in Tabish's car on the day of Binion's death. The evidence, taken as a whole, said Wall, pointed to Tabish being at Binion's home the day of the murder. Wall characterized Murphy and Tabish as liars and manipulators, whose primary interest was in obtaining Ted Binion's money and valuables.

"Ted Binion was [Murphy's] human ATM machine," Wall said. "No more sex . . . she saved that for her new lover . . . [Their] capacity for greed and deception is eclipsed only by their ability to blame everyone else."

The jury was charged with its obligations on May 10, 2000, and they began their deliberations. It was anyone's guess as to how long it would take them to decide Murphy and

Tabish's fate as one day turned into another. A few days into their deliberations, the jury asked to view Ted Binion's maid's testimony again, and at another point the jury foreman sent a note to Judge Bonaventure through the bailiff that they were making progress in the deliberations and were moving toward reaching a verdict. While the jury was out, it was reported that Sandy Murphy had begun making plans to have her hair done upon her acquittal so that she and Tabish could go out to dinner together afterward.

Rumors began circulating by Friday afternoon, May 19, 2000, after eight days of grueling deliberations, that the jury was getting closer to reaching a verdict. The rumor quickly brought news media from all over to the downtown courthouse, including Court TV. While waiting to see if the jury was actually coming back into the courtroom with their verdict, Court TV interviewed Nick Behnen, Ted Binion's brother-in-law. Among other things, Behnen voiced his feelings about Sandy Murphy and provided an interesting characterization of the accused murderer.

"Sandy was like a rabid dog on certain days," Behnen said. "You had to know her. On days when she was having a bad day, when I would call Ted or Ted would call me, she would put the phone down or tear it out of the wall and do all kinds of disparaging things."

According to what Behnen said to Court TV, Binion had told him basically the same thing that he had told James Brown, namely that "if I'm not alive this weekend, then Sandy killed me." He said that there was a lot of fear in Binion's voice the last time that they had spoken which had been on the night of September 16, at about 10:30 p.m.

"Ted is yelling over the phone, 'Nick, Nick, Nick,' and then the phone went dead," Behnen said. The phone had gone dead before, Behnen said, usually when Ted and Sandy had been "squabbling," when she would rip the phone out of the wall or hang up on him. He assumed that Sandy was home and they were fighting again. He said that he tried calling back about five or six times, but no one answered the phone that evening. Even though the information was available to the police, Behnen noted he was never asked about that conversation by anyone even though it corroborated James Brown's statements to investigators. He wasn't called to testify at the trial.

Behnen claimed that he had asked Binion to come to his and Becky's house, or even check into a hotel for the night. Binion had told him that he couldn't do that. He said that he couldn't leave the house, probably, Behnen speculated, because there was a lot of money inside the house and Sandy may have known where it was.

According to Behnen, Sandy called his home at about 1:30 a.m. on September 17, and spoke to Behnen's younger son, Jack. He said that she had asked Jack, "Is your father coming over this evening?" Jack had responded, "No, my dad is asleep." Behnen said that he wasn't informed of the phone call until the following day.

When one of the Court TV reporters asked him if there was anything else he knew that could have helped the prosecution, Behnen responded, "Yes. A scorcher, really."

Behnen said that although no one paid much attention to it, David Mattsen had told him in front of a reporter for the Las Vegas *Sun* that he was present at Binion's home when Ted was handcuffed. This would have been late on the night of September 16 or very early on the morning of September 17. He said Mattsen had related how Tabish had picked up Binion and had thrown him down on the floor, effectively knocking the wind out of him. Sandy then picked up the pair of handcuffs, according to what Mattsen had told Behnen and clasped them on Binion. The cuffs were the type that might be purchased at a porno shop, and they had rhinestones on them, which might account for the indentations and abrasions on Binion's wrists. At another point, said Behnen, Sandy picked up a gun and shoved it into Mattsen's face, threatening to kill his wife if he didn't leave right then and keep quiet about what he'd seen.

Ted, said Behnen, then begged Mattsen not to leave. After Mattsen went home, he called Binion's house several times that night and begged Tabish and Murphy not to kill Ted. The next morning, Behnen said Mattsen told him that he called and asked what had happened. Tabish purportedly said, "It's all over."

Later that day, according to Behnen, Mattsen met Tabish on Highway 160 at the top of the hill between Las Vegas and Pahrump. There was another man in the car with Tabish, who Tabish claimed was his alibi. When Tabish got into the car with Mattsen, he purportedly related to him some of the details of what had òccurred, even to the point of relating that Ted had said to Sandy, "Shoot Rick and I will give you a million dollars." Sandy had purportedly responded, "I can't do that, but I will do something else." She then had sex with Tabish in front of Binion.

Although it had been a shocking account of the supposed turn of events, Prosecutor David Roger later said that it couldn't have happened. There was a problem with the timeline surrounding Mattsen's claims.

"After hearing that David Mattsen told people that Binion was restrained with handcuffs on September 16, 1998, I knew that Mattsen was providing false information," Roger said. "Numerous witnesses saw Ted Binion on the evening of September 16, 1998 . . . and in the early morning hours of September 17, 1998 . . . common sense suggests that Binion's killers would not release Binion to allow him to go to the grocery store and then recapture him for the purpose of killing him."

Roger said that he intended to take statements from everyone who had spoken to Mattsen about the matter, but because of the large holes in Mattsen's story he wasn't considering it a priority.

It turned out that the rumors about the jury being ready to return a verdict were true. At about 4:30 p.m. they returned to Judge Bonaventure's courtroom and announced that they had rendered a verdict after eight long days of deliberations.

As they filed in and took their seats in the jury box, four
of them were wearing sunglasses, presumably because they
didn't want the defendants to see their eyes. Their verdict
came as a shock and a surprise to many, and as a relief to
others. They had found Tabish and Murphy guilty on all
counts. Although Tabish hung his head when the verdicts
were being read, neither he nor Murphy showed much emotion at the outcome.

Following the verdicts, the jury was thrust into the penalty phase of the trial. They faced the decision of sentencing
Tabish and Murphy to life in prison without parole, or to
life in prison with the possibility of parole. Prior to its beginning the difficult task. Murphy and Tabish were each
afforded the opportunity of making statements to the jury.

Tabish took the stand first and provided the following
unsworn statement:

"It's hard. It's hard on everybody. There's been so many
things that needed to come out, and I just can't talk," Tabish said.

"My heart's out to the Binion family, I mean that sin-
cerely," he continued. "I can look everybody in that front
row in the eye and tell you I am sorry. And please take
that from my heart because that's where it's coming from.

"I hope someday something can get rectified. The prosecution did their job. They put on a case. I'm not supposed
to talk about the case so I won't go there. . . . I know you
guys [the jury] had a big burden, and you did what you
had to do based on the evidence presented to you, and I
applaud you.

"Let's talk about who Rick Tabish is. Twenty months
have gone by. There's been a lot about Rick Tabish. Let
me tell you who I am. I'm proud of who I am. . . . I was
an overachiever. I should have listened to my father. He
told me all the time, learn how to walk before you run,
Rick. I never listened. I should have listened to my father.
I wouldn't be sitting here today.

"Old school has ruined me, because a handshake and

loyalty doesn't work anymore. It hasn't worked for me. Every time I've been in trouble . . . I've had trouble associating with my generation because they don't have oldschool values. Hit hard, run fast. I'm not about that.

"I'm not perfect by all means. I'm not standing here saying I'm perfect. I've made my mistakes. I've made my mistakes in this situation. . . . I have no real regrets about anything I did except getting involved in this situation. My heart's broke because everybody else is destroyed. If I could go spend the rest of my life in prison, or if I could give my life so that my mother, my two brothers that sat up here crying, could live their lives without knowing that their brother is going to prison for the rest of his life, I would do it. I'm not that selfish of a man.

"For every time I held my head up, for every time I smiled in this court, for every time I smiled for a news camera, for every bit of cocky attitude I had during this case, I'm ashamed of myself. I'm disgusted.

"I had the attitude nothing was good enough, and when the verdict came back, it was good enough. Everybody's worked for me. I've taken advantage of everybody's hard work. And I'm sorry, but in return what I have to say is I'm proud of who I am. You guys have returned a verdict on me, that's your decision. I'm going to live with that decision. I'm man enough to live with that decision.

"Some of the greatest lessons in life are hardship. . . . You don't learn until your hands are slapped," Tabish concluded.

When Rick Tabish stepped down from the witness stand, Sandra Murphy took his place and provided her statement often crying and sniveling as she read from handwritten notes. It was difficult to determine if the tears were for the victim and his family, or for herself.

"Hi, my name is Sandy Murphy, and I know you haven't had a chance to hear from me yet. But I've been very anxious to share the truth—the truth about what happened to Teddy. Regretfully, I did not testify, but now I can see that was a mistake. But instead of looking at what could have been, I can only look at what will be.

"So this will be the first and final time we get to know each other. I respect and sympathize with each and every one of you for the awesome task you have before you. As I look about the room today I see pain and suffering all around me. Bonnie for the loss of her father, Becky, Brenda, and Jack for the loss of their brother, the Fechsers and all the family and friends that were touched by Teddy's life. For the Tabish family, who have also suffered the loss of a son, a husband, a brother, and an uncle, and for Amanda and Kyle for the loss of their father. For my family, for my parents and my brothers and sisters, [crying and unintelligible] niece and a godmother, and for Tony and Ryan and the loss of their Aunty Sandy.

"For my friend, Rick Tabish, who whenever I called was always there, who stood by my side when no one did and who believed in me and was always there to lend a helping hand or an ear to listen to. For the life that he's lost and the one that will never come.

"For my loss, for the loss of my Teddy 'Ruxpin.' He was the man that swept me off my feet. I thought he was my fix-it man. I thought he would fill the hole in my heart. I thought he would always love and protect me. He bought me a wedding band, and the inscription read: 'With undying love, Teddy.' I miss the early mornings when he would wake me up to watch the sunrise, to play ball with Princess and take [unintelligible, crying and sniveling] and see the birds in the morning. The first thing that Teddy taught me was how to ride horses. We used to go to the farm in Pahrump and ride at sundown. We would watch countless hours of History, A&E, and Discovery Channel. He was like a sponge for knowledge. I miss the flowers that we would plant in the garden together on special days, all the romantic nights in front of the fireplace in our bedroom. I miss the talks on our bench under the tree that made heart-shaped leaves. Teddy was the kind of guy that had this smile, and no matter what he did or how angry you were at him, all he had to do was bat his eyes and smile. He always had me right where he wanted me. But most of all I miss his face, I miss his voice, and I miss his touch.

"I have loved and lost, but I have learned to just take the good memories and go on. I know you heard some ugly things about Teddy during these proceedings, but that was Teddy the heroin addict. There are trials and tribulations in every relationship, and sometimes we get lost and go astray, but that doesn't mean that we love each other any less. I love Teddy with all my heart, and I know he loves me just as much. You may have taken away my freedom, but no matter what goes on in these proceedings, or what anybody ever says about us, you can never take away the love we had for each other.

"I am so sad for all my hopes and dreams, for the family I will never have, the wedding that will never be, and my children that will never come. Last night I lay in bed thinking of what I wanted to say here today, and there was one thing that stuck out in my mind. There was something that I need to do for me. I want to say that I'm sorry to the Binion family, but most of all I'm sorry to Bonnie, and I'm sorry for the day I walked out that door on September 17th and left him there alone. And I'm sorry today for not being there when he needed me the most. And I'm sorry . . . Thank you."

On Wednesday, May 24, 2000, the jury that convicted Murphy and Tabish of murdering Ted Binion felt that there was a chance of rehabilitation for the two killers and recommended that they be sentenced to life in prison with the possibility of parole after serving twenty years. Judge Bonaventure set a formal sentencing date of September 15, 2000, to allow time for officials to submit a pre-sentence investigation (PSI) report.

The case of Sandra Murphy and Rick Tabish, however, was not over. Rick Tabish dismissed Louis Palazzo as his attorney and hired William Terry, claiming that Palazzo had provided ineffective counsel. Afterward, Terry and John Momet raised several issues that they felt warranted a new trial. Among the issues they brought to Judge Bonaventure's attention were: that Tabish and Murphy should have been tried separately; that the court erred by not requiring the jury to return a unanimous verdict; that there was insufficient evidence for the jury to have convicted the defendants on the crimes; ineffective counsel from Louis Palazzo; that so-called "Massiah" violations occurred prior to trial; that the state withheld exculpatory information in connection with FBI reports which showed that a possible hit was placed on Binion's life by mobsters; juror misconduct in that one juror had carried an electronic "Palm Pilot" with him to court and in the jury deliberation room; juror misconduct in that one juror said that she had initially voted not guilty but changed her verdict to guilty after hearing the term "depraved indifference" being discussed by other jurors in which, she said, it was pointed out to her that the defendants were guilty of murder if they just sat back and did nothing as another person died; that the group of jurors had a monetary interest in the case, as one of the jurors had discussed writing a book with a dental hygienist–turned–author and later, after trial, persuaded several other jurors to join in on the endeavor; that the jury had been influenced by the media by seeing a headline that state witness Kurt Gratzer had been arrested during the trial; that it was improper for the court to make photocopies of specific jury instructions at the jury's request without first consulting with the attorneys which, the attorneys contended, might have caused the jury to place more weight on the portions of the instructions that had been copied; that possible communication between the jury and a bailiff concerning the well-being of the jury was improper; that there was racial coercion among the jurors because one juror had asked another how she felt about being the token black person on the jury; that one of the jurors carried typewritten documents into the jury room that he had created on his computer at home; and that certain handwritten documents created by jurors contained errors that were prejudicial to the defendants. It was quite a list, enough to persuade Bonaventure to hold an evidentiary hearing to determine if there were sufficient grounds for a new trial.

The evidentiary hearing occurred in August 2000 over a period of four days. All twelve jurors were subpoenaed and brought back into the courtroom, this time to provide sworn testimony regarding all of the aforementioned issues. The attorneys were given stern warnings that under Nevada law they could not delve into areas that would force the jurors to reveal their thought processes during the deliberations process. After each juror answered the questions posed to him or her, Bonaventure released them "forever" from having to come forward again regarding the Binion trial.

FBI Special Agent Charles Maurer also testified regarding the exculpatory evidence that the defense attorneys alleged had been withheld from them regarding possible underworld hits on Binion's life. The report in question turned out to be the one in which Antone Davi had provided a statement to investigators regarding Herbie Blitzstein's murder and had provided information regarding the possible hit that had been planned against Ted Binion. It was shown that the report was available to any law enforcement agency that wanted it, as well as to the defense attorneys had they requested it. It was also pointed out that members of the defense team should have known the information since both Momet and Palazzo had represented certain aspects surrounding Blitzstein and the investigation into his murder.

When all was said and done, the evidentiary hearing failed to provide any relief for Murphy and Tabish, and was perceived by some as being an assault on the jury and the legal system in general. The most significant aspect of the hearing was that it preserved for the record a number of issues that will likely be filed in Murphy and Tabish's appeals to the Nevada Supreme Court and/or U.S. appellate courts.

On Friday, September 8, 2000, Judge Bonaventure denied all of the defense motions for a new trial, except for the issue of ineffective counsel regarding attorney Louis Palazzo, which had become moot after having been withdrawn prior to Bonaventure's decision.

CHAPTER 23

When Sandy Murphy and Rick Tabish entered Judge Joseph Bonaventure's courtroom through the rear door again on Friday, September 15, 2000, each was again dressed in the drab blue jail clothing that they had worn to court during pre-trial proceedings. They were also shackled, with their hands chained to their sides. Murphy looked haggard and worried, and appeared as if she had aged a good ten years since she first gained the community's, as well as the world's, attention nearly two years earlier. Gone were the smiles, the designer clothes, and the makeup, and the roots of her hair now clearly displayed that she was really a brunette. She was off to the big house, but she wouldn't be going far. She would soon be taking up residence at the women's prison in North Las Vegas. Tabish, on the other hand, would be going to the state prison system, likely the maximum security prison in Ely, located in the middle of the desert in White Pine County. Although each had stated that they were looking forward to getting on with their lives, neither looked like they really meant it. Before imposing sentence, Bonaventure gave Tabish and Murphy the opportunity to make statements.

Tabish stood up and addressed the court, stating that he regretted not testifying on his own behalf at the trial in May. "I pray to God that I get a new trial," he said, indicating that he would testify before a jury if a new trial was granted as a result of appeals. While Tabish announced that he took responsibility for his previous crimes, he never held himself accountable for Ted Binion's murder or the crimes associated with it. Instead, he portrayed himself as a friend of Binion's.

"Teddy was a friend of mine," Tabish said. "I'm the guy that he cried to, the guy that he told his problems to."

Tabish also denied trying to steal Binion's silver, saying that he didn't need it. He said that he had a number of friends and business associates who would have helped him overcome his financial troubles, and he could have easily sold off his equipment to solve some of his problems.

Because of the jury's determination, both Tabish and Murphy knew that they were going to be sentenced to life in prison with the possibility of parole. However, each also faced numerous additional years for their convictions on the other counts. Tabish, as well as his attorney, Bill Terry, made a plea for leniency in urging the judge not to tack on additional years. In that regard, Tabish provided a packet of photos of his children in an attempt to sway the judge in his favor.

"I want my parents to hold their heads up," Tabish said. "I want everybody who knows Rick Tabish to hold their heads up, because this is a good day. We're moving on. I accept my punishment for twenty years. I'm not telling you I am a victim."

When it was Sandra Murphy's turn to speak, she was nervous and hesitant at first, as she apparently tried to decide whether to read from a prepared statement or just to say what was on her mind. She opted for the latter and, as was her custom, she cried and wiped tears from her eyes throughout much of her statement.

Murphy denied killing Binion, and refuted the prosecution's contention that she was with Binion only for his money. She described in detail how she had met and fallen in love with Binion, and recounted many of the things, such as fishing, that they used to do together. She said that she didn't ask Binion for money or expensive clothes, but she bought the expensive items that she became known for because he told her to.

"I'm a bad person because I did that?" Murphy asked.

She went on to say that she did not strive for greater things in life, that she did not want to be a doctor, lawyer, or judge. Instead, she said, she wanted to be like her stepmother, and that was her dream, as simple as it was. She compared herself to her stepmother by relating how she had cared for Binion by cooking for him, turning down his bed at night, trimming his toenails and fingernails, and cutting his hair.

"I just wanted to be what my mom was," Murphy said. "I loved doing it, and that was all I really wanted to do, was have a family."

In an attempt to explain her foul-mouthed, materialistic behavior on the videotape made of Binion's home the day after his death, Murphy said that her grief had turned to anger because she believed Binion's estate was stealing from her.

"I took a couple of his Xanax and drank a couple of glasses of wine," she said. "I was angry. I was furious that they were in my house, stealing my things." She never mentioned taking the wine glass with her.

"I don't think I should even be here to begin with," Murphy stated. "I have never hurt or stolen anything from anyone in my entire life, and I never will. No matter what happens here, I'll get along ... I believe I was wrongly convicted. I loved Teddy very much and I would never hurt him."

At the conclusion of Murphy's statement, Judge Bonaventure shuffled through a stack of papers. As he meted out Murphy and Tabish's sentences, he also delivered the following powerful admonishment to the two convicts:

"This is the time set for entry of judgment and imposition of sentences as to Sandra Murphy and Rick Tabish," Bonaventure said. "Here it is, almost two years to the day of Mr. Binion's murder, and we all wish we were not here today. Unfortunately due to the cowardly acts of the two defendants, we are. The many lives they have ruined will never be the same.

"As I indicated, on behalf of the victims in this case, the court has received letters from Leo Casey, Jack Binion, and Bonnie Binion. Leo Casey writes this court that he is sixty-five years old and has had everything he owned stolen from him by Rick Tabish. In addition, he suffers from severe neck pain, blurred vision, and chronic fatigue due to the beating he suffered at the hands of Mr. Tabish. He states that Mr. Tabish has ruined his life and that Rick Tabish is a vicious hardened criminal hoodlum thug, hell-bent on crime. He asks for justice.

"In a heart-wrenching letter to this court, Bonnie Binion tries to explain the unforgivable harm that has been done to her, a harm which can never be undone. She asks how the knowledge of these horrific events can ever fully leave her. The court can do many things. Unfortunately it cannot heal Bonnie's hurt, for the images she has of her father's murder will permeate every aspect of her young life; indeed, she writes, her past and future relationships are marred forever. Mr. Tabish and Ms. Murphy, by murdering this young lady's father you forever stole her innocence and peace of mind. Bonnie Binion asks for justice.

"The greatest injustice to Bonnie Binion is that this court, in doling out justice, cannot bring back her father. Ms. Binion writes that her health as well as her schooling has suffered from the acts of the defendants, and she has expressed such sadness, forever living with the notion that she will never have an adult relationship with her father. This court realizes that her pain must be indescribable, one that others who have never known it cannot fully understand.

"The jury has spoken in regard to Ted Binion's murder and has sentenced the defendants to life in prison with the possibility of parole after twenty years. Most disheartening to this court, Bonnie Binion writes that she is forever haunted by the unbearable weight this horrible tragedy has left with her. This court asks that Bonnie accept that none of us can help the things that life has done to us, and to not let your grief and pain harden your heart and steal your soul forever. If you allow that to happen, the defendants will have succeeded in also taking your life. Remember the words of Robert Anderson, 'Death ends a life, not a relationship.' Finally, this court looks to Jack Binion's grief-stricken letter. He writes that it was pure greed that drove the defendants to kill his brother. Greed most surely played a part, for greed corrupts and poisons all those who fall prey to it. However, what most concerns this court in the defendants' actions is the disregard of Mr. Binion; for it is clear that Mr. Binion was truly in love with the defendant Ms. Murphy, and that he had befriended Mr. Tabish. What a horrendous image this court envisions, when it conjures up the picture of a man who so completely entrusts his confidences to his loved one, to only then be a victim of her ultimate betrayal. It is the sad irony of Ted Binion's life that whatever caused him to devote his love to Ms. Murphy, also started the spiral of his demise. The disdain that our society has for individuals who gain the trust of others only to cause them harm, is far greater than the aversion we have for criminals who carry out their crimes upon complete strangers.

"However, the jury, after an extensive trial and penalty hearing felt that these defendants were deserving of parole after twenty years in prison. This court is here now to see that justice be given to the estate of Ted Binion and to Leo Casey, given the fact the crimes occurred in three separate phases: the extortion, the actual murder, and the taking of seven million dollars' worth of silver from the estate of Ted Binion.

"This court now looks to Richard Tabish in deciding what penalty to set for the crimes he has been found guilty of in addition to the murder sentence of which the jury has set forth. This court looks to the pre-sentence investigation report from the Department of Parole and Probation and weighs the particular circumstances of the offenses as well as the character of the defendant.

"Mr. Tabish, there are more victims in this case than . . . just Ted Binion and Leo Casey. In addition to the families of the victims who must live with what you have caused upon their loved ones, there is your family, of which this court has observed firsthand, one which seems to be of fine and caring caliber. A family who looks upon their brother and son and wonders what went wrong, a family who looks upon you and wonders if there was something they could have done to protect you from this situation. A family who is now forever shattered by your actions. Your young wife and two children forced to go forward without their husband and father, forced to forever be apart from you because of your deeds. All lives destroyed by your acts.

"The letters this court has received on your behalf, as well as what has been perceived by this court over the many months, show an individual who is friendly and personable towards others. This is not surprising to this court as you are a con man, one who gains the trust of others only to then betray them for your own personal gain.

"Additionally, what is most striking to this court is that you come from a family of some prominence and stability. In fact, you yourself were making a decent, fair, and honest living, one which most people would be content with having. It was a life that you decided to give up to satisfy the most primal of your desires. There is no justification that you could bring to this court for your actions, as you are here by your own choice. Your lack of remorse and your ramblings as to the guilt of others is clearly an indication that you have not yet acquired the ability to take responsibility for your own actions.

"Your prior felony history shows that you do not learn from your mistakes. You chose to steal that which is not yours, and now you must live with the results. You chose to beat up a sixty-three-year-old man, and now you must live with the outcome. You chose to betray and kill your friend, and now you must live with the consequences.

"Therefore, in recognizing the mitigating and aggravating circumstances, as well as your statements here today, and taking into consideration the Department of Parole and Probation PSI report, this court sentences Richard Bennett

Tabish to the following: In addition to the $25 Administrative Assessment and $250 DNA Analysis fees payable to the Clark County Clerk, the defendant RICHARD BENNETT TABISH, to be sentenced as follows:

"Count I—CONSPIRACY TO COMMIT ROBBERY: To a maximum term of Seventy-Two months with the minimum parole eligibility of TWENTY-EIGHT months in the Nevada Department of Prisons.

"Count II—CONSPIRACY TO COMMIT EXTORTION: To a term of ONE year in the Clark County Detention Center to be served concurrently with Count I. And pay $7,000 restitution jointly and severally with co-defendant.

"Count III—CONSPIRACY TO COMMIT KIDNAPPING: District Attorney dismissed.

"Count IV—FALSE IMPRISONMENT WITH USE OF A DEADLY WEAPON: To a maximum term of SEVENTY-TWO months with the minimum parole eligibility of TWENTY-EIGHT months, in the Nevada Department of Prisons to be served concurrently with Count II.

"Count V—ASSAULT WITH A DEADLY WEAPON: To a maximum term of SEVENTY-TWO months with the minimum parole eligibility of TWENTY-EIGHT months in the Nevada Department of Prisons, to be served concurrently with Count IV.

"Count VI—EXTORTION WITH THE USE OF A DEADLY WEAPON: To a maximum term of ONE-HUNDRED TWENTY months with the minimum parole eligibility of EIGHTEEN months in the Nevada Department of Prisons, plus an equal and consecutive maximum term of ONE HUNDRED TWENTY months with the minimum parole eligibility of EIGHTEEN months in the Nevada Department of Prisons for the use of a deadly weapon. It is further recommended that Count VI be served concurrently with Count V.

"Count VII—MURDER OF THE FIRST DEGREE: Set by jury verdict, as LIFE with the possibility of parole, with eligibility for parole beginning when a minimum of TWENTY years has been served. It is recommended that the defendant pay $10,992.68 jointly and severally with Sandra Renee Murphy, and that Count VII be served concurrently with Count VI.

"Count VIII—ROBBERY: To a maximum of ONE HUNDRED EIGHT (108) months with the minimum parole eligibility of SEVENTY-TWO months in the Nevada Department of Prisons. Count VIII to be served concurrently with Count VII.

"Count IX—CONSPIRACY TO COMMIT BURGLARY: To a term of ONE year in the Clark County Detention Center to be served concurrently to Count VII.

"Count X—BURGLARY: To a maximum term of ONE-HUNDRED TWENTY months with the minimum parole eligibility of TWENTY-FOUR months in the Nevada Department of Prisons. Count X to be served consecutively with Count VII.

"CounT XI—GRAND LARCENY: To a maximum term of ONE HUNDRED TWENTY months with the minimum parole eligibility of FORTY-EIGHT months in the Nevada Department of Prisons. Count XI to be served concurrently with Count IX.

"The defendant shall submit to a test to determine genetic markers.

"This court now looks to Sandra Murphy in deciding what penalty to set for the crimes that she has been found guilty of, in addition to the murder sentence of which the jury has set forth. This court looks to the PSI report from the Department of Parole and Probation and weighs the particular circumstances of the offenses as well as the character of the defendant.

"Ms. Murphy, your involvement in these crimes is horrific and strikes at the very core of trust between significant others. Through your greed and betrayal you plotted an elaborate scheme to kill Mr. Binion and steal his money, as well as swap him for a younger boyfriend. You presented yourself as a caring and loving girlfriend only to lure your victim into a trap which ultimately cost him his life. You too have not only ruined the lives of the relatives of Ted Binion, people who took you into their lives and trusted you, but also those of your own family. The pain and grief you have caused them must be immense, to sit and watch their daughter be found guilty of murdering the man with whom she attested her love to must be unpalatable.

"This court has witnessed firsthand your disdain for the laws of our society and particularly of this jurisdiction. No record could perpetuate your scowl of resentment or bland indifference toward these proceedings that this court has witnessed. Your attitude reflects that of one who shows little respect for these proceedings and of the system of law. The public must be protected from individuals like yourself, for you do not display the telltale signs of the criminal actor. Your feigned innocence permeated this court, as if you are oblivious to the predicament you are in. Your façade is of no concern, as you are to receive just punishment for your offenses. You chose to steal that which is not yours, and now you must live with the aftermath. You chose to betray and kill your lover, and now you must live with the consequences. It is this court's hope that after your period of incarceration, you will have awoken from the 'Alice in Wonderland' dream-like state you have attempted to portray in this courtroom and will have finally gained the understanding of what the law intends to do when certain lines are crossed and broken.

"Therefore, in recognizing the mitigating and aggravating circumstances, as well as your statements here today, and taking into consideration the Department of Parole and Probation PSI Report, this court sentences Sandra Renee Murphy to the following: In addition to the $25 Administrative Assessment and $250 DNA Analysis fees payable to the Clark County Clerk, the defendant, SANDRA RENEE MURPHY, be sentenced as follows:

"Count I—CONSPIRACY TO COMMIT MURDER: To a maximum of Seventy-Two months with the minimum parole eligibility of TWENTY-EIGHT months in the Nevada Department of Prisons.

"Count VII—MURDER IN THE FIRST DEGREE: As determined by jury. LIFE with the possibility of parole with eligibility for parole beginning when a minimum of TWENTY years has been served. It is further recommended that the defendant pay $10,992.68 restitution jointly and severally with Richard Bennett Tabish, and that Count VII be served concurrently with Count I.

"Count VIII—ROBBERY: To a maximum term of ONE HUNDRED EIGHTY months with the minimum parole eligibility of SEVENTY-TWO months in the Nevada Department of Prisons. Count VIII to be served concurrently with Count VII.

"Count IX—CONSPIRACY TO COMMIT BURGLARY: To a term of ONE year in the Clark County

Detention Center. Count IX to be served concurrently to Count VIII.

"Count X—BURGLARY: To a maximum term of ONE HUNDRED TWENTY months with the minimum parole eligibility of TWENTY-FOUR months in the Nevada Department of Prisons. Count X to be served consecutively with Count VII.

"Count XI—GRAND LARCENY: To a maximum term of ONE HUNDRED TWENTY months with the minimum parole eligibility of FORTY-EIGHT months in the Nevada Department of Prisons. Count XI to be served concurrently with Count IX.

"The defendant shall submit to a test to determine genetic markers.

"As far as this court is concerned, this sentencing brings this case to its final chapter. It is this court's desire that the victims and the families of the victims will also find some closure. Hopefully, they will be able to resume some semblance of normalcy as they move forward in their lives. As this case has garnered much media attention in this community and around the world, this court is cognizant of the fact that this community was very much affected by this case and its outcome. Now that the case has been resolved, it is hoped that Las Vegas will also find a sense of closure and return to more important matters that affect this great community. Justice, though due the accused, is due the accuser also. Justice has been served.

"This case is closed."

EPILOGUE

This case, however, was not closed. On Monday, July 14, 2003, the Nevada Supreme Court overturned the murder convictions that had been leveled against Rick Tabish and Sandra Murphy in connection with Ted Binion's death after hearing arguments by celebrated criminal lawyer Alan Dershowitz. The court also overturned the convictions of Tabish and Murphy for conspiracy, robbery, and grand larceny arising out of the removal of the silver from Binion's underground vault. The high court stated that Tabish and Murphy's trial was flawed and unfair.

At issue was the fact that the murder and robbery charges against Tabish and Murphy were tried along with the charges that Tabish had extorted Leo Casey, with whom he had shared the sand pit business, and kidnapped and beat him. The Supreme Court ruled that the largely unrelated Casey charges should have been severed from the murder charges and the silver robbery charges. By trying all the charges together both Tabish and Murphy were prejudiced. However, given what the Court found to be the "strong and more than substantial evidence" presented against Tabish and the Casey charges, the joinder of the claims was found to be not prejudicial and his conviction on those charges was affirmed.

The original trial court's error in trying all the charges together "was especially prejudicial in Murphy's case, although it was manifestly prejudicial to Tabish's trial on the other counts as well," the court stated in a majority opinion.

Also at issue on the appeal was the fact that the jury was allowed to hear a statement that Ted Binion had allegedly made to attorney James J. Brown prior to his death: "Take Sandy out of the will if she doesn't kill me tonight. If I'm dead, you'll know what happened," Brown had testified at trial. The Supreme Court decided that Clark County District Judge Joseph Bonaventure erred by allowing Brown's statement into evidence without providing a limiting instruction with regard to how much credence Brown's statement should carry as possible evidence.

As a result of its decisions, the Nevada Supreme Court ordered a new trial for Tabish and Murphy on the murder and silvery robbery charges.

Following a six-week retrial in which the prosecution focused heavily on the circumstantial evidence of the case, the jury decided that there was too much reasonable doubt surrounding the manner in which Ted Binion died. As a result, on Tuesday, November 23, 2004, jurors acquitted both Tabish and Murphy of the charges that they had killed Ted Binion. The jury did, however, find them guilty of conspiring to commit burglary and/or larceny, and also found them guilty of burglary and grand larceny.

On Friday, March 11, 2005, District Judge Joseph Bonaventure sentenced Rick Tabish and Sandra Murphy each to one to five years in prison in the theft of Binion's silver and ordered each to pay a $1,000 fine. Bonaventure also ordered Tabish's sentence to begin after he has finished the remaining sentence stemming from the kidnapping and extortion conviction regarding Leo Casey. Bonaventure credited Murphy for 1,406 days that she had served in prison for the murder conviction that was overturned, and she will remain out of custody pending an appeal.

"I feel relieved," Murphy said to reporters following the sentencing hearing. "I'm ready to go home. I respect the sentence, but I'll be satisfied when the Supreme Court acquits me of all the charges."

APPENDIX

Richard Tabish and Sandra Murphy appealed their convictions. On July 14, 2003, the Supreme Court of Nevada reversed Judge Bonaventure's decision (set forth below) and granted a new trial on these counts. Ultimately, after the new trial, Tabish and Murphy were acquitted on all murder charges.

CLARK COUNTY DISTRICT COURT JUDGE JOSEPH BONAVENTURE'S DENIAL FOR A NEW TRIAL

This is the time set for this Court to rule on Sandra Murphy and Rick Tabish's Motion for New Trial and Motion for Judgment Not Withstanding the Verdict in Case #C161663 *State of Nevada* v. *Tabish & Murphy*.

As to the Defense contention that this Court erred by not requiring the jury to return a unanimous verdict as to the cause of death of Mr. Binion. Such issue has been ruled upon at trial and is not for this court to decide upon in a Motion for New Trial as District Court Rule 13 (7) explains. This issue is therefore preserved in the record. It is this Court's prior reasoning that the jury was required to find beyond a reasonable doubt that the defendants killed Ted Binion. The jury did not have to be unanimous on the facts or theory of how the Defendants killed Ted Binion. Therefore, by their verdict, the jury found that the prosecution proved beyond a reasonable doubt that the Defendants killed Ted Binion. The Constitution requires nothing more.

As to the Defense position that the two defendants should have been tried separately, once again, such issue has been ruled upon at trial and is not for this court to decide upon in a Motion for New Trial as District Court Rule 13 (7) explains. This issue is therefore preserved in the record.

As to the Defense claim that there was insufficient evidence for the jury to have convicted the defendants on crimes so charged, this Court, aware of the many days of conflicting testimony regarding the medical certainty as to the cause of Mr. Binion's death, notes that at most trials the experts from each side disagree, and find there is sufficient evidence to support the jury's verdict. As we stated in *United States* v. *Nelson* 419 F.2d 123 (9th Cir. 1969), juries constantly convict, and the convictions are duly affirmed, on evidence upon which none would hesitate to act but which cannot be said to exclude as a matter of inexorable logic, every reasonable hypothetical consistent with innocence. Therefore, the Motion for New Trial based on Sufficiency of the Evidence is DENIED.

The Defense originally raised the issue of ineffective assistance of counsel as to Mr. Palazzo. As this was a joint defense, the court had some difficulty in the determination as to where Mr. Palazzo's role ended and Mr. Momot's role continued. The tightrope of legal perplexity would have been a treacherous one to follow, should a hearing on such matters have taken place. However, the defense has since withdrawn their claims against Mr. Palazzo in light of this Court's ruling, and the Nevada Supreme Court's affirmation, as to the testimony of attorneys in defense of their profession. Therefore the issue of Ineffective assistance of Counsel is MOOT.

The Defense alleges that Massiah violations occurred prior to trial, particularly that the District Attorney's office or the Clark County Detention center conspired to place David Gomez in a jail cell nearest to Mr. Tabish, in order to glean information on the trial strategy or to circumvent the Attorney client Privilege. Prior to trial, this court held an extensive evidentiary hearing allowing Defendants to explore the alleged Massiah violations. At the conclusion of the hearing, this court concluded that Defendant failed to establish that law enforcement engaged in any wrongdoing. The Defendants' desire to relitigate their motion to dismiss, claiming that David Gomez is now willing to testify at an evidentiary hearing. This Court stated that it would allow a new evidentiary hearing based solely upon Mr. Gomez's new allegation. However, when it came time for this four-time felon to testify, he took the Fifth Amendment, just as he did in the pre-trial hearing. Therefore, since the Defendants have failed to provide the court with any credible evidence that the State conspired with David Gomez to steal Defendants' paperwork or any other new revelation concerning Mr. Gomez, The Defendants' Motion for New Trial based on Massiah violations is DENIED.

The Defense has claimed that the state withheld exculpatory information in violation of *Brady* v. *Maryland*. Specifically, FBI reports, which confirm a possible hit was put on Mr. Binion's life by organized crime. Such a hit was to be carried out by means of an overdose of heroin.

In order to make a *prima facie* showing that the prosecution withheld evidence in violation of the Defendant's [sic] due process rights as set forth in *Brady* v. *Maryland*, 373 U.S. 83 (1963), the defense must establish that the prosecution suppressed favorable and material evidence in its possession. Additionally, the prosecution does not have an obligation to provide exculpatory evidence that it does not possess or of which it is unaware. *U.S.* v. *Monroe*, 943 F.2d 1007 (9th Cir. 1991). Also, an accused cannot complain that exculpatory evidence has been suppressed by the prosecution when the information is known to him. *U.S.* v. *Dupuy*, 760 F.2d 1492, 1501 (9th Cir. 19?5) [sic] or as stated in *U.S.* v. *Brown*, 562 F.2d 1144 (9th Cir. 1977) it is of no concern whether defendant negligently failed to discover exculpatory evidence in its possession or deliberately withheld vital information from the court, in either event the accused cannot complain that the prosecution suppressed evidence.

As evidenced by the testimony at the post-trial hearing, the defense has always contended that Ted Binion's death was suicidal or accidental and that the Defendant Sandra Murphy was present when Ted Binion died. It would seem that such a memo would fly in the very face of the defense's entire case. However, it is not for this Court to determine pre-trial strategy that may have resulted from the awareness of one memo.

The Court is more impressed with the fact that there was not a joint investigation between the District Attorney's office and The FBI. There was no working relationship between the two agencies. Additionally, the State did not possess the FBI report. Also, the fact that the State made a good faith attempt to obtain reports by sending a letter to the U.S. Attorney.

Moreover, as evidenced by the numerous affirmations to this Court by both defense investigators and attorneys as to their knowledge of alleged underworld plots against Mr. Binion's life and the defense pre-trial motion to the State to provide such documents, as well as both Mr. Palazzo and Mr. Momot's prior representation of these very individuals, it is clear to this court that the Defendants were aware or should have been aware of this information. Consequently, as stated in *Brown*, the Defendant cannot now complain that they did not have access to any potential exculpatory evidence.

It is this Court's ruling that the defendants are found not to have been prejudiced by any failure to receive such FBI reports due to the showing that the defense was not "surprised" by such information. The State was not in possession of such information and the State made a good faith effort to provide such information. It has been shown that the defense had otherwise been aware of the undisclosed evidence, or should reasonably have known it existed. Also, this Court is of the opinion that if the defense had used such documents, it would have opened the door for the State to bring in evidence of Mr. Tabish's alleged ties to organized crime. Additionally, this Court finds that any defense knowledge of such evidence would not have been likely to result in a significant change in trial strategy or the effectiveness of the defense. Therefore, it is the Order of this Court that the defense Motion for a New Trial based upon Brady violations is DENIED.

Turning now to the area to which this Court finds some merit in, Juror Misconduct. Juror Misconduct is an especially distasteful area for this Court. This Court holds juries in the highest regard. For our judicial system asks twelve individuals from all walks of life, complete strangers, to put their daily lives on hold, to overcome any personality conflicts, and in a joint effort of the functioning of their several minds to ferret out the truth and ultimately decide upon the fate of another human being. As evidenced by the fact that this jury was the most secure and protected jury Clark County has ever seen, and this Court's awareness that they gave up two months of their lives for this trial, having jurors testify on the witness stand is not something that this Court takes any solace in.

However, Mr. Wall's impassioned homily to save this jury from the rigors of testifying is understandable considering his stake in this trial. But, it is misplaced. For when a jury has decided that two individuals must spend twenty years to life behind bars and then those same jurors decide to reveal the sanctity of their deliberations on the Internet for the entire world to read, or contact defense attorneys about improper influences, or submit affidavits alleging that improper rules of law were used to determine guilt or bring electronic devices into the jury room that are capable of downloading extraneous material; all of their deserved commendations do not make them immune from the rules of law.

The Sixth Amendment to the United States Constitution guarantees the accused the right to a trial by an impartial jury. Extraneous information that has a prejudicial effect on a jury's verdict denies the accused their Sixth Amendment guarantees. Consideration is needed to whether the extraneous information was improperly brought to the attention of the jury and whether the information would have affected the decision of an average responsible juror.

Courts hold evidentiary hearings to consider the prejudicial effect of such information and allow jurors to testify whether the extraneous information reached the jury, but prohibit jurors from testifying whether the information affected their deliberations or thought processes. The origin of the common-law rule derives from Lord Mansfield's opinion in *Vaise* v. *Delaval*. See *McDonald* v. *Pless*, 238 U.S. 264 (1915). The rule attempts to discourage the losing party from harassing jurors, to encourage free and open discussions among the jurors, to reduce incentives for jury tampering, and to maintain the viability of the jury, thereby promoting verdict finality and integrity.

Extraneous information includes a jury's consideration of evidence not admissible in court and communications between jurors and third parties. However, case law in this State shows that reviewing courts have looked more harshly upon a conviction when the trial court fails to conduct an evidentiary hearing.

The common-law rule prohibits the use of juror testimony concerning information to impeach a jury verdict in order to promote verdict finality. To preserve the right to a fair trial, an exception to the verdict finality rule permits juror testimony for the sole purpose of showing that extraneous information improperly reached the jury. Our judicial system has required that the jury's decision in a case should be reached based only on evidence received in open court, where a defendant could exercise his Sixth Amendment rights.

The standard most commonly articulated is whether in a given case there is "Such a probability that prejudice will result that the verdict is deemed inherently lacking in due process."

In *US* v. *Vasquez*, 597 F.2d 192 (1979) a 9th Circuit case, the Court held that it is a fundamental principle that the government has the burden of establishing guilt solely on the basis of evidence produced in the courtroom and under circumstances assuring the accused all the safeguards of a fair trial. Judicial control of the jurors' knowledge of the case pursuant to the laws of evidence is fundamental to the prevention of bias and prejudice. Our rules of evidence are designed to exclude from consideration by the jurors those facts and objects which may tend to prejudice or confuse. Evidence presented under the exclusionary rules is subject to cross-examination and rebuttal. It is therefore necessary that all evidence developed against an accused "come from the witness stand in a public courtroom where there is full judicial protection of the defendant's right of confrontation, of cross-examination, and of counsel."

Indeed, however, the Nevada Supreme Court in *Revuelta* v. *State*, 86 Nev. 587 (1970) quoted the US Supreme Court in *Bruton* when it stated that not every admission of inadmissible hearsay or other evidence can be considered to be reversible error unavoidable through limiting instructions; instances occur in almost every trial where inadmissible evidence creeps in, usually inadvertently. 'A defendant is entitled to a fair trial but not a perfect one.' It is not unreasonable to conclude that in many such cases the jury can and will follow the trial judge's instructions to disregard such information."

This Court will first address the defense contention that the jury was prejudiced by influence form the media. The Court finds this issue to be without merit. As stated in *Arndt* v. *State*, 93 Nev. 671 (1977), the question of any exposure to outside media influence is whether there's been a prejudicial effect on the substantial rights of the Defendant. Two jurors testified that they had inadvertently heard something to the effect that Kurt Gratzer had been arrested during the trial. Kurt Gratzer was a witness for the State and any arrest of Kurt Gratzer would tend to diminish his believability in the eyes of the jury, thereby gaining favor for the defense. This Court finds any exposure to such a report would not have prejudiced the defendants in any way.

Additionally, it is the defense contention that the jurors disregarded this Court's lengthy admonition to them. The record belies such a contention. In *US* v. *Steele*, 785 F.2d 743 (1986) a 9th Circuit case, the Court held that absent some indication to the contrary, we must assume the jury followed the judge's instructions. There is nothing in the record of the examinations of each juror which indicates that the jury intentionally disregarded the court's instructions.

The Defense contends that it was improper for this Court to make photocopies of specific jury instructions, as requested by the jurors, without first consulting the attorneys. Also, that a possible communication between the bailiff and the jury concerning their well-being was improper and is cause for a new trial.

As a matter of course during a trial there will usually be contact between the jurors and bailiff since the bailiff is normally in charge of the jury. It is not unusual for the bailiff to have extensive interpersonal relations with members of a jury during a trial since the jury ordinarily orders lunch through the bailiff and is directed around the courthouse by the bailiff. Misconduct occurs, however, depending on what the court officer says to the jurors and how it relates to a particular case. In this case, the bailiff was in control of this jury from the moment they arrived at the Courthouse to the moment they left. Additionally, the jurors were given the bailiff's cell phone number should any of them encounter any security or personal problems regarding the trial while away from court. It would be likely that the Bailiff would have developed a concern for the jury as he had spent the past seven weeks with them, so any concern on his part for their well-being is understandable. The defendants' contention is that the bailiff committed reversible error when he asked the jury foreman about his well-being. In *People* v. *Kirk*, 76 Ill. App. 3d 459, (1979) the Illinois Supreme Court held that while such inquiries might be erroneous, any error was not reversible since "it can not be said that they interfered with the deliberations of the jurors to the prejudice of plaintiff, or that they hastened the verdict." The record belies such an accusation, if any improper communication occurred, it was on the 3rd day of deliberations, the jury was not hastened in any respect, as they took five more days to reach a verdict.

The defense asks this Court to speculate that "there is possibility the jury could have given greater weight to those instructions that were photocopied," and thus, in their minds, "lessened the burden placed upon the prosecution by the court and by the law." There is nothing in the record which would support an inference that the jury did such an act. The record of the evidentiary hearing demonstrates that there is not reasonable possibility that the jury's use of photocopies of official Court instructions affected the verdict. Reversal on the basis of this conjecture would find no support in the record and be contrary to the law of this state.

The defense contends that racial coercion among the jurors affected the verdict. During the evidentiary hearing it was revealed that juror #4, while laughing, asked juror #10 how she felt about being the token black on the jury. A totally inappropriate comment in this Judge's eyes and one that has no place in this society. But does such a remark rise to the level of prejudice to warrant a new trial? In *United States* v. *Blackburn*, 446 F.2d 1089, a Fifth Circuit case, after the jury returned a verdict of guilty, defense counsel moved for a new trial alleging that one of the jurors had telephoned an associate of defendant and had told her that the jury foreman had "harassed them pretty strong." The court found that the jury's verdict of guilty cannot be impeached by the fact that a juror may have been influenced by the improper remark of a fellow juror. As inappropriate a remark as this was, the jury should not be exposed to post-verdict fishing expeditions into their mental processes with the hope that something will turn up.

The Defense alleges that the jury had a monetary interest in the verdict and was therefore not impartial. First, it is the defense contention that because a majority of the jurors appeared on *Dateline* and a local NBC affiliate, they had a monetary interest in the verdict. The media coverage surrounding this trial was immense, in fact it would be hard to compare such a frenzy with any other recent trial other than that of O. J. Simpson. The jurors were harassed from the moment they left the courthouse after reaching their verdict, in fact some jurors' homes were being staked out by reporters. Logic prevails that in order to return to some semblance of normal life, an interview would be a necessary step to avoid further intrusion into their private lives. This was not an act of greed, it was one of self-preservation and this Court sees no merit in the defense position.

Secondly, it is the defense position that the jury had a monetary position in the trial due to Juror #3 speaking to a dental assistant turned book publisher. And, by this conversation, the verdict was impartial. This Court would be hard pressed to reason that if a jury found the defendants guilty, that would sell more books than if they found them not guilty. Suffice to say one only has to look at the amount of juror books that came out of the O. J. Simpson trial for a good example. Additionally, while disturbing to the Court that a dental assistant would attempt to interfere with a criminal trial, the testimony evidenced that the only conversation the juror had with this woman was that she had a proposition for her when the trial was over. Moreover, during trial it was revealed that Juror #2 had remarked about the possibility of writing a book, such information was brought to the attention of the Defense attorneys and even after the court advising it would remove Juror #2, the defense logged no objection to her continuing as a juror. The court finds such actions do not rise to the level of prejudice to the defendant.

The defense claims that the use of fugitive documents, specifically "Witnesses, Charges, & Instructions Binion Case," were erroneous and infected the jury room as to taint the verdict. In *People* v. *Martinez*, 82 Cal. App. 3d 1 (1978) the Court held that whether a defendant has been injured by jury misconduct in receiving evidence outside of court necessarily depends upon whether the jury's impartiality has been adversely affected, whether the prosecution's burden of proof has been lightened and whether any asserted defense has been contradicted. If the answer to any of these questions is in the affirmative, the defendant has been prejudiced and the conviction must be reversed. On the other hand, since jury misconduct is not *per se* reversible, if a review of the entire record demonstrates that the appellant has suffered no prejudice from the misconduct, a reversal is not compelled.

Juror #12 brought typewritten pages of the previously entitled documents into the jury room. Such documents were

typewritten on his personal home computer from his handwritten notes. He testified that he did so as an aid or a guide
for himself to help him decipher the reams of information
and as a reference to the official court instructions. Testimony revealed that the other jurors found them helpful and
utilized them for the obvious purpose of aiding the jury to
evaluate that which had been presented at trial.

In the year 2000, Courts are faced with many challenges,
from handheld electronic devices to cell phones as small as
a credit card. Had this juror handwritten these documents
instead of typing them, most likely more errors would have
occurred. Also, what if, instead of typing the documents,
the jurors made huge handwritten charts within the jury
room? Would that be misconduct? In this ever-changing
world of technology, people look for ways to make their
tasks more convenient. While not condoning the use of an
outside computer this Court sees no prejudicial harm in the
jury having the benefit of such documents to aid in its understanding of the trial. Having said that, future juries
would be wise to ascertain the Court's permission, before
embarking on such an ambitious project.

Secondly, the defense claims that errors on these handwritten documents prejudiced the defendants. The pre-
sumption of prejudice is clearly rebutted by the record.
First, there is little inconsistency between that presented at
trial and that depicted on the documents; the documents
merely bring such into clearer focus.

This court must now take the few errors into account, and
look to find if such errors lighten the prosecution's burden
of proof in any manner. This Court looks to Jury Instruction
#33, as that goes to the heart of the prosecution's burden.
The handwritten instruction indicates that "First degree
murder must be beyond a shadow of a doubt for first degree
murder." In actuality, the Court's instructions for #33,
while lengthy, contain in part that Murder in the First De-

gree must be proven beyond a reasonable doubt. Clearly, to this court "a shadow of a doubt" increases the burden on the prosecution and causes no prejudice to the defendants. In taking into account the other nine differences between the official Court instructions and the handwritten ones, this Court looks to the testimony of the jurors themselves. The jurors testified that such documents were used as an index, a guide, a tool, an aid, a reference or as a paraphrasing of the Court's official instructions. The inconsistencies can be explained by the jurors who used them. While it would be easy for an outsider to look upon them to decide their conformity, the jurors testified that they were used as a reference to the Court's official instructions, additionally, any errors did not prejudice the defendants or lighten the prosecution's burden.

Presumably, the foreman believed that the documents would help the jury to ascertain the truth. The items depicted on the documents did not impeach the defense witnesses or contradict the defense case. Nor can it be argued that the documents contained information which would cause a bias among the jurors against the defendants.

As stated by the US Supreme Court in *Remmer* v. *United States*, 350 U.S. 377 (1950), Though a judge lacks the insight of a psychiatrist, the Court must reach a judgment concerning the subjective effects of facts without the benefit of couch-interview introspections. As this Court is not allowed to delve into the mental processes of the jurors, it is the Court's determination that no prejudice resulted from such documents and any breach to the defendants was harmless.

This court now looks to the use of the Palm Pilot during the course of this trial and during deliberations. Juror number twelve revealed to the surprise of this Court that he had used a Palm Pilot notebook-type device during the trial.

Additionally, Juror number twelve revealed that he had used the calendar function, the calculator function and a list of 800 numbers on the Palm Pilot. Quite frankly, prior to this issue being raised, this Court had no idea what a Palm Pilot was. This Court has since become quite versed in its capabilities. The Court was extremely disturbed when it first was brought to the Court's attention in defense counsel's motion. The new generation of these models have the capability of downloading information off of the Internet without the benefit of a phone line, something that clearly would be disallowed in a jury room.

However, upon the Court's receipt of juror #12's Palm Pilot, my staff ascertained that this model could only be used for the simplest of tasks. Downloading e-mail, storing names, addresses and telephone numbers, and as a calculator or calendar. This Court cannot understand how a juror, after being admonished by this court as to the importance of this trial and what is allowed inside a jury room, could have reasoned that the use of such an item was proper without prior court approval. To have such a device in a jury room with the potential to download foreign information, should have raised a red flag in this juror's mind. If cell phones are not allowed in the jury room, Palm Pilots would certainly be a cause of concern.

However, this Court must look to whether such conduct was prejudicial to the defendants and if so, to order a new trial. Juror number 12 testified that he used the calculator function, the calendar function and a list of 800 numbers. The 800 number he was looking for was contained in evidence in the jury room, which was later confirmed by the juror. There is no case law regarding a juror bringing a Palm Pilot into a jury room, so this Court must look to cases dealing with jurors independently researching facts. In *US* v. *Steele*, 785 F. 2d 743 (1986) 9th Circuit case, a juror brought a dictionary in to the deliberations, the Court found that there was no prejudice to the defendant due to the way the dictionary was utilized.

Additionally, in *People* v. *Phillips*, 122 Cal. App. 3d 69 (1981) the trial court observed that a juror's independent experiment was one of fairly common knowledge and the matter to which it related was, in light of all the evidence, tangential rather than critical to the case.

The result in *Phillips* of the juror's independent investigation was not such as to adversely affect the juror's impartiality, lighten the prosecution's burden of proof, or contradict any asserted defense.

This court so finds that Juror #12's use of a Palm Pilot to look up a date, perform some math functions, and retrieve an 800 number could not have prejudiced the defendants' right to a fair trial. Any one of these items the Court could have taken judicial notice of. Also, a calendar had been entered into evidence as well as the 800 number the juror looked up. The research merely confirmed what any reasonable juror already knew. Additionally, the mere presence of the device in the jury room would not constitute *per se* prejudice, juror #12 testified he only downloaded personal e-mail having nothing to do with the trial.

Having ruled upon the Palm Pilot issue and finding no prejudice to the defendants, this Court would be remiss if it did not issue a word of caution. The Court system is slow to change and sometimes altogether adverse to it. However, electronic communication devices are becoming smaller and smaller and their capabilities more powerful as well as being more commonplace in society. In light of the future prospect of declaring a mistrial due to the unauthorized use of such devices, this Court is in the process of working with Court administration to devise a set of instructions to better inform jurors of what can be brought into a jury room. Such instructions will encompass the changing world of technology, in order to ensure defendants a fair trial and to avoid the expense of two trials.

The Court must now consider the Defendants' Motion for New Trial based on the term "Depraved Indifference" being introduced into the jury deliberations room. Once again, this Court is somewhat surprised that such a term was discussed in the jury room. Having done an extensive nationwide search of case law, as well as the State and Defense Counsel not providing this Court with any cases on point, it is clear to this Court that this issue is one of first impression. It does not seem there has been a case where a jury has been properly instructed by the Court on the law that applies to the case, given the jury instructions to be taken back into the deliberation room, only then to have the jury discuss a term of law not applicable to the jurisdiction of which the case is being tried. In fact, "Depraved Indifference" is a term that was not used during the entire two-month trial. As uncomfortable as that may seem, this Court's obligation is to follow the case law which controls the deliberations of jurors. This Court looks to the prevailing case law based upon extraneous information being received by a jury.

It is the Defense position that the term "Depraved Indifference" infected the sanctity of the Jury deliberations and ultimately, the verdict. Five jurors testified that such a term was heard in the jury room. Two jurors describe the term as a "mind set," one stated it was "self-explanatory," one said "it was to sit back when you had an opportunity to make a difference," and one described it as "if you are in the house when a person dies and you do nothing." The other seven jurors do not recall the phrase being used at all. Testimony revealed that Juror #11 first introduced the term into the jury room from her own past experiences living in New Jersey where evidently the term is common to the vocabulary. While it is not clear how the jurors used the term during deliberations, the evidence established that the jury did not conduct independent research to define the term "depraved indifference." The testimony revealed that the term was heard before the trial and that it was brought in from the juror's prior experience, with juror #2 even commenting that she thought she heard it years ago on an old *Perry Mason*–type show.

As stated in *United States* v. *Bagnariol*, 665 F.2d 877, a 9th Circuit 1981 case, the introduction of outside influences into the deliberative process of the jury is inimical to our system of justice. The defendant is entitled to a new trial if there existed a reasonable possibility that the extrinsic material could have affected the verdict.

However, well-established case law forbids the eliciting of juror testimony regarding the jury's mental processes, or the influences that any particular evidence had upon the jury's conclusion. As stated in *McDonald* v. *Pless*, 238 US 264 (1915), "The evolved law represents an accomodation of conflicting policies, on the one hand, the interest in stability of jury verdicts and the protection of jurors from harassment, on the other hand, the prevention of injustice arising from an unfair trial." As Judge Friendly remarked in *Miller* v. *US*, 403 F.2d 83, "While existing law can be criticized as forbidding inquiry into the subject most truly pertinent, it represents a pragmatic judgment how best to attempt reconciliation of the irreconcilable."

The State asks this Court to strike the affidavits of the jurors, claiming that they deal with the mental processes of the jurors.

And our own Nevada Supreme Court has consistently declined to allow a jury to impeach its verdict even when the defense has claimed that the jury disregarded the court's instructions on the law. *ACP Reno Associates* v. *Airmotive*, 109 Nev. 314 (1993); *Weaver Brothers* v. *Misskelley*, 98 Nev. 232 (1982).

The US Supreme Court stated in *Mattox* v. *US*, 146 US 140,

"Public policy forbids that a matter resting in the personal consciousness of one juror should be received to overthrow the verdict, because being personal it is not accessible to other testimony; it gives to the secret thought of one the power to disturb the expressed conclusions of twelve; its tendency is to produce bad faith on the part of a minority; to induce tampering with individual jurors subsequent to the verdict. But as to overt acts, they are accessible to the knowledge of all the jurors; if one affirms misconduct, the remaining eleven can deny; one cannot disturb the action of the twelve; it is useless to tamper with one, for the eleven may be heard."

Additionally, The Supreme Court in *McDonal* v. *Pless*, 238 US 264, held that "it is, of course, necessary to prevent instability of verdicts, fraud, and harassment of jurors, and on the other hand, it is desirable to give the losing party relief from wrongful conduct by the jury. And, after discussing these policies and stating that the wrong to the individual was the lesser of two evils, the Court concluded that as a general rule the affidavits of jurors should be excluded but that there might be instances where the rule could not be applied without 'violating the plainest principles of justice.' "

Under this view of the law the affidavits were properly received. They tended to prove something which did not essentially inhere in the verdict, an overt act, open to the knowledge of all the jury, and not alone within the personal consciousness of one. And while this Court did not consider the mental processes of the jurors, the record will stand with the affidavits in their complete form. However, this Court has found no case law which supports the proposition that an affidavit by a private investigator alleging testimony of a witness should be allowed to be considered, and therefore it is the order of the Court that all affidavits by such private investigator shall be stricken from the record.

This Court has looked long and hard at what such an introduction into the jury room of this term could have endeavored and if there existed a reasonable possibility that it could have affected the verdict.

The defendant complains that one or more jurors, by using the term "Depraved Indifference," attempted to secure a greater weight for an opinion by referring to his or her background and experience in the use of such a word. However, the mere fact that certain jurors expressed an opinion to other members of the jury cannot be considered to be misconduct, since that is the nature of deliberation. As stated in *United States* v. *Howard*, 506 F.2d 865, a 5th Circuit decision,

"This Court must look to whether there was any reasonable possibility of prejudice to the defendants. Modern day trials are factually presented in open court before the iron curtain descends upon the jury room. We cannot tolerate prejudicial factual intrusion into the sanctum lest our courts return to darker days of our jurisprudential history. The dagger of hidden evidence must not be taken from its scabbard for the first time in the jury room to wound the defendant; and unless its piercing effect is only skin deep and without prejudice to the anatomy of the trial, we must apply a constitutional salve."

When determining what is proper and what is improper discussion among jurors, regard must be had for the fact that the jury are men and women of different walks of life, avocation, and necessarily views that would be affected by their past experiences and situations. They could hardly arrive at a solution of their differences without discussion of the facts before them, and each man's or woman's discussion would necessarily be tinged or affected by his own viewpoint and experiences.

It is of course "the very stuff of the jury system" for the jury to exercise its collective wisdom and experience in dissecting the evidence properly before it; and in this process the cross-pollination of opinion, viewpoint, and insight into human affairs is one of the jury's strengths. As was stated in *Farese* v. *United States*, 428 F.2d 178 (1970).

The verdict in this case represents "the merger of a variety of ideas, reflections and sentiments; a compound in which only the omniscient could identify the component parts and accurately ascribe to each its relative influence generating the ultimate product. No one but the jurors can tell what was put into it, and the jurors are not permitted to say."

Here, the jurors' testimony as to the term "Depraved Indifference" goes, not to the motives or methods or processes by which they reached the verdict, but merely to the existence of conditions or the occurrence of events bearing on the verdict from their own experiences.

The Nevada Supreme Court in *Lopez* v. *State*, 105 Nev. 68 (1989) stated that limitation on juror misconduct represent sound judicial policy as observed by one court: "It must be, too, that in their deliberations jurors more or less generally recall experiences in their own lives, and if new trials were commonly granted for such a reason there would be no end to litigation."

Even assuming that the term "Depraved Indifference" played any role in the deliberations—and there was no competent proof of when exactly it was related to the other jurors—in a larger sense it was no more than a small item of "background experience," possession of which is an important, highly valued, and expected strength of a jury.

In persuading one another to their respective viewpoints, and indeed in resolving their own doubts, jurors, like other people, employ the products of their education and experience, frequently argue by analogy and commonly make comparisons with things at hand. That is essentially all that happened in the case. Consequently, if the juror episode here is to contaminate the verdict, hardly any determination of facts, by Judge or jury, would be impervious to such attack.

For, it is a mistake to underestimate the intelligence of a jury, which, when all is said and done, is a collective body with the unique advantage of having the brightest twelve at its disposal at all times. Instead, whatever was said about the term undoubtedly ranked no higher than the experience-based arguments that inevitably punctuate jury deliberations. Under all these circumstances, by no means can it be equated with the jury disregarding this Court's instructions to follow the law as it was laid out for them.

Accordingly, it is this Court's view that juror number 11 was but "spontaneously drawing on a common everyday situation with which she was familiar in order to more easily convey her opinion to the other members of the jury." The jurors indicated that they had not taken the term into consideration when reaching their verdict. The fact that other jury members found it helpful to use such a term did not adversely affect the jurors' impartiality, nor did it lighten the prosecution's burden of proof and most importantly, it did not prejudice the defendants.

This Court's failure to uphold the case law in this area would either help sap the jury system of its vitality or encourage the blinking of normal and sensible conduct. As stated in *United States* v. *Bagnario*, 665 F.2d 877, 9th Circuit (1981), "we must accept the jury as a rational body, fully capable of making the fine distinctions necessary to the fact-finding process. We are not called upon to isolate, examine, and negate each of the possible and irrational constructions on which a jury conceivably could rely.

Based on the foregoing, it is the order of this Court that Defendants Sandra Murphy and Richard Tabish's Motion for a New Trial and Motion for Judgment Not Withstanding the Verdict be DENIED. All evidence and testimony is to be preserved for any future appeal. The defendants are to be sentenced on September 15, 2000 at the hour of 9:30 a.m.

Honorable Joseph Bonaventure
Eighth Judicial District Court
Clark County, NV USA
September 8, 2000

Al Lasso
Law Clerk